The Global Economy

The Global Economy

Version 2.4

NYU Stern
Department of Economics

This document was created for the Global Economy course at New York University's Stern School of Business by a team that includes Dave Backus, Gian Luca Clementi, Tom Cooley, Joe Foudy, Kim Ruhl, Tom Pugel, Kim Schoenholtz, Laura Veldkamp, Venky Venkateswaran, Paul Wachtel, Mike Waugh, and Stan Zin. The cover was designed by Alexa Zin.

This version was created December 29, 2017.

David K. Backus
1953-2016

We dedicate this book to our friend,
colleague and coauthor, David K. Backus.
His clear thinking and elegant writing echo
throughout these pages.

Contents

Preface

This document evolved from a set of notes developed for the Global Economy course at New York University's Stern School of Business. The idea behind the course is to use the tools of macroeconomics to assess the economic performance of countries and the challenges facing businesses operating in them. We emphasize data; virtually every chapter includes links to data sources. The book is designed as background reading for the in-class experience. The focus is on tools, leaving us to spend most of our class time on applications.

All of the materials related to this book are available upon request to others with similar interests in the hope that they will reciprocate. "We" here means the Global Economy team: Dave Backus, Gian Luca Clementi, Tom Cooley, Joe Foudy, Kim Ruhl, Tom Pugel, Kim Schoenholtz, Laura Veldkamp, Venky Venkateswaran, Paul Wachtel, Mike Waugh, and Stan Zin.

This set of notes is available online at

http://www.stern.nyu.edu/GEMatter.

The online version of the notes includes color graphs and an extensive collection of links. An inexpensive black-and-white printed version is also available through Amazon, self-published through their CreateSpace facility, which we were delighted with.

We're equally interested in your thoughts: on the course, the materials, teaching macroeconomics, or anything else that crosses your mind. Send us an email, we're easy to track down.

One last request: Please pass on any typos or other glitches you find. Your efforts will help us improve future versions.

Part I
Preliminaries

1
Mathematics Review

Tools: Exponents and logarithms; growth rates and compounding; derivatives; spreadsheets; the FRED database.

Key Words: Production function; demand function; marginal product; marginal cost.

Big Ideas:

- Macroeconomics is a quantitative discipline; ditto business.

- Mathematics and data analysis are essential tools.

Mathematics is a precise and efficient language for expressing quantitative ideas, including many that come up in business. What follows is an executive summary of everything you'll need in this course: functions, exponents and logarithms, derivatives, and spreadsheets, each illustrated with examples.

1.1   Functions

In economics and business, we often talk about relations between variables: Demand depends on price; cost depends on quantity produced; price depends on yield; output depends on input; and so on. We call these relations *functions*. More formally, a function f assigns a (single) value y to each possible value of a variable x. We write it this way: $y = f(x)$. Perhaps the easiest way to think about a function is to draw it: Put x on the horizontal axis and plot the values of y associated with each x on the vertical axis. In a spreadsheet program, you might imagine setting up a table with a grid of values for x. The function would then be a formula that computes a value y for each value of x.

Example: Demand functions. We may be interested in the sensitivity of demand for our product to its price. If the quantity demanded is q and the price p, an example of a demand function relating the two is

$$q \ = \ a + bp,$$

where a and b are "parameters" (think of them as fixed numbers whose values we haven't bothered to write down). Sensitivity of demand to price is summarized by b, which we'd expect to be negative (demand falls as price rises).

Example: Production functions. In this class, we'll relate output Y to inputs of capital K and labor L. (In macroeconomics, capital refers to plant and equipment.) It'll look a little strange the first time you see it, but a convenient example of such a function is

$$Y \ = \ K^{\alpha} L^{1-\alpha},$$

where α is a number between zero and one (typically, we set $\alpha = 1/3$). This is a modest extension of our definition of a function—Y depends on two variables, not one—but the idea is the same.

Example: Bond yields. The price p and yield y for a one-year zero-coupon bond might be related by

$$p \ = \ \frac{100}{1+y},$$

where 100 is the face value of the bond. Note the characteristic inverse relation: high yield, low price.

1.2   Exponents and logarithms

Exponents and logarithms are useful in many situations: elasticities, compound interest, growth rates, and so on. Here's a quick summary.

Exponents. Exponents are an extension of multiplication. If we multiply x by itself, we can write either $x \times x$ or x^2, where 2 is an exponent (or power). In general, we can write x^a to mean (roughly) "x multiplied by itself a times," although this language may seem a little strange if a isn't a positive whole number such as 2 or 3. We can, nevertheless, compute such quantities for any value of a we like as long as x is positive. (Think about how you'd do this in a spreadsheet.)

The most useful properties of exponents are

$$
\begin{aligned}
x^a x^b &= x^{a+b} \\
x^a y^a &= (xy)^a \\
(x^a)^b &= x^{ab} \\
x^{-a} &= 1/x^a.
\end{aligned}
$$

You can work these out for yourself using our multiplication analogy.

Logarithms. By logarithm, we mean the function "LN" in Microsoft Excel, OpenOffice Calc, or Google spreadsheets, sometimes called the *natural logarithm.*

The natural logarithm of a number x comes from the power of a number e, a mathematical constant that is approximately 2.718. If $x = e^y$, then y is the logarithm of x, expressed $y = \ln x$. There are other logarithms based on powers of other numbers, but we'll stick with e. Some people use log to mean ln, but that's a story for another time. In this class, including assignments and exams, we *always* use ln and LN, not log or LOG.

Suppose that you know that y is the logarithm of x. How do you find x? From the definition, apparently $x = e^y$. In Excel, this is written "exp(y)." As a check, you might verify that $\ln 6 = 1.792$ and $\exp(1.792) = 6.00$.

The most useful properties of logarithms are:

$$
\begin{aligned}
\ln(xy) &= \ln x + \ln y \\
\ln(x/y) &= \ln x - \ln y \\
\ln(x^a) &= a \ln x \\
\ln(\exp(x)) &= x \\
\exp(\ln x) &= x \\
\ln(1 + x) &\approx x, \quad \text{when } x \text{ is small.}
\end{aligned}
$$

The wiggly equals sign means "approximately equal to." That's true for the last equation when x is close enough to zero: a number like 0.1 rather than 0.9 or 1.2 or 10. In short, logarithms convert multiplication into addition, division into subtraction, and "exponentiation" into multiplication. In each case, an operation is converted into a simpler one: Addition, for example, is simpler than multiplication.

Example: Demand functions. A more useful demand function is $q = ap^b$, which is linear in logarithms:

$$
\ln q = \ln a + b \ln p.
$$

This follows from the first and third properties of logarithms. Here, b is the price elasticity of demand you may have learned about in a microeconomics class.

Example: Production functions. Understanding differences in output per worker (across production units, firms, countries) is a central question in macroeconomics and this course. Using the production function discussed above, we can use properties of exponents to arrive at an expression suitable for this analysis. Using the production function

$$Y = K^\alpha L^{1-\alpha},$$

use the first and last property of exponents to obtain

$$
\begin{aligned}
Y &= K^\alpha L L^{-\alpha} \\
  &= K^\alpha L (1/L^\alpha).
\end{aligned}
$$

Combining the terms with the α exponent and then using the second property of exponents, we have

$$Y = (K/L)^\alpha L.$$

Finally, dividing both sides by L leaves us with the expression

$$Y/L = (K/L)^\alpha.$$

In words, output per worker equals capital per worker to the exponent α.

1.3   Growth rates

Growth rates are frequently used in this class, in the business world, and in life in general. We will use two types — sorry, it can't be avoided. The first is a *discretely-compounded growth rate*. For a time interval of one year, this is analogous to an annually-compounded interest rate. The second is a *continuously-compounded growth rate*. This is analogous to a continuously-compounded interest rate, in which interest is compounded over a very short time interval. The former is more natural in some respects, but the latter leads to simpler expressions when compounding is important.

Discretely-compounded growth rates

The simplest growth rates are those that are compounded each period t at discrete time intervals. If the time period is a year (which will frequently be the case), then this corresponds with annual compounding. The annually compounded growth rate relates variable x across time periods as

$$x_{t+1} = (1 + g)x_t,$$

where lower case g will denote the discretely-compounded growth rate.

Notation note: We will always denote the discretely-compounded growth rate as g.

To compute this growth rate from data on x, one can use the formula

$$g = (x_{t+1}/x_t) - 1 = (x_{t+1} - x_t)/x_t.$$

If we want to express this growth rate as a percent, we multiply it by 100.

Example: The FRED database reports that annual US real Gross Domestic Product (GDP) (measured in 2009 dollars) in 2010 was 14,779.4 billion. For 2011, annual US real GDP was 15,052.4 billion. The annual (discrete compounded) growth rate of US real GDP between 2010 and 2011 was

$$g = \frac{15052.4}{14779.4} - 1 = 0.0185.$$

To express this growth rate as a percent, multiply 0.0185 by 100 to obtain 1.85 percent.

Multi-period growth. The formula above is for the growth rate from period t to $t + 1$. The formula for the average growth rate over many periods is a natural extension:

$$x_{t+n} = (1 + g)^n x_t,$$

which follows from repeatedly multiplying x by $(1 + g)$ and the first property of exponents discussed above. To calculate the average growth rate based upon data on x, one can use the formula

$$g = \left(\frac{x_{t+n}}{x_t}\right)^{1/n} - 1.$$

If we want to express this growth rate as a percent, we multiply it by 100.

Example: The FRED database reports that annual US real GDP (measured in 2009 dollars) in 2011 was 15,052.4 billion. Annual US real GDP in 1947 was 1,937.6 billion. The average annual growth rate of US real GDP between 1947 and 2011 was

$$g = \left(\frac{15052.4}{1937.6}\right)^{1/(2011-1947)} - 1 = 0.0326.$$

To express this growth rate as a percent, multiply 0.0326 by 100 to obtain 3.26 percent.

Note the difference in the average growth rate of 3.26 percent for the US over the post-WWII time period versus the recent annual growth rate of 1.85 percent in the previous example.

Continuously-compounded growth rates

For many purposes in this course, it will be easier to use continuously compounded growth rates. Mathematically, this device is simply an extension of the discrete growth rate discussed above when the time interval becomes infinitesimal. While this growth rate is difficult to conceptualize, it has very useful features, which we discuss below.

The continuously compounded growth rate relates variable x across time periods as

$$x_{t+1} = \exp(\gamma)x_t.$$

Notation note: We will always denote the continuously compounded growth rate as γ.

To compute this growth rate from data on x, one can use the formula

$$\gamma = \ln x_{t+1} - \ln x_t,$$

which follows from the properties of logarithms listed above. If we wish to express this growth rate as a percent, we multiply it by 100.

Example: We can compute the continuously-compounded growth rate using the same data described above. Recall that the FRED database reports that annual US real GDP (measured in 2009 dollars) in 2010 was 14,779.4 billion. For 2011, annual US real GDP was 15,052.4 billion. The continuously-compounded growth rate is

$$\gamma = \ln 15052.4 - \ln 14779.4 = 0.0183.$$

To express this growth rate as a percent, multiply 0.0183 by 100 to obtain 1.83 percent. Note the similarity of the continuously compounded growth rate and the annually compounded growth rate (1.85 percent). This similarity is not a coincidence, as we discuss below.

Continuous compounding has three useful features for measuring growth rates:

1. **Continuously-compounded growth rates approximate discretely-compounded growth rates.** In the example above, the continuously-compounded growth rate and the annually-compounded growth rate are very similar. The similarity reflects the final property of logarithms listed above. Specifically,

$$\ln(1 + a) \quad \approx \quad a \text{ when } a \text{ is small,}$$

where $\approx$ means "approximately equal to" and the value of a is small (less than 0.10 is a good rule of thumb). In words, the logarithm of one plus a is approximately equal to a, when a is small.

In the context of growth rates, take logarithms of both sides of the discrete compounded growth formula $[x_{t+1} = (1 + g)x_t]$ giving us

$$\ln x_{t+1} \quad = \quad \ln(1 + g) + \ln x_t,$$

which follows from the first property of logarithms. Rearranging and applying the approximation discussed above yields

$$\ln x_{t+1} - \ln x_t \quad = \quad \ln(1 + g) \approx g \text{ when } g \text{ is small.}$$

Notice that $\ln x_{t+1} - \ln x_t$ *is* the continuously compounded growth rate, γ. Putting this information together shows that when the growth rate is small, the discrete compounded growth rate g will be approximately the same as the continuously compounded growth rate γ.

2. **Continuously compounded growth rates are additive.** Suppose that you're interested in the growth rate of a product xy. For example, x might be the price deflator and y real output, so that xy is nominal output. Using our definition:

$$\gamma_{xy} \quad = \quad \ln\left(\frac{x_{t+1}y_{t+1}}{x_t y_t}\right) \quad = \quad \ln\left(\frac{x_{t+1}}{x_t}\right) + \ln\left(\frac{y_{t+1}}{y_t}\right) \quad = \quad \gamma_x + \gamma_y.$$

They add up! Thus, the growth rate of a product is the sum of the growth rates. Mathematically, this result follows from the first two properties of logarithms discussed above. In the same way, the growth rate of x/y equals the growth rate of x minus the growth rate of y.

This additive feature of continuously compounded growth rates is the primary reason we use continuous compounding.

3. **Averages of continuously compounded growth rates are easy to compute.** Suppose that we want to know the *average* growth rate of x over n periods:

$$\gamma \quad = \quad \frac{(\ln x_t - \ln x_{t-1}) + (\ln x_{t-1} - \ln x_{t-2}) + \cdots + (\ln x_{t-n+1} - \ln x_{t-n})}{n}.$$

This expression is the average of the one-period growth rates ($\ln x_t - \ln x_{t-1}$). Now, if you look at this expression for a minute, you might notice that most of the terms cancel each other out. The term $\ln x_{t-1}$, for example, shows up twice, once with a positive sign, once with a negative sign. If we eliminate the redundant terms, we find that the average growth rate is

$$\gamma \;=\; \frac{\ln x_t - \ln x_{t-n}}{n}.$$

In other words, the average growth rate over the full period is simply the n-period growth rate divided by the number of time periods n.

Example: We can compute the average continuously compounded growth rate for post-WWII GDP data. The average annual growth rate of US real GDP between 1947 and 2011 was

$$\gamma \;=\; \frac{\ln 15052.4 - \ln 1937.6}{2011 - 1947} \;=\; 0.0320.$$

In percent terms, the average annual growth rate for the US is 3.20 percent. Note, again, that because the growth rate is small, its value is similar to the discretely-compounded growth rate $g = 0.0326$ calculated in the previous example.

1.4   Slopes and derivatives

The slope of a function is a measure of how steep it is: the ratio of the change in y to the change in x. For a straight line, we can find the slope by choosing two points and computing the ratio of the change in y to the change in x. For some functions, though, the slope (meaning the slope of a straight line tangent to the function) is different at every point.

The *derivative* of a function $f(x)$ is a second function $f'(x)$ that gives us its slope at each point x if the function is continuous (no jumps) and smooth (no kinks). Formally, we say that the derivative is

$$\frac{\Delta y}{\Delta x} \;=\; \frac{f(x + \Delta x) - f(x)}{\Delta x}$$

for a "really small" Δx. (You can imagine doing this on a calculator or computer using a particular small number, and if the number is small enough your answer will be pretty close.) We express the derivative as $f'(x)$ or dy/dx and refer to it as "the derivative of y with respect to x." The d's are intended to be suggestive of small changes, analogous to Δ but with the understanding that we are talking about infinitesimal changes.

So the derivative is a function $f'(x)$ that gives us the slope of a function $f(x)$ at every possible value of x. What makes this useful is that there are some

Table 1.1: Rules for computing derivatives.

Function $f(x)$	Derivative $f'(x)$	Comments
Rules for Specific Functions		
a	0	a is a number
$ax + b$	a	a, b are numbers
ax^b	bax^{b-1}	a, b are numbers
ae^{bx}	bae^{bx}	a, b are numbers
$a \ln x$	a/x	a is a number
Rules for Combinations of Functions		
$g(x) + h(x)$	$g'(x) + h'(x)$	
$ag(x) + bh(x)$	$ag'(x) + bh'(x)$	a, b are numbers
$g(x)h(x)$	$g(x)h'(x) + g'(x)h(x)$	
$g(x)/h(x)$	$[g'(x)h(x) - g(x)h'(x)]/[h(x)]^2$	$h(x) \neq 0$
$g[h(x)]$	$g'[h(x)]h'(x)$	"chain rule"

relatively simple mechanical rules for finding the derivative f' of common functions f (see Table 1.1).

Example: Marginal cost. Suppose that total cost c is related to the quantity produced q by

$$c = 100 + 10q + 2q^2.$$

Marginal cost is the derivative of c with respect to q. How does it vary with q? The derivative of c with respect to q is

$$dc/dq = 10 + 4q,$$

so marginal cost increases with q.

Example: Bond duration. Fixed-income analysts know that prices of bonds with long maturities are more sensitive than those with short maturities to changes in their yields. They quantify sensitivity with duration D, defined as

$$D = -\frac{d \ln p}{dy}.$$

In words, duration is the ratio of the percent decline in price (the change in the log) over the increase in yield for a small increase. Two versions follow from different compounding conventions. With annual compounding, the price of an m-year zero-coupon bond is related to the yield by $p = 100/(1 + y)^m$. Therefore,

$$\ln p = \ln 100 - m \ln(1 + y),$$

and duration is $D = m/(1 + y)$. With continuous compounding, $p = 100 \exp(-my)$, $\ln p = \ln 100 - my$, and $D = m$. In both cases, it's clear that duration is higher for long-maturity bonds (those with large m).

Example: Marginal product of capital. Suppose that output Y is related to inputs of capital K and labor L by

$$Y = K^\alpha L^{1-\alpha}$$

for α between zero and one. If we increase K holding L fixed, what happens to output? We call the changes in output resulting from small increases in K the marginal product of capital. We compute it as the derivative of Y with respect to K holding L constant. Since we're holding L constant, we call this a *partial derivative* and write it:

$$\frac{\partial Y}{\partial K} = \alpha K^{\alpha-1} L^{1-\alpha} = \alpha \left(\frac{K}{L}\right)^{\alpha-1}.$$

Despite the change in notation, we find the derivative in the usual way, treating L like any other constant.

1.5   Finding the maximum of a function

An important use of derivatives is to find the maximum (or minimum) of a function. Suppose that we'd like to know the value of x that leads to the highest value of a function $f(x)$, for values of x between two numbers a and b. We can find the answer by setting the derivative $f'(x)$ equal to zero and solving for x. Why does this work? Because a function is "flat" (has zero slope) at a maximum. (That's true, anyway, as long as the function has no jumps or kinks in it.) We simply put this insight to work.

Fine points. Does this always work? If we set the derivative equal to zero, do we always get a maximum? The answer is no. Here are some of the things that could go wrong: (i) The point could be a minimum, rather than a maximum. (ii) The maximum could be at one of the endpoints, a or b. There's no way to tell without comparing your answer to $f(a)$ and $f(b)$. (iii) There may be more than one "local maximum" (picture a wavy line). (iv) The slope might be zero without being either a maximum or a minimum: for example, the function might increase for a while, flatten out (with slope of zero), then start increasing again. An example is the function $f(x) = x^3$ at the point $x = 0$. [You might draw functions for each of these problems to illustrate how they work.] If you want to be extra careful, there are ways to check for each of these problems. One is the second-order condition: A point is a maximum if the second derivative (the derivative of $f'(x)$) is negative.

While all of these things can happen, in principle, we will make sure they do not happen in this class.

Example: Maximizing profit. Here's an example from microeconomics. Suppose that a firm faces a demand for its product of $q = 10 - 2p$ (q and p being quantity and price, respectively). The cost of production is 2 per unit. What is the firm's profit function? What level of output produces the greatest profit?

Answer. Profit is revenue (pq) minus cost ($2q$). The trick (and this isn't calculus) is to express it in terms of quantity. We need to use the demand curve to eliminate price from the expression for revenue: $p = (10 - q)/2$ so $pq = [(10 - q)/2]q$. Profit (expressed as a function of q) is, therefore,

$$\text{Profit}(q) = [(10 - q)/2]q - 2q = 5q - q^2/2 - 2q.$$

To find the quantity associated with maximum profit, we set the derivative equal to zero:

$$\frac{d\text{Profit}}{dq} = 3 - q = 0,$$

so $q = 3$. What's the price? Look at the demand curve: If $q = 3$, then p satisfies $3 = 10 - 2p$ and $p = 7/2$.

Example: Demand for labor. A firm produces output Y with labor L and a fixed amount of capital K, determined by past investment decisions, subject to the production function $Y = K^\alpha L^{1-\alpha}$. If each unit of output is worth p dollars and each unit of labor costs w dollars, then profit is

$$\text{Profit} = pK^\alpha L^{1-\alpha} - wL.$$

The optimal choice of L is the value that sets the derivative equal to zero:

$$\frac{\partial \text{Profit}}{\partial L} = p(1 - \alpha)(K/L)^\alpha - w = 0.$$

(We use a partial derivative here, denoted by ∂, to remind ourselves that K is being held constant.) The condition implies that

$$L = K \left[\frac{p(1 - \alpha)}{w} \right]^{1/\alpha}.$$

You can think of this as the demand for labor: Given values of K, p, and w, it tells us how much labor the firm would like to hire. As you might expect, at higher wages w, labor demand L is lower.

1.6   Spreadsheets

Spreadsheets are the software of choice in many environments. If you're not familiar with the basics, here's a short overview. The structure is similar in Microsoft Excel, OpenOffice Calc, and Google documents.

The first step is to make sure that you have access to one of these programs. If you have one of them on your computer, you're all set. If not, you can download OpenOffice at www.openoffice.org or open a Google spreadsheet at docs.google.com. Both are free.

In each of these programs, data (numbers and words) are stored in tables with the rows labeled with numbers and the columns labeled with letters. Here's an example:

	A	B	C
1	x1	x2	
2	3	25	
3	8	13	
4	5	21	
5			

The idea is that we have two (short) columns of data, with variable x1 in column A and variable x2 in column B.

Here are some things we might want to do with these data, and how to do it:

- Basic operations. Suppose that you want to compute the natural logarithm of element B2 and store it in C2. Then, in C2 you would type: =LN(B2). (Don't type the period, it's part of the punctuation of the sentence.) The answer should appear almost immediately. If you want to add the second observation (row 3) of x1 and x2 and put in C3, then in C3 you type: =A3+B3. We have expressed functions (LN) and addresses (A3) with upper-case letters, but lower-case letters would do the same thing.

- Statistics. Suppose that you want to compute the sample mean and standard deviation of x1 and place them at the bottom of column A. Then, in A5 type: =AVERAGE(A2:A4). That takes the numbers in column A from A2 to A4 and computes the sample mean or average. The standard deviation is similar: in A6 you type =STDEV(A2:A4). Finally, to compute the correlation between x1 and x2, you type (in any cell you like): =CORREL(A2:A4,B2:B4).

If you're not sure what these functions refer to, see the links to the Khan Academy videos at the end of this chapter.

1.7   Getting data from FRED

We will use data extensively in this course. One extraordinarily useful source
— for this course and beyond — is FRED,

http://research.stlouisfed.org/fred2/,

an online economic database supported by the Federal Reserve Bank of St.
Louis. It's one of the best free tools you'll ever run across. All of the series
used in this book are listed in what FRED calls a Published Data List:

http://research.stlouisfed.org/pdl/649,

Names of relevant variables are listed at the end of every chapter.

FRED allows you to graph data, transform it (compute growth rates, for
example), and download it into a spreadsheet. They also have an Excel "add-
in" that allows you to download data directly into an Excel spreadsheet.
FRED mobile apps allow you to graph data on your phone or tablet.

To get started using FRED, go to the main FRED page and graph US
real GDP (You'll know what that is shortly.) Click on "Category," then
"National Accounts," then "National Income and Product Accounts," then
"GDP/GNP," and finally "Real Gross Domestic Product" (also known as
GDPC1). The graph of GDPC1 will then appear with quarterly data be-
ginning in 1947:Q1. Notice that recessions are shaded on the graph. Once
you know the variable code — namely, GDPC1 — you can enter it in the
FRED search box on the main page and do this in one step.

If you return to the Category page, you'll see the wide variety of data that
FRED makes available. Try exploring some of these categories to familiarize yourself with popular data series. Each data series has a name (e.g.,
GDPC1 for US real GDP). As an exercise, find and graph the consumer
price index (CPIAUCSL), total nonfarm payroll employees (PAYEMS), and
the monthly US/Euro foreign exchange rate (EXUSEU). If you find the categories confusing, simply type what you're looking for into the search box
on the upper right: "real GDP," "consumer price index," and so on.

We have posted a series of FRED tutorials on the NYUSternGE YouTube
channel. In addition to FRED basics, they explain how to format and
download graphs for course assignments that use FRED. In addition, the
St. Louis Fed offers a series of tutorials that show how to make and alter
FRED graphs. You can change the graph type, add data series, change
the observation period or frequency, and transform the data (e.g., percent

change, percent change from a year ago, percent change at an annual rate). You can also alter the graph characteristics (e.g., size, background, color, font, and line style).

Review questions

If you're not sure you followed all this, give these a try:

1. Growth rates. Per capita income in China was 439 in 1950, 874 in 1975, and 3425 in 2000, measured in 1990 US dollars. What were the annual growth rates in the two subperiods?

    Answer. The average continuously compounded growth rates were 2.75 percent and 5.46 percent. The discrete (annually compounded) growth rates are 2.79 percent and 5.62 percent, so there's not much difference between them.

2. Derivatives. Find the derivative of each of these functions:

    (a) $2x + 27$ [2]
    (b) $2x^2 + 3x + 27$ [$4x + 3$]
    (c) $2x^2 + 3x - 14$ [$4x + 3$]
    (d) $(x - 2)(2x + 7)$ [$4x + 3$]
    (e) $\ln(2x^2 + 3x - 14)$ [$(4x + 3))/(2x^2 + 3x - 14)$]
    (f) $3x^8 + 13$ [$24x^7$]
    (g) $3x^{2/3}$ [$2x^{-1/3} = 2/x^{1/3}$]
    (h) $2e^{5x}$ [$10e^{5x}$]

    Answers in brackets [ ].

3. Capital and output. Suppose output Y is related to the amount of capital K used by

    $$Y = 27K^{1/3}.$$

    Compute the marginal product of capital (the derivative of Y with respect to K) and describe how it varies with K.

    Answer. The marginal product of capital is MPK $= 9K^{-2/3} = 9/K^{2/3}$, is positive, and falls as we increase K. We call this *diminishing returns*: The more capital we add, the less it increases output.

4. Find the maximum. Find the value of x that maximizes each of these functions:

    (a) $2x - x^2$ [$f'(x) = 2 - 2x = 0$, $x = 1$]
    (b) $2\ln x - x$ [$f'(x) = 2/x - 1 = 0$, $x = 2$]

(c) $-5x^2 + 2x + 11$ $[f'(x) = -10x + 2 = 0, x = 1/5]$

Answers in brackets [ ].

5. Spreadsheet practice. You have the following data: 4, 6, 3, 4, 5, 8, 5, 3, 6. What is the mean? The standard deviation? (Use a spreadsheet program to do the calculations.)

Answer. 4.889, 1.616.

6. FRED practice. Use the FRED website to construct the following graphs:

(a) Civilian unemployment rate (UNRATE) from January 1971 through July 2012.

(b) Percent change from a year ago of personal consumption expenditures price index (PCEPI) from January 1960 to the present. What is the most recent data point?

(c) US Gross Private Domestic Investment (GPDI) as a share of GDP (GDP) from 1960Q1 to the present. What is the most recent data point?

(d) Based on these graphs, how are recessions reflected in these three series?

Helpful hints: Usually you will be asked to find the data yourself, so you should familiarize yourself with the various categories of data on FRED. For this exercise, you can find the data by typing the series name (e.g., PCEPI) into the search box on the FRED website. Doing so will produce a simple graph of the entire series. Set the date range using the start and end boxes above the graph. To alter the graph settings, click "Graph Settings." The dropdown box provides options to change the graph type, font, font size, and other aspects of the graph. Or, you can click "Edit Data Series 1" to alter the line style, line width, mark type/width, color, frequency, and units. For example, to graph the percentage change from a year ago, change the "Units."

To graph the ratio of two series, graph the first series and click "Add Data Series" and choose "Modify Existing Series." Search for the second series, and click "Add Series." Under "Edit Data Series 1," click "Create your own data transformation," then type "a/b" in the formula box and click "Apply."

If you're looking for more

If these notes seem mysterious to you, we recommend the Khan Academy. They have wonderful short videos on similar topics, including logarithms (look for "Proof: ln a ..."), calculus (look for "Calculus: Derivatives ..."), and statistics (start at the top). For spreadsheets, the Google doc tutorial is quite good.

Symbols and data used in this chapter

Table 1.2: Symbol table.

Symbol	Definition
Y	Output
K	Stock of physical capital
L	Quantity of labor
g	Discrete compounded growth rate
γ	Continuously compounded growth rate
ln	Natural logarithm (inverse operation of exp)
exp	Exponential function (inverse operation of ln)
$f(x)$	Function of x
Δx	Infinitesimal change of x
$f'(x)$	Derivative of $f(x)$
dy/dx	Derivative of $f(x)$
$\partial F(x,y)/\partial x$	Partial derivative of $F(x,y)$ with respect to x

Table 1.3: Data table.

Variable	Source
Real GDP	GDPC1
consumer price index	CPIAUCSL
Nonfarm employment	PAYEMS
US$/Euro exchange rate	EXUSEU
Unemployment rate	UNRATE
Personal consumption expenditures price index	PCEPI
Gross private domestic investment	GPDI
Nominal GDP	GDP

To retrieve the data online, add the identifier from the source column to
http://research.stlouisfed.org/fred2/series/. For example, to retrieve
real GDP, point your browser to http://research.stlouisfed.org/fred2/
series/GDPC1

2
Macroeconomic Data

Tools: GDP; accounting identities; price and quantity indexes.

Key Words: GDP; value added; real; nominal; index; deflator.

Big Ideas:

- GDP is three things at once: production (value added by production units), income (payments to labor and capital), and expenditure (consumption, investment, government spending, net exports).

- Current price variables (such as nominal GDP) can be decomposed into measures of price and quantity. There are several ways to do this, but none of them are perfect.

Gross Domestic Product (GDP) is our primary measure of macroeconomic performance: the total value of output produced in a particular economy over some period of time (typically a year or a quarter). Countries with high GDP per person are said to be rich, and those in which GDP has gone down are said to be in recessions. But what is GDP and how is it measured? We review its definition and construction below. Along the way, we also note connections among output, income, and expenditures, and explain how we separate changes in quantities from changes in prices.

The system that produces GDP and related numbers is known as the National Income and Product Accounts (NIPA). The national accounts are analogous to financial statements: They give us a picture of an economy, just as financial statements give us pictures of firms. Similar methods are used in most countries, so the numbers are (in principle) comparable.

2.1 Measuring GDP

GDP is the total value of goods and services produced in a given region, typically a country. In the US, for example, GDP was 15,533.8 billion US dollars in 2011: 15.5 trillion dollars. With a population of 312 million (average for the year), that amounts to nearly $50,000 per person. But where does this number come from? What does it mean?

The standard approach to measuring GDP is to add up the value produced by every firm or production unit in the economy. The question is how we separate value produced by one firm from value produced by another in an economy in which the value chain typically involves many firms. Walmart, for example, has enormous sales, but most of the value is already built into products by suppliers. As a concrete example, consider a fictional firm that assembles PCs from parts made by someone else. Its only other expense is labor. Let's say that the firm's income statement looks like Table 2.1.

The question is how we measure this firm's contribution to output. The straightforward answer is 40m, the total value of its sales. But if we think about this a minute, we realize that 6m of this was produced somewhere else, so it shouldn't be counted as part of the firm's output. A better answer is 34m, the value the firm has added to the parts. That, in fact, is the accepted answer: We base GDP on *value added* , not on sales. To get GDP for the whole economy, we sum the value added of every production unit.

Another way to compute value added is to sum payments to labor and capital. In this case, we add 20m paid to workers (labor) to 14m net income paid to owners of the firm (capital). That gives us total payments of 34m, the same number we found above using a different method. Since this approach is based on the income received by labor and capital, we see that the value of production and income are the same. More on this in the next section.

Usually, when we compare the GDPs of two countries, we presume that the country with the larger GDP produces more in some useful sense. But

Table 2.1: PC assembler's simple income statement.

Sales revenue	40,000,000
Expenses	26,000,000
Wages	20,000,000
Cost of goods sold (parts)	6,000,000
Net Income	14,000,000

suppose that they produce different goods: Country A produces 10 billion apples and country B produces 10 billion bananas. Which produces more? We generally assume that if apples are worth more than bananas, then country A produces more. The idea is that market prices tell us which goods are more valuable, apples or bananas. The same idea underlies our measurement of value added.

To make this concrete, suppose the 40m sales of our fictitious company consists of 20,000 PCs at $2,000 each. Our presumption is that the market price of $2,000 reflects economic value, and we use it as part of our calculation of GDP. In some cases, this isn't so obvious. In, say, North Korea, prices do not generally reflect market forces, so it's not clear how we would calculate economic value. There are also some subtle issues in market economies about how to value non-market activities, such as washing your own clothes, and "bads," such as pollution. Typically, neither is valued in the national accounts. We don't claim this is right, but it's what we do.

Example (salmon value chain). A fisherman catches a salmon and sells it to a smokehouse for $5. After smoking it, the smokehouse sells it to Fairway for $10, which, in turn, sells it to a restaurant for $15. The same restaurant buys lettuce from a farmer at Union Square for $3. The restaurant puts the lettuce and salmon together on a plate and sells it to an NYU student for $25. How much does each production unit contribute to GDP? What is the overall contribution to GDP?

Answer. The contributions (value added) are $5 each for the fisherman, smokehouse, and Fairway, $3 for the farmer, and $7 for the restaurant, for a total of $25.

Note that we could have computed GDP by counting only the value of the final good in the value chain. This is true in general: GDP can be computed as the total value of final goods produced in the economy. Intermediate products (salmon, lettuce, PC parts) must then be ignored, as their value shows up at the end of the value chain.

We'll finish this section with two subtle issues. One is the treatment of government services. We generally treat government as a producer of value added and measure its output at cost. If we pay the mayor $100,000, that's counted as $100,000 of value added whether she does a good job or not. The other is that capital expenditures are not treated as intermediate inputs. Basically, we ignore them when we compute the value added of a firm. Why? Because the expense is balanced by an equal addition to the firm's value. With firms, financial statements do something similar: We spread the expense out over time in the form of depreciation. Here, we measure

Table 2.2: PC assembler's complicated income statement.

Sales revenue	40,000,000
Expenses	32,000,000
Wages	20,000,000
Cost of goods sold	6,000,000
Interest	2,000,000
Depreciation	4,000,000
Net income	8,000,000

output gross of depreciation, so we ignore capital expenditures altogether as expense. It sounds a little strange, but that's what the national income and product accounts do.

2.2   Identities

Since every transaction has both a buyer and a seller, we can often approach any measurement problem from (at least) two directions. This gives rise to *identities*: relations that hold as a matter of accounting truth. They do not depend on any particular economic theory and, for that reason, are extremely useful.

Income (Gross Domestic Product = Gross Domestic Income). We've seen the first identity already: output and income are equal. Let's go back to our PC assembler to see this in action, adding a few things to make the example more realistic. In Table 2.2 we add two new expenses, interest and depreciation. These categories are counted as capital income. In the previous section, we computed (its contribution to) GDP as value added of 34m. Here, we compute GDI (I for Income) from payments to labor (20m) and capital (14m). Capital payments include the net income paid to owners of the firm, interest income paid to the debt holders, and depreciation. Adding labor income and capital income, we arrive at GDI of 34m. The answer, of course, is the same.

Since we include depreciation in our measures of output and income, we refer to them as *gross* — gross of depreciation. In principle, we could compute Net Domestic Product by subtracting depreciation, but most people stick with GDP because economic depreciation (as opposed to what shows up on financial statements and tax returns) is difficult to measure.

The national income and product accounts do this at the aggregate level: namely, measure output by adding up payments to inputs. By construction, then, output and income are the same. To give you a sense of what real numbers look like, we report the income for the US economy in Table 2.3. The statistical discrepancy is a reminder that the measurement system isn't perfect.

Table 2.3: Income components of US GDP.

Compensation of employees	9,704.1
Proprietor's income	1,376.8
Corporate profits	1,702.3
Rental income	659.6
Net interest income	693.2
Taxes and miscellaneous	1,323.6
Depreciation	2,830.8
Gross domestic product	18,290.3
Statistical discrepancy	-253.7

The numbers are for 2015, billions of US dollars, from the BEA's NIPA Table 1.10.

Expenditures (Gross Domestic Product = Gross Domestic Expenditure). Our second identity comes from the perspective of expenditures on final goods—the last stage in the value chain. We distinguish both who buys them (consumers, firms, governments, or foreigners) and whether they are consumption or investment. The most common decomposition of this sort is: GDP equals consumer expenditures C by households plus business and residential investment I plus government purchases of goods and services G plus net exports NX; in more compact notation,

$$Y \;=\; C + I + G + NX. \tag{2.1}$$

We refer to this as the *expenditure identity*. On the left, Y is the letter we use for GDP. (It's not clear where the letter Y comes from, but we follow a long tradition in using it this way.) On the right are the expenditure components of GDP. The point is that the two are equal: Everything that's produced is sold — to someone. (And if it's not sold, we call it an addition to inventories and include it in I. The idea is that firms produce the output and sell it to themselves.)

We refer to C as (personal or household) consumption. Investment (I) is accumulation of capital by firms and households: for example, construction of new buildings or houses, purchase of new machines. Investment also includes, as noted, additions to the stock of inventories, a category that is small, on average, but highly variable.

Government purchases G consist of spending on goods and services (mainly wages) for both consumption and investment purposes. They do not include government outlays for social security, unemployment insurance, or medical care. We think of them, instead, as transfers since no goods or services are involved. It also omits interest payments on government debt, which we track separately. Net exports (*NX*) are exports minus imports: the trade balance, in other words.

Some recent numbers for the US are reported in Table 2.4.

Table 2.4: Expenditure components of US GDP.

	$ billions	$ billions	Percent of GDP
Consumption	12,283.7		68.1%
Durable goods		1,355.2	
Nondurable goods		2,656.9	
Services		8,271.6	
Gross private investment	3,056.6		16.9%
Nonresidential		2,311.3	
Residential		651.9	
Change in inventories		93.4	
Government	3,218.3		17.8%
Net exports of goods and services	−522.0		−2.9%
Exports		2,264.3	
Imports		2,786.3	
Gross domestic product	18,036.6		100.0%

The numbers are for 2015, from the BEA's NIPA Table 1.1.5.

Example (salmon value chain, continued). Suppose, in our example, that the salmon is imported from Norway. Then you'd think — and you'd be right — that it shouldn't count as US GDP. How does that work?

On the income side of the accounts, the contributions to GDP are the same as before: the contributions are $5 each for the fisherman, smokehouse, and Fairway, $3 for the farmer, and $7 for the restaurant, for a total of $25. But when the salmon is imported, $5 is attributed to Norway's GDP and only $20 to US GDP.

What if we looked at this from the perspective of expenditures on final goods? The final sale ($25) is the same as before, but the imported salmon is now subtracted to give us a contribution to GDP of $20. Why subtracted? We need to subtract imports from GDP, because purchases of imported goods do not reflect local production. That's what net exports does in the expenditure identity: it's a correction for the difference between domestic production and domestic expenditures.

Flows of funds.   The expenditure identity follows the goods, but you can also follow the "money" (the financial funds) that goes along with the goods. For households, you might think about how income compares to consumption. If it's higher, we call what's left saving, which is a source of funds that can be used by others. We might also think about how firms finance investment in new plant and equipment. They might, for example, raise funds in capital markets from households.

Let's be specific. We'll look at two similar relations, both based on the expenditure identity. One is

$$S \;=\; Y - C - G \;=\; I + NX, \tag{2.2}$$

where S is (gross domestic) saving.   This is a consolidated measure of saving in which we subtract both household and government expenditures from income. It's also a gross measure since income (GDP) includes depreciation. Investment is also gross, so the two sides of the relation balance. The other relation separates household and government activities:

$$S_p + S_g \;\equiv\; (Y - T - C) + (T - G) \;=\; I + NX,$$

where T is taxes collected by the government net of transfer payments and interest, $S_p = Y - T - C$ is (gross) private saving; and $S_g = T - G$ is government "saving" (the negative of the government deficit). Clearly, S_p and S_g are two components of national saving S. Most countries report a further breakdown of saving by households, governments, and firms, but this will be enough for us.

We refer to both versions as *flow of funds identities*. What do they tell us? Roughly speaking, the left side is a source of funds and the right a use of funds, and sources and uses balance. In the first version, saving is a source of funds that can be used to purchase domestic securities (which finance new domestic investment) or foreign securities (which finance a trade deficit by the rest of the world if NX is positive). If net exports are negative, it's the reverse, of course: We sell securities to the rest of the world, which is then a source of funds. In the second version, household saving can also be used to purchase government securities (if government saving is negative).

Example (PC assembler, continued). Suppose that 10m of the 40m in sales are sold abroad. If this is the only firm in the economy, what are Y, NX, C, and S? Assume that investment and the government deficit are zero.

Answer. GDP remains 34m: production hasn't changed. Net exports equal exports (10m) minus imports (6m) or 4m. With no investment or government deficit, the 30m of local sales must be consumption. Saving is, therefore, 4m = 34m – 30m (income minus consumption). The flow-of-funds identity then tells us that saving of 4m is used to purchase 4m in foreign securities. Stated differently, the rest of the world (everyone but us) must have a trade deficit of 4m, which they finance by borrowing from us (the saving we mentioned).

2.3   Distinguishing prices from quantities

You'll see various versions of the terms *real* and *nominal* GDP. Nominal GDP measures output in dollars (or local currency units), and real GDP measures the quantity of output once overall changes in prices have been (somehow) taken out.

A *price index* or *deflator* is a measure of the overall level of prices — what we call the *price level*. If the price level rises over time, we say that the economy experiences inflation; if the price level decreases, the economy experiences deflation.

The question for this section is how we separate changes in quantities (real GDP growth) from changes in prices (inflation). The former is good (we have more stuff), but the latter is bad (prices are going up), so it makes some difference to us which we have. Like sales, GDP and related objects are values: products of price and quantity. You might well ask: How much of a change in value is a change in quantity, and how much a change in price? With one product, the answer is easy. With more than one, you need to average the prices or quantities somehow, and (sad to say) there's no obvious best way to do this. There are, instead, many ways to do it, and they give us different answers. We'll charge ahead anyway, but it's something to keep in mind.

One difficulty in separating prices and quantities is that prices of specific products change in different ways, and it's not clear how to average them to get a measure of "overall" prices. Two sensible approaches, known as fixed-basket and fixed-weight, respectively, give different answers. In practice, this isn't a huge problem (the answers usually aren't much different), but it adds another element of fuzziness to macroeconomic data. The issue is that the economy has many goods and services whose prices and quantities change by different amounts over time. If all prices rose by ten percent between last year and this year, we would say that inflation is ten percent and divide this year's nominal output by 1.10 to get real output. But when prices of different products change by different amounts, things aren't that easy.

The consumer price index (CPI) is based on a fixed-basket approach which measures the change in the price level as the change in the total cost of a given basket of products (two quarts of milk, one hamburger, five news-papers, etc). The difficulty here is that people change what they consume over time, partly in response to price changes and partly because tastes and products change. Should we use last year's typical basket or this year's? The GDP deflator is based on a fixed-weight approach, and is constructed in two steps. We first compute a measure of real GDP by evaluating (typically different) expenditure quantities at constant prices. The price deflator is then the ratio of nominal to real GDP. The difficulty is, again, that prices change over time. So, should we use last year's prices or this year's?

Fixed-basket approach. The CPI indicates the change in the total cost of a basket of goods and services that is representative of a typical household's spending habits at a given date. Such a basket might include, say, five gallons of gasoline, one haircut, two pounds of chicken, three bottles of soda, and so on. Government statistical agencies do this by sending people to stores to check the prices of all the products in the basket. The CPI is the cost of the whole basket, normalized to equal 100 at some date. It's the same idea, really, as the Dow Jones Industrial Average or the S&P 500. Producer price indexes apply a similar methodology to goods purchased by firms. An example shows how the fixed-basket approach works.

Example (fish and chips). Consider an economy with two goods, fish and chips. At date 1, we produce 10 fish and 10 chips. Fish sell for 25 cents and chips for 50 cents. At date 2, the prices of fish and chips have risen to 50 cents and 75 cents, respectively. The quantities have changed to 8 and 12. We summarize the data in Table 2.5.

Table 2.5: Price and quantity data.

Date	Chips Price	Chips Quantity	Fish Price	Fish Quantity
1	0.5	10	0.25	10
2	0.75	12	0.50	8

Note that the two prices have not gone up by the same amount: the price of fish has doubled, while chip prices have gone up by only 50 percent. Another way to say the same thing is that the relative price of chips to fish has fallen from 2 ($= .50/.25$) to 1.5 ($= .75/.50$). What is the inflation rate?

Answer. We construct the CPI using date 1 quantities. The index is shown in Table 2.6.

Table 2.6: consumer price index computation.

Date	CPI
1	$7.50 = .50 \times 10 + .25 \times 10$
2	$12.50 = .75 \times 10 + .50 \times 10$

The inflation rate by this measure is $\pi = 12.50/7.50 - 1 = 0.667 = 66.7\%)$. Since nominal GDP growth is 73.3 percent, real GDP growth is 4 percent:

$$g_Y = \frac{1 + g_{PY}}{1 + \pi} - 1 = \frac{1 + 0.733}{1 + 0.666} - 1 = 0.04.$$

By convention, the CPI in the base year (year 1 in this case) is normalized to 100. Normalizing is straightforward: Just divide all the values of the CPI by its value in the base year and multiply by 100. In our example, the index is 100 in year 1 and 166.7 in year 2.

Fixed-weight approach.   Price deflators are typically computed from the ratio of GDP (or one of its other expenditure components) at current- and base-year prices (these are called nominal and real GDP.) Over several periods, this fixed-weight approach applies a constant set of prices to changing quantities. As before, this is easiest to see in an example.

Example (fish and chips, continued).   We compute GDP at current prices and date 1 prices in Table 2.7. The GDP deflator (the ratio of nominal to real GDP) is 1.0 in year 1. This is trivial, as nominal and real GDP must coincide in the base year. In year 2, the deflator is $1.625 = 13/8$, implying an inflation rate of 62.5 percent. Note the difference from the inflation rate computed with the CPI. In short, different approaches lead to

Table 2.7: Nominal and real GDP computation.

Date	Nominal GDP (current prices)	Real GDP (date 1 prices)
1	$7.50 (= .50 \times 10 + .25 \times 10)$	$7.50 (= .50 \times 10 + .25 \times 10)$
2	$13.00 (= .75 \times 12 + .50 \times 8)$	$8.00 (= .50 \times 12 + .25 \times 8)$

different measures of inflation. The conceptual difficulty with both methods is that it's not clear how to measure the price level when relative prices are changing. What can we do? We content ourselves with the knowledge that the differences are typically small and remind ourselves that macroeconomic measurement (like financial accounting) is as much art as science.

2.4   Fine points

Some other issues you may run across:

Causality. You might be tempted to interpret identities as saying that one side of an identity causes the other. Don't be. For example, you might hear someone say that low consumption is causing low output ("We need consumers to spend more."). However, the identity says only that if output goes down, then so must one or more of its components. No causality is implied. We could as easily say that consumption falls because output did. The point is not that there is no causal connection, but that no such connection is built into the identity.

Underground economy. Standard GDP figures do not include the value of goods and services produced by the so-called "underground" economy. This term generally refers to businesses that are not licensed to operate, such as sellers of counterfeit CDs in the streets of Bangkok, and businesses evading either income or social security taxes, such as Southern Spain's farms employing illegal immigrants as day laborers. Such activity is generally not reported and, therefore, does not show up in official statistics. In advanced economies such as the US and Japan, the size of the underground economy is thought to be small. But in developing countries, such as Peru and Lebanon, it has been estimated to be as large as 50 percent of official estimates of GDP.

Capital gains. We've seen that GDP reflects income, but there are kinds of income that are not included in GDP. The prime example is capital gains. They are part of your income, but do not show up in GDP because they do not reflect (at least not directly) the production and sale of current output. And since they're not in GDP, they're not in saving either. One curious result is that net worth can rise even when saving is zero. In the US, capital gains are a larger fraction of changes in net worth than saving. For similar reasons, GDP does not include interest on government debt. Why? Because it isn't a payment made for producing goods and services.

GDP v. GNP. While GDP measures output produced within the borders of a given country, Gross National Product (GNP) measures output produced by inputs owned by the residents of that country. For example, to compute Bangladesh's GNP, we need to add to GDP the income paid to Bangladeshi capital invested abroad and subtract income paid to capital installed in Bangladesh but owned by citizens of other countries. Similarly, with labor, we need to add the wages earned abroad by Bangladeshi people and subtract the wages earned in Bangladesh by foreign nationals. Thus, GNP is a measure of the income received by "locally-owned" labor and capital. In most countries, the differences between GDP and GNP are small.

One exception is Ireland, where a large amount of foreign capital makes GNP significantly smaller than GDP (by about 20 percent last time we looked).

Net exports vs. current account. You may hear people refer to the US "current account" deficit. What are they talking about? The current account (we'll label this *CA* later in the course) is net exports (the trade balance) plus net receipts of foreign capital and labor income plus miscellaneous transfers from abroad. In the US, there's usually little difference, but Ireland is a different story. We'll generally use the terms current account, net exports, and trade balance as synonyms. Current account sounds a little cooler; you can use it to make people think you're an expert.

Chain weighting. The US — and many other countries, too — now uses a method that's somewhere between fixed-weight and fixed-basket methods: chain-weighting. It mitigates some of the problems of applying the same prices over long periods of time (when relative prices often change dramatically), but doesn't eliminate them. If we told you exactly what it is, your eyes would glaze over. But trust us, it's an improvement.

Prices and quality change. Many people feel that price indexes do not adequately account for increases in product quality. As a result, price increases are (slightly) overstated, and quantity increases are understated. Separating prices from quantities is particularly difficult with services because the quantity produced is inherently difficult to measure. (It sounds like the start of a joke: How can you tell when a lawyer is more productive?) Our best guess is that this adds less than 1 percent to the inflation rate: that is, inflation is probably 0.5 percent to 1 percent lower than reported. Not a lot, but it adds up over time.

Expenditure deflating. In most countries, real GDP is computed by applying price deflators to final goods, typically using the expenditure components. This isn't real GDP; it's real GDE (gross national *expenditure*). The two are often similar, but need not be if production is largely exported. As an extreme example, Saudi Arabia produces oil for export. If we adjust GDP for changes in prices of Saudi purchases (food, shelter, imported cars, and electronic equipment), then an increase in the price of oil can lead to an increase in real GDP, even if the quantity of oil produced hasn't changed. An alternative is to adjust production quantities directly for price changes, which some countries do.

PPP-adjusted data. When we compare output across countries, people have noticed that if (say) the euro increases in value relative to the dollar, then it appears that Europeans have become richer than Americans. We say "appears" because we haven't taken into account that dollar prices of non-tradable goods, such as, haircuts and car-washes, are typically higher in Europe when the euro is strong. In other words, this is a change in prices, not quantities. A similar issue arises when comparing GDPs of a rich country such as Germany, and a developing country, such as Botswana. If we use local prices and simply convert them to dollars or euros at the spot exchange rate, Botswana will look poorer than it actually is because local prices of many basic goods are much lower in Botswana. The state-of-the-art way to address this issue is to apply the same prices to output in both locations to produce real GDP based on "purchasing power parity" (PPP). The logic is the same as with the GDP deflator, but the comparison is across countries rather than across time.

Seasonal adjustment.   Quarterly or monthly data often exhibit systematic variations by season. Quarterly GDP, for example, typically has a sharp increase in the fourth quarter (holidays). Most macroeconomic data have been smoothed to eliminate this seasonal variation. The same thing happens with business data: Analysts often report changes relative to the same period the year before, which will help eliminate any seasonal effect.

Revisions. NIPA data are revised frequently and significantly. In the US, the "advance estimate" of real GDP is released in the first month following each quarter (month t, say). The fourth quarter estimate, for example, is released in late January. This estimate is revised in each of the next two months (months $t + 1$ and $t + 2$) as additional data becomes available. Subsequent revisions occur annually, as more new data (such as tax revenues) appears and as seasonal factors are updated. In addition, roughly every five years, a benchmark revision updates the base year for calculating real GDP. The current base year of 2009 was established in the July 2013 benchmark revision. Benchmark revisions also typically include technical improvements in the measurement of past economic activity. For example, the 2013 benchmark altered NIPA history all the way back to 1929. The idea was to capture more accurately the impact of R&D on investment, in addition to other less significant modifications.

NIPA revisions matter greatly to business decision makers and government policymakers who are making decisions in real time. It's an unfortunate fact of life that they're working with imperfect information. The standard deviation of revisions between each of the initial real GDP releases (in months t, $t + 1$, and $t + 2$) and the most recent estimate was 1.6% for the 1983-2009 period. This represents a sizable uncertainty about the current state of the economy. It means that economic forecasters must first "backcast" GDP revisions.

By way of example, consider economic activity in the third quarter of 1990 as contemporary observers viewed it. The initial report of third-quarter

1990 real GDP showed quarter-to-quarter annualized growth of 1.8%. Two years later, the revised reading showed a decline of 1.6%. With the benefit of hindsight, the National Bureau of Economic Research Business Cycle Dating Committee estimates that a mild recession began in July 1990, but NIPA data released in 1990 and 1991 did not show it. Moreover, the Federal Reserve did not respond by easing monetary policy until the fourth quarter of 1990. As of August 2015, the latest estimate for the third quarter of 1990 was a change of 0.1%.

Executive summary

1. GDP measures the total value of production measured at market prices, the sum of value-added by every production unit in the economy.

2. Identities.

   - Output (GDP) = Income (payments to labor and capital, gross of depreciation).

   - Output (GDP) = Expenditures (purchases of goods): $Y = C + I + G + NX$

   - Flow of funds (How is investment financed?): $S = I + NX$

3. We use magic to separate changes in quantities from changes in prices:

   - Quantity indexes, such as real GDP, measure the overall movement of quantities.

   - Price indexes measure the overall movement of prices.

Review questions

1. Value added. Company A sells four tires to Company X for $400. Company B sells a CD player to Company X for $300. Company X installs both in a car, which it sells for $5000. What is the total contribution to GDP of these transactions?

   Answer. The contribution to GDP is $5000: $400 from A, $300 from B, and the rest from X.

2. Expenditures. Place each transaction into the appropriate expenditure component of US GDP:

   (a) Boeing sells an airplane to the Air Force.

   (b) Boeing sells an airplane to American Airlines.

   (c) Boeing sells an airplane to Virgin Atlantic airline.

(d) Boeing sells an airplane to Halle Berry.

(e) Boeing builds an airplane but fails to sell it.

(f) Airbus sells a plane to Delta Air Lines.

Answer.

(a) G: It's a government purchase, as the Air Force is part of the Federal Government.

(b) I: It's investment, as American Airlines will use the aircraft as capital good.

(c) NX: It's export, since Virgin Atlantic is incorporated in the United Kingdom.

(d) C: It's consumption (durable consumption), because Halle Berry will use the plane for her personal travel.

(e) I: It's investment, because the plane will increase Boeing's inventory of unsold products.

(f) I and $-NX$: It's an investment and an import, so the net is zero.

3. Prices and quantities. The following data describe the NYU economy:

	Prices			Quantities		
Year	PCs	Pizza	Beer	PCs	Pizza	Beer
2000	100	10	5	25	100	250
2005	50	20	15	50	125	200
2010	25	30	30	100	150	150

(a) Compute real and nominal GDP and the GDP deflator using 2000 as the base year.

(b) Compute the CPI using 2000 quantities as your basket.

Answer. The numbers are

Year	Nominal GDP	Real GDP	Deflator	CPI	Base = 100
2000	4750	4750	100.00	4750	100.00
2005	8000	7250	110.34	7000	147.37
2010	11500	12250	93.88	11125	234.21

The point is that different methods give different answers. This is most striking if we compare the fourth and last columns. The last one is the CPI, indexed so that it's value is 100 in 2000. Note that the deflator has prices going down in 2010, and the CPI has prices rising—a lot! The reason is that the CPI has a fixed basket and doesn't account for the substitution effect: our tendency to buy more PCs as their price falls.

4. Investment and depreciation. This problem was suggested by Frederic Bouchacourt, MBA 09. The issue is how we deal with investment and depreciation; we need to make sure that they show up in output, expenditures, and income in the same way so that we get the same GDP number all three ways. Imagine an economy with three companies, named D, E, and F, which operate over years 1 and 2 as follows:

- D produces apples and sells them to F for $10 in years 1 and 2. This $10 is paid to workers.

- E builds a machine to can apples and sells it for $10 to F in year 1 and does nothing in year 2. It pays its workers $10 in year 1, nothing in year 2.

- F buys apples from D for $10 in years 1 and 2 and buys a machine to can apples from E for $10 in year 1. F pays its workers $10 each year. With the help of this machine, F produces canned apples in years 1 and 2 that are sold to final consumers for $30 in each year. The machine is amortized equally over the two years: $5 per year.

In this economy:

(a) What is GDP in years 1 and 2?

(b) What are consumption and investment?

(c) What are capital and labor income?

(d) What is net domestic product in each year (GDP minus depreciation)?

Answer.

(a,b) We can find GDP two ways: as value added (summed across producers) or as expenditures (summed across categories). If we compute value added for each firm and sum, we have

	Year 1	Year 2
Firm D	10	10
Firm E	10	0
Firm F	20	20
GDP	40	30

Note that investment does not count as part of the cost of materials: That's the way the national accounts work. It's similar to financial accounting in that we don't consider new plant and equipment ("capex") an expense, although we may include depreciation of existing capital. The latter doesn't show up here because we measure output gross of depreciation.

If we look at the expenditure identity, we have consumption C of $30 each year (canned apples) and investment I of $10 in the first year only. Expenditures add to $40 the first year, $30 the second, so we get the same answer.

(c) Value added is payments to capital and labor. Since we know value added and payments to labor, payments to capital are the difference. Payments to labor are $30 in year 1, $20 in year 2. In year 1, capital receives $(10 - 10) + (10 - 10) + (20 - 10) = \$10$, of which $5 is depreciation. In year 2, capital receives $(10-10)+0+(20-10) = \$10$, of which $5 is depreciation.

(d) Net domestic product is GDP minus depreciation. Since depreciation is 5 each year, NDP is $35 (=40–5) the first year, $25 (=30–5) the second. Effectively, we've subtracted off the cost of the investment, but unlike other material costs, we do it over time rather than all at once. That's the logic of amortization: to spread the cost over time, since the benefits are presumably spread the same way. You can also calculate net domestic income just as we did gross domestic income, except that you subtract depreciation from capital income each period. That way, net domestic product equals net domestic income.

5. Real-world data. Find the appropriate data for US income and expenditures from the Bureau of Economic Analysis (BEA) online interactive tables, particularly Tables 1.10 and 1.1.5.

(a) What are the expenditure components of GDP? How does the official version differ from ours? What is the share of consumption in Gross Domestic Product?

(b) What are the components of Gross Domestic Income? How does the official version differ from ours? What is the share of labor compensation in Gross Domestic Income?

(c) Are Gross Domestic Product and Gross Domestic Income the same? Why or why not?

If you're looking for more

Most macroeconomics textbooks cover similar material. If you're interested in how measurement issues affect international comparisons, here are some particularly interesting papers on the subject:

• Ben Bernanke, "Economic measurement," relates GDP to measures of "economic well-being" and "happiness."

• Rob Feenstra, Hong Ma, Peter Neary, and Prasada Rao, "Who shrunk China?" describe the impact of various measurement issues on estimates of China's GDP.

- Chad Jones and Pete Klenow, "Beyond GDP," look at the relation between GDP per person and various other measures of individual welfare.

Symbols and data used in this chapter

Table 2.8: Symbol table.

Symbol	Definition
Y	Gross domestic product ($=$ Expenditure $=$ Income)
C	Private consumption
I	Private investment (incl. residential and business investment)
G	Government purchases of goods and services (not transfers)
X	Exports
M	Imports
NX	Net exports ($= X - M$)
S	Gross domestic saving ($= Y - C - G = I + NX$)
S_p	Private saving ($= Y - T - C$)
S_g	Government saving ($= T - G$)
T	Taxes collected net of transfer payments and interest
$\pi = g_P$	Discretely-compounded growth rate of price index (inflation)
g_Y	Discretely-compounded growth rate of real GDP
g_{PY}	Discretely-compounded growth rate of nominal GDP

Table 2.9: Data table.

Variable	Source
Nominal GDP	GDP
Compensation of employees	GDICOMP
Proprietor's income	PROPINC
Corporate profits after tax	W273RC1Q027BEA
Taxes on corporate profits	A054RC1Q027SBEA
Gross domestic income	GDI
Rental income	RENTIN
Depreciation	COFC
Consumption	PCE
Durable goods	PCDG
Nondurable goods	PCND
Services	PCESV
Gross private domestic investment	GPDI
Nonresidential investment	PNFI
Residential investment	PRFI
Change in inventories	CBI
Government consumption	GCE
Net exports of goods and services	NETEXP
Exports	EXPGS
Imports	IMPGS
Gross private savings	GPSAVE
Gross government savings	GGSAVE
GDP deflator	GDPDEF
Consumer price index	CPIAUCSL
Nominal GNP	GNP
Current account	BOPBCA

To retrieve the data online, add the identifier from the source column to http://research.stlouisfed.org/fred2/series/. For example, to retrieve nominal GDP, point your browser to http://research.stlouisfed.org/fred2/series/GDP

Part II
Long-Term Economic Performance

Long-Term Overview

This outline covers key concepts from the first part of the course: long-term economic performance. It is not exhaustive, but is meant to help you (i) anticipate what is coming and (ii) organize your thoughts later on.

The Aggregate Production Function

Tools: Cobb-Douglas production function.

Key Words: Productivity (TFP); constant returns to scale, diminishing marginal product, capital, labor.

- A production function relates output (real GDP) to inputs (capital and labor). Ours have three essential properties: (i) more inputs lead to more output; (ii) diminishing returns to capital and labor; (iii) constant returns to scale.

- The Cobb-Douglas production function is a specific form that we'll use throughout.

- Total factor productivity (TFP) is the overall efficiency with which inputs are transformed into outputs.

The Solow Model

Tools: Capital accumulation dynamics; Cobb-Douglas production function.

Key Words: Investment; saving; depreciation; steady state; convergence.

Big Ideas:

- The Solow model connects saving and investment with economic growth.

- In the Solow model without productivity (TFP) growth, capital accumulation does not generate long-run growth. The reason is diminishing returns to capital: the impact of additional capital declines the more you have. As a result, differences in saving rates have only modest effects on output per worker and none at all on its long-run growth rate.

- TFP growth generates long-run growth in output per worker.

Sources of Economic Growth

Tools: Cobb-Douglas production function; level and growth accounting; continuously-compounded growth rates.

Big Ideas:

- Level and growth accounting allow us to *quantify* the sources of growth: the contributions of capital, labor, and total factor productivity (TFP) to growth in real GDP.

- TFP accounts for most of the cross-country differences in output per worker and in differences in the growth rate of output per worker.

Institutions and Policies

Key Words: Institutions; governance; time consistency; property rights; markets.

Big Ideas:

- Cross-country differences in productivity (TFP) are connected to differences in institutions that shape productivity and policy.

- Good institutions include good governance; time consistency; rule of law; property rights; open and competitive markets.

Labor Markets

Tools: Labor supply and labor demand diagrams; simple model of unemployment dynamics.

Key Words: Labor force; employment; unemployment; vacancies; accessions and separations.

Big Ideas:

- Employment and unemployment rates summarize the labor market status of the adult population.

- Labor market institutions and policies affect employment, unemployment, and job creation.

- Unemployment and vacancy rates tell us about excess supply and demand in labor markets. Unemployment arises from the time it takes to match a worker and with an appropriate job and firm.

Financial Markets

Key Words: Time consistency; information asymmetry.

Big Ideas:

- Effective financial markets require strong institutional support.

- Good institutions deal with information asymmetries and time consistency issues.

International Trade

Tools: Ricardo's model of trade; consumption and production possibility frontiers.

Key Words: Absolute advantage; comparative advantage; autarky.

Big Ideas:

- Trade is a positive-sum game: both countries benefit.

- Gains from trade are similar to increases in TFP: trade increases aggregate consumption opportunities.

- Trade creates winners and losers, but the winners win more than the losers lose. Trade affects the kind of jobs that are available, not the number of jobs.

3
The Production Function

Tools: Cobb-Douglas production function.

Key Words: Productivity (TFP); constant returns to scale, diminishing marginal product, capital, labor.

- A production function relates output (real GDP) to inputs (capital and labor). Ours have three essential properties: (i) more inputs lead to more output; (ii) diminishing returns to capital and labor; (iii) constant returns to scale.

- The Cobb-Douglas production function is a specific form that we'll use throughout.

- Total factor productivity (TFP) is the overall efficiency with which inputs are transformed into outputs.

We want to understand why some countries are richer than others, in the sense of having higher GDP per capita. Since rich means they produce more output, the question becomes where the output comes from. Here we describe a tool for answering that question: a *production function* that relates the quantity of output produced to (i) the quantities of inputs and (ii) the efficiency or productivity with which they're used. Doing this for an entire economy takes a leap of faith, but the reward is a quantitative summary of the sources of aggregate economic performance.

3.1 The production function

Economic organizations transform inputs (factories, office buildings, machines, labor with a variety of skills, intermediate inputs, and so on) into outputs. Boeing, for example, owns factories, hires workers, buys electricity and avionics, and uses them to produce aircraft. American Express's credit card business uses computers, buildings, labor, and small amounts of plastic to produce payment services. Pfizer hires scientists, MBAs, and others to develop, produce, and market drugs. McKinsey takes labor and information technology to produce consulting services.

For an economy as a whole, we might think of all the labor and capital used in the economy as producing real GDP, the total quantity of goods and services. A production function is a mathematical relation between inputs and output that makes this idea concrete:

$$Y \;=\; AF(K, L),$$

where Y is output (real GDP), K is the quantity of physical capital (plant and equipment) used in production, L is the quantity of labor, and A is a measure of the productivity of the economy. We call A *total factor productivity*. More on each of these shortly.

The production function tells us how different amounts of capital and labor may be combined to produce output. The critical ingredient here is the function F. Among its properties are

1. **More input leads to more output.** In economic terms, the marginal products of capital and labor are positive. In mathematical terms, output increases in both K and L:

$$\frac{\partial Y}{\partial K} > 0, \;\; \frac{\partial Y}{\partial L} > 0.$$

2. **Diminishing marginal products of capital and labor.** Increases in capital and labor lead to increases in output, but they do so at a decreasing rate: The more labor we add, the less additional output we get. You can see this in Figure 3.1. For a given capital stock $\bar{K}$, increasing labor by an amount Δ starting from L_1 has a larger effect on output than increasing labor by the same amount starting from $L_2 > L_1$. That is: $AF(\bar{K}, L_1 + \Delta) - AF(\bar{K}, L_1) > AF(\bar{K}, L_2 + \Delta) - AF(\bar{K}, L_2)$. This condition translates into properties of the second derivatives:

$$\frac{\partial^2 Y}{\partial K^2} < 0, \;\; \frac{\partial^2 Y}{\partial L^2} < 0. \tag{3.1}$$

3. **Constant returns to scale.** This property says that if we (say) double all the inputs, the output doubles, too. More formally, if we multiply both

Figure 3.1: The production function.

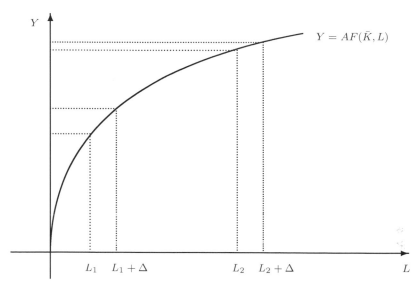

inputs by the same number $\lambda > 0$, then we multiply output by the same amount:

$$AF(\lambda K, \lambda L) = \lambda AF(K, L). \tag{3.2}$$

Thus, there is no inherent advantage or disadvantage of size.

These properties are more than we need for most purposes, but we mention them because they play a (sometimes hidden) role in the applications that follow.

Our favorite example of a production function is $F(K, L) = K^\alpha L^{1-\alpha}$, which leads to

$$Y = AK^\alpha L^{1-\alpha} \tag{3.3}$$

for a number ("parameter") α between zero and one. Circle this equation so that you remember it! It's referred to as the *Cobb-Douglas* version of the production function to commemorate two of the earliest people to use it. (Charles Cobb was a mathematician. Paul Douglas was an economist and later a US senator.) Let's verify that it satisfies the properties we suggested. First, the marginal product of capital and labor are

$$\partial Y/\partial K = \alpha AK^{\alpha-1}L^{1-\alpha} = \alpha Y/K$$
$$\partial Y/\partial L = (1-\alpha)AK^\alpha L^{-\alpha} = (1-\alpha)Y/L.$$

Note that both are positive. Second, the marginal products are both decreasing. We show this by differentiating the first derivatives to get second derivatives:

$$\partial^2 Y/\partial K^2 \;=\; \alpha(\alpha-1)AK^{\alpha-2}L^{1-\alpha}$$
$$\partial^2 Y/\partial L^2 \;=\; -\alpha(1-\alpha)AK^\alpha L^{-\alpha-1}.$$

Note that both are negative. Finally, the function exhibits constant returns to scale. If we multiply both inputs by $\lambda > 0$, the result is

$$A(\lambda K)^\alpha(\lambda L)^{1-\alpha} \;=\; A\lambda^\alpha K^\alpha \lambda^{1-\alpha}L^{1-\alpha} \;=\; \lambda AK^\alpha L^{1-\alpha},$$

as needed. We will typically use $\alpha = 1/3$. If you'd like to know why, see the "Review questions" at the end of the chapter.

3.2 Capital input

The capital input (or capital stock) K is typically measured as the total amount of physical capital used in production. In order to arrive to this total, we value different kinds of capital (machines, office buildings, houses, computers) at their base-year prices, just as we do with real GDP in the National Income and Product Accounts. It's somewhat heroic to combine so many different kinds of capital into one number, but that's the kind of people we are.

Fine points:

- **How does capital change over time?** Typically, capital increases with investment (purchases of new plant and equipment) and decreases with depreciation. Mathematically, we might write

$$K_{t+1} \;=\; K_t - \delta_t K_t + I_t, \tag{3.4}$$

where δ_t is the rate of depreciation between t and $t+1$. On average, the capital stock depreciates about 6 percent a year, but this is an average of depreciation rates for structures (which depreciate more slowly) and equipment (for example, computers, which depreciate more quickly). In practice, we use (3.4) to construct estimates of the capital stock from investment data.

Digression. Note that we've used a different timing convention than financial accountants. Capital at time t is the amount available for production during the period. We use the amount available at the start of the period, which in financial statements would be the end of the previous period. Why do we do this? Because, otherwise, current production would depend on last period's capital stock, which seems a little strange. Note, too, that for a period like a year, this is a moving target: The amount of capital available in December is likely to be different from the amount available in March. That's not a big deal, because the capital stock is slow to change, so any changes within a period are likely to be small relative to the total.

- **Quality.** In principle, we want to take into account changes over time in the quality of capital. Computers, for example, are more productive than they were ten years ago, so a computer today should count as more capital than a computer ten years did. Ideally, this happens when we construct our real investment series: the national income and product accountants consider changes in quality when they divide investment into price and quantity components. In recent times, the effect of this has been a sharp decrease in the price of investment goods, particularly equipment, so that a given dollar expenditure results in greater additions to capital than in the past.

- **Wars and natural disasters.** Wars can have an impact on the capital stock—natural disasters, too, although their impact is rarely as big. Experts estimate that the German and Japanese capital stocks declined by about 50 percent between the start and end of World War II. In modern times, the impact is almost always negligible. September 11 and Hurricane Katrina, for example, had enormous effects on New York City and New Orleans, respectively, but the impact on the US capital stock was tiny in both cases.

- **Does land count?** The short answer: No. In principle, maybe it should, but in modern economies, land is far less important than plant and equipment. For very poor agricultural economies, land and livestock are important inputs to production, but they're not typically included in our measures of the capital stock.

- **Intangibles.** Our definition of capital here consists solely of physical capital. In particular, we do not include "investments" in such things as research and development, patents, brands, and databases. This is mostly a practical matter, rather than one of principle – for most countries, these newer forms of capital aren't yet part of published measures of capital yet, but there's been some progress towards including them.

3.3 Labor input

The next component of our production function is labor. The first-order approximation is simply the number of people employed (L), which is a number we can find for most countries. (It's not as easy as you might think to measure employment, especially in countries with a large informal sector.) In some cases, we also include measures of the quality of labor ("human capital" H) and hours worked (h). If we include both, our measure of labor input becomes hHL.

The starting point for the labor input is, of course, the population. Populations of countries differ not only in quantity, but also in their age distribution and its evolution. Right now, for example, China has a relatively young population, but with a low birth rate, it is aging rapidly. The US has a younger population than Europe or Japan, the result of a higher birth rate (more young people!) and a higher immigration rate (immigrants tend to be young, too). These demographic issues are interesting in their own right. They play an important role in government policy—many countries have state-supported pension and health-care systems, for example, so changes in the age distribution can have a significant impact on government budgets. They're also a critical input in product decisions, telling you, for example, whether you should be selling diapers or walkers.

Our focus, however, is on the quantity and quality of labor. There's no question that individuals differ in skill. Derek Jeter's skills earn him $15m a year as a shortstop for the New York Yankees baseball team, but most of us would be worth far less in the same job. American workers earn more than Mexican and Chinese workers, in part because their skills are better. There are many skills we might want to measure. One that's relatively easy to measure is the level of education of the workforce. In 2013, the average Korean worker had 11.8 years of schooling, and the average Mexican worker had 8.5 years. We know that individuals with more education have higher salaries, on average, so we might guess that Koreans have higher average skills than Mexicans. We call this school-based difference in skill human capital and take it into account by putting it into our production function:

$$Y = AF(K, HL),$$

where H is a measure of human capital.

There are two common measures we could use, both tied to the number of years of school S of the workforce. The first is to set human capital equal to average years of school:

$$H = S.$$

This seems to be a relatively good approximation for most purposes, but it leads to unreasonably large percentage increases in H at low levels of schooling. For example, workers in India had an average level of schooling of 1.7 years in 1960, so one additional year of school increases H by 59 percent. Another approach, based on a huge body of evidence, is to credit each year of school with (say) a given percentage increase in skill. Mathematically, we might say

$$H = \exp(\sigma S),$$

where σ is the extra value of a year of school. A good starting point is $\sigma = 0.07$, which means that every year of school increases human capital by 7 percent.

A second refinement of our measure of labor input focuses on quantity: the number of hours worked. Curiously enough, there are substantial differences in average hours worked across countries. If we use h to represent hours worked, our state-of-the-art modified production function is

$$Y = = AF(K, hHL) = AK^\alpha(hHL)^{1-\alpha}. \tag{3.5}$$

3.4   Productivity

The letter A in the production function plays a central role in this course. We refer to it as total factor productivity or TFP, but what is it? Where does it come from?

The word productivity is commonly used to mean several different things. The most common measure of productivity is the ratio of output to labor input, which we'll call the *average product of labor*. This is typically what government agencies mean when they report productivity data. It differs from the *marginal product of labor* for the same reason that average cost differs from marginal cost. *Total factor productivity*, the letter A in the production function, measures the overall efficiency of the economy in transforming inputs into outputs.

Mathematically, the three definitions are:

$$
\begin{aligned}
\text{average product of labor} &= Y/L \\
\text{marginal product of Labor} &= \partial Y/\partial L \\
\text{total factor productivity} &= Y/F(K, L).
\end{aligned}
$$

For the Cobb-Douglas production function they are:

$$
\begin{aligned}
\text{average product of labor} &= A(K/L)^\alpha \\
\text{marginal product of Labor} &= (1-\alpha)A(K/L)^\alpha \\
\text{total factor productivity} &= A.
\end{aligned}
$$

Holding A constant, the first two increase when we increase the ratio of capital to labor. Why? You can be more productive if you have (say) more equipment to work with. TFP is an attempt to measure productivity independently of the amount of capital each worker has. That allows us to tell whether the US is more prosperous than India because it has more and better capital (higher K) or uses the labor and capital it has more effectively (higher TFP A).

In practice, we measure total factor productivity as a residual: We measure A by taking a measure of output (real GDP Y) and comparing it to measures of capital and labor inputs. In the simplest case (without corrections to labor), we solve

$$A = Y/(K^\alpha L^{1-\alpha}).$$

As a result, anything that leads the same inputs to produce more output results in higher TFP. What kinds of things might do this? One example is innovation. If we invent the computer chip or a drug that cures cancer, they will clearly increase measured productivity (or one would hope they would). But there are many other examples. Another example is security. If we establish personal safety and security, then individuals can spend more time working productively, and less time worrying about being robbed or murdered. Another is competition. If the economic system reallocates resources from less-productive to more-productive firms, that will lead to an increase in country-wide productivity. Capital and labor-market laws and regulations play a clear role here. In short, anything that affects the allocation of resources can have an impact on total factor productivity.

3.5   Marginal products

In competitive markets, labor and capital are paid their marginal products. We could show that, but for now would prefer to simply take it on faith. That, in turn, tells us where payments to labor and capital come from.

Consider payments to labor. Firms hire workers until the marginal product of an additional unit of labor equals its cost, the wage w. We'll go into this in more detail when we study labor markets, but for now note that this bit of logic can be represented mathematically by

$$w = \text{MPL} \equiv \partial Y/\partial L,$$

where MPL means the marginal product of labor. With our basic Cobb-Douglas production function (3.3), this becomes

$$w = (1-\alpha)AK^\alpha L^{-\alpha} = (1-\alpha)A\,(K/L)^\alpha = (1-\alpha)Y/L.$$

We can now ask ourselves: What do we need to generate high wage rates? The answer: High total factor productivity and/or high capital-labor ratios. In words, workers are more productive, at the margin, if TFP is high and if they have more capital to work with.

Note that high wages are a good thing for an economy: they reflect (for example) high productivity. Often, countries with high TFP also have high capital per worker, so the two terms drive wages in the same direction. It doesn't seem fair, but it happens because the same productivity that makes workers valuable also raises the return on capital, as we see next.

The market return on capital (r, say) equals the marginal product of capital. In this case, there's an additional adjustment for depreciation, so we have

$$r = \text{MPK} = \alpha A \left(K/L \right)^{\alpha-1} - \delta = \alpha Y/K - \delta.$$

The right-hand side here is the net marginal product of capital—net because we have netted out depreciation. Without that term, we have the gross marginal product of capital, because our measure of output is gross of depreciation (the G in GDP).

In short, the productive value of labor and capital (ie, their marginal products) depends in large part on total factor productivity. To understand this, it's important that you be able to distinguish between total factor productivity (the letter A in the production function) and the marginal products of labor and capital.

Executive summary

1. A production function links output to inputs.

2. Inputs include physical capital (plant and equipment) and labor (possibly adjusted for skill and hours worked).

3. Total Factor Productivity (TFP) is a measure of overall productive efficiency.

Review questions

1. Components of the production function. A small country invests a large fraction of GDP in a major infrastructure project, which later turns into a "white elephant" (that is, it's not used). How does this affect the components of the production function?

   Answer. The investment will raise the stock of capital K, but since it's not used, we would expect no increase in output Y. We would, therefore, expect measured productivity to fall.

2. Computing TFP. Suppose an economy has the production function

$$Y = AK^{1/4}L^{3/4}.$$

   If $Y = 10$, $K = 15$, and $L = 5$, what is total factor productivity A?
   Answer. $A = Y/(K^{1/4}L^{3/4}) = 1.520$.

3. Diminishing returns. Suppose the production function is

$$Y = 2K^{1/4}L^{3/4}$$

and $K = L = 1$. How much output is produced? If we reduced L by 10 percent, how much would K need to be increased to produce the same output?

Answer. With $K = L = 1$, $Y = 2$. If L falls to 0.9, $K = 1/0.9^3 = 1.372$ (a 37 percent increase in K). The reason for the difference between the magnitudes in the changes in K and L is the difference in their exponents in the production function.

4. Human capital 1. Worker 1 has ten years of education, worker 2 has 15. How much more would you expect worker 2 to earn? Why?

Answer. If $H =$ years of education, then one hour of worker 2's time is equivalent to 1.5 $(= 15/10)$ hours of worker 1's time, so we'd expect her to be paid 50 percent more. A more complex answer is that skill may increase in a more complicated way with years of education, and that types of education may differ in their impact on earning power (an MBA may be worth more in this sense than a PhD in cultural anthropology, however interesting the latter may be).

5. Human capital 2. Consider the augmented production function

$$Y = K^{1/3}(HL)^{2/3}.$$

If $K = 10$, $H = 10$, and $L = 5$, what is the average product of labor ? How much does the average product increase if H rises to 12?

Answer. Output is $Y = 29.24$ so $Y/L = 5.85$. If H rises to 12, $Y/L = 6.60$.

6. Production function conditions. Conditions 2 and 3 [equations (3.1) and (3.2)] seem to contradict each other. One says increases in inputs have a declining impact on output, while the other says that proportional increases in capital and labor lead to the same proportional increase in output. What's going on here?

Answer. This is a subtle issue, but the answer is that the conditions are different. Condition 2 concerns increases in one input, *holding constant the other input*. Condition 3 concerns increases in both inputs at the same time. Different concepts, different properties.

7. One-third. Why does $\alpha = 1/3$?

Answer. If we look at the income side of the National Income and Product Accounts, about two-thirds is paid to labor and one-third to capital. We'll see later that firms will hire labor until its marginal product equals the wage. For our Cobb-Douglas production function,

$$w = \text{MPL} = (1 - \alpha)AK^\alpha L^{-\alpha}.$$

Total payments to labor are the product of the wage and labor:

$$wL = (1 - \alpha)AK^\alpha L^{1-\alpha} = (1 - \alpha)Y.$$

So we set $1 - \alpha = 2/3$, as stated.

If you're looking for more

The methodology described in this chapter has been applied, with lots of variations, to countries, industries, and even firms. The biggest challenge in most studies is coming up with a good measure of the aggregate capital stock. For cross-country data, a good source are the Penn World Tables. If you're interested, and can't find the data online, send us an email.

Lots of other organizations do their own calculations. Two of the most useful public sources are

- The Bureau of Labor Statistics. They report what they call "multifactor productivity," both levels and growth rates, for the US private business sector and a number of industries:

  http://www.bls.gov/bls/productivity.htm.

- The Conference Board. Their Total Economy Database includes growth rates of aggregate TFP for a number of countries:

  http://www.conference-board.org/data/economydatabase/.

Symbols used in this chapter

Table 3.1: Symbol table.

Symbol	Definition
Y	Output (real GDP)
A	Total factor productivity (TFP)
K	Stock of physical capital (plant and equipment)
L	Quantity of labor (number of people employed)
$F(K,L)$	Production function of K and L
$\partial F(K,L)/\partial K$	Partial derivative of $F(K,L)$ with respect to K
$\partial F(K,L)/\partial L$	Partial derivative of $F(K,L)$ with respect to L
Δ	Infinitesimal number
$\overline{K}$	Given capital stock
λ	Constant
α	Exponent of K in Cobb-Douglas production function ($=$ capital share of income)
δ	Rate of depreciation of physical capital
I	Investment (purchases of new plant and equipment)
H	human capital
h	Hours worked
hHL	Volume of labor input
S	Years of school of workforce
σ	Extra value of a year of school
w	Wage
r	market return on capital (or rental cost of capital)

4

The Solow Model

Tools: Capital accumulation dynamics; Cobb-Douglas production function.

Key Words: Investment; saving; depreciation; steady state; convergence.

Big Ideas:

- The Solow model connects saving and investment with economic growth.

- In the Solow model without productivity (TFP) growth, capital accumulation does not generate long-run growth. The reason is diminishing returns to capital: the impact of additional capital declines the more you have. As a result, differences in saving rates have only modest effects on output per worker and none at all on its long-run growth rate.

- TFP growth generates long-run growth in output per worker.

We see large differences in saving and investment rates across countries, with (for example) the US investing 20 percent of GDP, China 40 percent, and India 30 percent in recent years (ratios of real investment to real GDP from the Penn World Tables). How important are these differences to the long-run growth rates of countries? The answer: not important at all. Why? Because diminishing returns to capital means (in practice) that additional capital generates smaller and smaller additions to output. This insight comes from work by Robert Solow, who received the 1987 Nobel Prize in economics for his work. His model is also a useful tool for extrapolating current trends and pointing out the critical inputs to any such exercise.

4.1   The model

Solow's model has four relatively simple components. The first is our friend
the production function:

$$Y_t \;=\; A_t F(K_t, L_t) \;=\; A_t K_t^{\alpha} L_t^{1-\alpha}. \tag{4.1}$$

Changes in output, therefore, come from changes in (total factor) productivity, capital, and/or labor. Recall that one of the properties of this production
function is diminishing returns to capital — each additional unit of capital
leads to a smaller addition to output. This is the critical ingredient in what
follows. The second component is a link between investment and saving.
You'll recall that the flow identity, $S = I + NX$, linked saving to investment
and net exports. Solow ruled out the last one (we can put it back later if
we like), giving us

$$S_t \;=\; I_t.$$

Lurking behind the scenes here is the expenditure identity. Ignoring government expenditure (or treating it as part of consumption for the moment),
this is $Y = C + I$.

The third component is a description of saving behavior: people save a
constant fraction s of their income,

$$S_t \;=\; sY_t,$$

where the saving rate s is a number between zero and one. This is a little
simplistic — you might expect saving to depend on the rate of return and/or
expectations of future income — but there is a lot to be said for simplicity.
For our purposes, s is really the investment rate (the ratio of investment to
GDP), but since saving and investment are the same here, we can call it the
saving rate. Finally, the capital stock depreciates at a constant rate δ, so
that

$$K_{t+1} \;=\; (1 - \delta)K_t + I_t, \tag{4.2}$$

where the depreciation rate δ is a number between zero and one.

The model consists of these four equations. This seems kind of simple for a
Nobel Prize, but they really are good equations. Now let's see where they
lead.

4.2   Capital dynamics

Let's think about how the model behaves if the labor input L and productivity A are constant. Analysis of the model in this case consists of describing

Table 4.1: Output dynamics in the Solow model.

Date t	Capital Stock K	Output Y
0	250.0	135.7
1	252.1	136.1
2	254.2	136.5
3	256.0	136.8
4	257.8	137.1
5	259.4	137.4
6	261.0	137.7
7	262.4	137.9
8	263.8	138.2
9	265.0	138.4
10	266.2	138.6

how the capital stock evolves through time. Other variables follow from their relations to the capital stock. We can find output from the production function, saving (= investment) from output, and consumption (should we need it) from the expenditure identity ($C = Y - I$).

The key step is to describe how the capital stock changes from one period to the next. To do that, we add time subscripts to the equations that don't have them already. Then, with a little work, we see that the capital stock behaves like this:

$$
\begin{aligned}
K_{t+1} &= (1 - \delta)K_t + I_t \\
&= (1 - \delta)K_t + S_t \\
&= (1 - \delta)K_t + sY_t \\
&= (1 - \delta)K_t + sAK_t^\alpha L^{1-\alpha}.
\end{aligned}
\tag{4.3}
$$

Note that each step follows from one of the components of the model. The result is a formula for computing K_{t+1} from K_t and some other stuff. If we have numerical values for the parameters (A, α, s, δ), we can do the computations in a spreadsheet or other program and see how K moves through time.

Example. A numerical example will show you how this works. Let $L = 100$, $A = 1$, $s = 0.2$, $\delta = 0.1$, and $\alpha = 1/3$. (We'll use the same parameters throughout.) If the initial capital stock is 250, we can compute future values of the capital stock by applying equation (4.3) repeatedly. We then compute output from the capital stock using the production function. The results for this case are summarized in Table 4.1. [Suggestion: Try to reproduce a few periods of the table to make sure you understand how it works. If you get

stuck, read the last two pages again. The trick is to set up formulas that tie
each period to the previous one.]

You can see in the table that capital and output both increase over time.
Will they increase forever? The answer is no, but it takes a little work
to show. (Alternatively, you could extend the simulation and see what
happens.) This is an important conclusion, because it tells us saving and
capital formation can't be the reason (in this model, anyway) that some
countries grow faster than others. More on this soon.

The dynamics of the capital stock reflect a balance of two factors: (i) saving
tends to increase the capital stock by financing new investment and (ii) depreciation tends to reduce it. A modest change to equation (4.3) makes this
clear:

$$\Delta K_{t+1} \quad \equiv \quad K_{t+1} - K_t \quad = \quad sAK_t^\alpha L^{1-\alpha} - \delta K_t. \tag{4.4}$$

(The equal sign with three lines means that the equation defines the expression that comes before it, in this case ΔK_{t+1}.) You can see that the change
is zero (the capital stock doesn't change) when

$$K_{ss} \quad = \quad \left(\frac{sA}{\delta}\right)^{1/(1-\alpha)} L,$$

where K_{ss} is the "steady-state" capital stock. This is a little complicated,
but remember: it's just a formula. In our example, $K_{ss} = 282.8$, so we have
a ways to go before the model reaches its steady state.

What happens if we are above or below K_{ss}? You can get a sense of the
dynamics from Figure 4.1. The top line is output, which is related to the
capital stock through the production function. The next line is saving, a
constant fraction of output and the first expression on the right side of equation (4.4): $sAK^\alpha L^{1-\alpha}$. The third line is depreciation, a constant fraction δ
of the capital stock and the second object on the right side of equation (4.4):
δK. Diminishing returns to capital gives the saving line its curvature. It
leads to higher saving than depreciation at low values of the capital stock, so
the capital stock is increasing. Similarly, saving is lower than depreciation at
high values of the capital stock, so the capital stock falls. The crossing point
is K_{ss}, where saving is just enough to make up for depreciation, leaving the
capital stock unchanged.

4.3   Convergence

The central feature of the model is what we call the convergence property:
If countries have the same parameters, they will eventually converge to the

Figure 4.1: The Solow model.

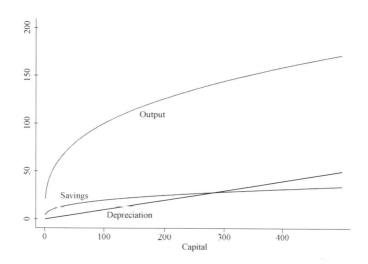

same level of output per worker. We haven't quite shown this yet, but the only thing missing is the "per worker" qualification.

Consider, then, a version of the model in per-worker terms. The first step is to divide both sides of (4.3) by L. If $k \equiv K/L$ is capital per worker (or the capital-labor ratio), the equation becomes

$$k_{t+1} = (1 - \delta)k_t + sAk_t^{\alpha}$$

or

$$\Delta k_{t+1} \equiv k_{t+1} - k_t = sAk_t^{\alpha} - \delta k_t. \tag{4.5}$$

You'll note a resemblance to equation (4.4).

Figure 4.2 illustrates the model's dynamics. It's based on the same parameter values as our earlier example: $A = 1$, $s = 0.2$, $\delta = 0.1$, and $\alpha = 1/3$. The line marked "saving per worker" is the first expression on the right side of equation (4.5): sAk^{α}. The line marked "depreciation per worker" is the second expression on the right side of equation (4.5): δk. For small values of k, saving per worker is greater than depreciation per worker, so k increases. For large values of k, saving per worker is less than depreciation per worker, so k decreases. The two lines cross at the steady state, where the capital-labor ratio is constant. We can find the steady-state value of k from equation (4.5) by setting $\Delta k_{t+1} = 0$. This leads to

$$k_{ss} = \left(\frac{sA}{\delta}\right)^{1/(1-\alpha)},$$

Figure 4.2: The impact of the saving rate in the Solow model.

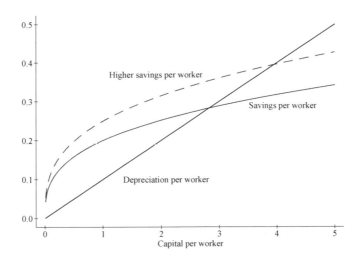

a minor variant of our earlier expression for the steady-state capital stock.

We have shown that the capital-labor ratio eventually converges to its steady-state value. What about output per worker? The production function in per worker form is $Y/L = Ak^\alpha$, so steady-state output per worker depends on steady-state capital per worker:

$$(Y/L)_{ss} \;\; = \;\; Ak_{ss}^\alpha \;\; = \;\; A\left(\frac{sA}{\delta}\right)^{\alpha/(1-\alpha)} \;\; = \;\; A^{1/(1-\alpha)}\left(\frac{s}{\delta}\right)^{\alpha/(1-\alpha)}. \quad (4.6)$$

Similarly, the steady-state capital-output ratio is

$$(K/Y)_{ss} \;\; = \;\; \left(\frac{s}{\delta}\right).$$

The algebra isn't pretty, but it tells us how the steady state depends on the various parameters. The last equation tells us, for example, that countries with higher saving rates also have higher steady-state capital-output ratios — that is more saving leads to more capital. Equally important, the existence of a steady state tells us that if two countries have the same parameter values, they will converge to the same output per worker. We refer to this as the convergence property. In this model, any long-term differences between countries must come from differences in their parameters.

4.4   Impact of saving and investment

We can return to the question we began with: What is the impact of saving and investment rates on growth and income? The long-run impact of saving on growth is zero; the steady-state growth rate is zero, regardless of the saving rate. But there is an effect of saving on steady-state output per worker.

Consider our example. From equation (4.6), we see that steady-state output per worker is 1.4142. What if we increase the saving rate s from 20 percent to 25 percent? Then, steady-state output rises to 1.5811, an 11 percent increase. This isn't irrelevant, but it's a relatively modest increase for a substantial increase in saving. It clearly does not explain much of the enormous differences in GDP per capita that we see around the world.

We can see the same thing in Figure 4.2. The line marked "saving per worker" is based on a saving rate of $s = 0.20$, or 20 percent. If we raise the saving rate to 25 percent, the saving line shifts up, as shown by the dashed line marked "higher saving per worker." Why? Because sAk^α is higher at every value of k. With this new line, the steady-state value of capital per worker (where the saving line crosses the depreciation line) is higher, as shown.

4.5   Growth

If saving doesn't generate growth, what does? We add growth in the labor force and (critically) growth in total factor productivity with two goals in mind. The first goal is to account for the growth rate of output, showing how it depends on the growth rates of our two inputs. The second is to show that the economy approaches what we call a balanced growth path in which output and capital grow at the same rate. As before, the capital-output ratio approaches a constant, the features of which we can easily summarize. We do this with a striking example in mind: We know that China invests an astounding 40 percent of its GDP. Is this too much? A hint is that capital intensity (measured by the capital-output ratio) depends not only on the investment rate (which tells us how much new capital is added), but also on the growth rate (how fast the denominator is changing). A fast-growing economy needs a high investment rate simply to maintain a given capital-output ratio.

The new inputs into our analysis are growth in the labor force and productivity. Let us say, to be concrete, that labor and productivity grow at constant rates:

$$L_{t+1} = (1 + g_l)L_t$$
$$A_{t+1} = (1 + g_a)A_t.$$

How fast do output and capital grow? Let's guess that output and capital grow at the same rate g_y, to be determined. (Why? Because we're good guessers.) From the production function, we then know that

$$(1 + g_y) = Y_{t+1}/Y_t$$
$$= (A_{t+1}/A_t)(K_{t+1}/K_t)^{\alpha}(L_{t+1}/L_t)^{1-\alpha}$$
$$= (1 + g_a)(1 + g_y)^{\alpha}(1 + g_l)^{1-\alpha}.$$

The growth rate, is therefore,

$$(1 + g_y) = (1 + g_a)^{1/(1-\alpha)}(1 + g_l).$$

Just a formula, but it says that output growth is tied to the growth rates of productivity and labor. The saving rate does not affect this growth rate. Similarly, the growth rate in output per worker is

$$(1 + g_y)/(1 + g_l) = (1 + g_a)^{1/(1-\alpha)},$$

which depends only on productivity growth. If α is positive, the growth rate of output per worker is higher than the growth rate of productivity, because the exponent $1/(1 - \alpha)$ is greater than one. In words, the direct impact of productivity on output is magnified by the growth in the stock of capital; see the production function (4.1). This ties in with a remark we made earlier: That capital accumulation tends to reinforce the impact of productivity growth. Countries with high productivity also have a lot of capital.

What about capital — do countries with higher saving rates have more capital, relative to the size of their economies? Consider, again, a steady state in which capital and output grow at the same rate g_y. Then $K_{t+1} = (1 + g_y)K_t$ and equation (4.3) becomes

$$K_{t+1} = (1 - \delta)K_t + sY_t$$
$$(1 + g_y)(K_t/Y_t) = (1 - \delta)(K_t/Y_t) + s.$$

Solving for K/Y gives us the steady-state capital-output ratio:

$$(K/Y)_{ss} = \left(\frac{s}{\delta + g_y}\right).$$

To return to our goal of understanding the sources of capital intensity, note the impact of growth on the steady-state capital-output ratio. For a given saving/investment rate s, countries with higher growth g_y will have relatively less capital per unit of output. Why? Because when output is growing quickly, you need to invest a lot to keep capital growing at the same rate.

Example. Here are some numbers based loosely on the US: $g_l = 0.005$ (0.5%), $g_a = 0.01$ (1%), $s = 0.15$, and $\delta = 0.06$. What is the growth rate of output? The steady-state capital-output ratio? The growth rate satisfies

$$1 + g_y \;=\; (1 + g_a)^{1/(1-\alpha)}(1 + g_l) \;=\; 1.015 \times 1.005 \;=\; 1.0201.$$

Here, we've used $\alpha = 1/3$, as usual. Using the same parameters as our earlier examples, the steady-state capital-output ratio is

$$1.872 \;=\; \frac{0.15}{0.06 + 0.020}.$$

Now consider numbers based on China. We keep $g_l = 0.005$ and $\delta = 0.06$, but change the others to $g_a = 0.04$ and $s = 0.40$. The growth rate is now $g_y = 0.0659$ and the capital-output ratio is 3.17. Note the moderate increase, despite the near tripling of the saving/investment rate. Is China investing too much? Perhaps not. Their capital-output ratio (by this calculation) is not much different from that of the US, so the 40% investment rate isn't delivering excessive capital intensity by this measure. They need to invest a lot simply to keep up with the growth of their economy.

Executive summary

1. Solow's model bases growth on saving and investment.

2. Saving affects steady-state GDP per worker, but not its growth rate. In this sense and others, saving is secondary to long-term economic performance.

3. Fast-growing countries must invest more to maintain the same capital-output ratio.

Review questions

1. The basics. Suppose $A = L = K = 1$, $\alpha = 1/3$, $\delta = 0.06$, and $s = 0.12$.
   (a) What is output Y?
   (b) What are saving S and investment I?
   (c) What is next period's capital stock?

Answer.

(a) $Y = AK^{1/3}L^{2/3} = 1$.

(b) $S = I = sY = 0.12$.

(c) Put t's on everything so far. Then $K_{t+1} = (1 - \delta)K_t + I = 0.94 + 0.12 = 1.06$.

2. Example, continued. For the numerical example in the text:

(a) Suppose that the economy starts with the steady-state capital stock. What are the steady-state levels of output, investment, and consumption?

(b) If 25 percent of the capital stock is destroyed in a war, how long does it take the economy to eliminate half the fall in output?

Answer.

(a) The steady-state capital stock is (as we've seen) $K_{ss} = 282.8$. Using this value, the production function tells us that output is 141.4. Investment equals the depreciation of the capital stock, 28.3. We can find consumption in two ways. The first is through the expenditure identity: $Y = C + I$. We know Y and I, so C is 113.1. The second is through the flow identity. Saving is fraction s of output, so consumption is fraction $1 - s$, $0.8 \times 141.4 = 113.1$.

(b) This requires a simulation. Let the capital stock fall to 212.1, 75 percent of its steady-state value. Then, output is 128.5, 90.9 percent of its steady-state value. We recover half the fall if output rises to 135.0. If we simulate the model, we see that it reaches 135.1 in 10 periods (years).

3. Government. We've ignored government so far. Suppose, instead, that the government purchases goods and services equal to a constant fraction of GDP (say, $G = dY$ for some fraction d) and collects taxes equal to the same fraction of output. Individuals have after-tax income of $(1 - d)Y$ and save a fraction s of it. With these changes, how would the analysis of the basic Solow model change?

Answer. The critical ingredient here is the fraction of output allocated to investment. Investment here is $I = S = s(1 - d)Y$. Effectively, d reduces the saving rate from s to $s(1 - d)$ and takes resources away from investment. If the government invests, we'd have to include that, but we'd also have to decide how useful the investment was (does it count the same as other investment?).

If you're looking for more

This material is covered in many macroeconomics textbooks. Our favorites are

- Tyler Cowen and Alex Tabarrok, *Modern Principles: Macroeconomics*, ch 7.

- N. Gregory Mankiw, *Macroeconomics (6th edition)*, chs 7-8.

Any editions will do, but the chapter numbers may vary.

Goldman Sachs has used the Solow model (and some heroic assumptions about fundamentals) to forecast the importance of the BRICs (Brazil, Russia, India, and China) to the world economy in 50 years. See "Dreaming with BRICs." It's a good example of how assumptions about productivity, population growth, and education can be used to generate plausible scenarios for the sizes of economies in the distant future. (The equations on their page 18 should look familiar.) This doesn't make forecasting any less hazardous, but it tells you what the critical inputs are. The key one here, of course, is productivity growth.

Symbols used in this chapter

Table 4.2: Symbol table.

Symbol	Definition
Y	Output (real GDP)
A	Total factor productivity (TFP)
K	Stock of physical capital (plant and equipment)
L	Quantity of labor (number of people employed)
$F(K, L)$	Function of inputs K and L in production function
α	Exponent of K in Cobb-Douglas production function (= capital share of income)
S	Saving
I	Investment
C	Consumption
s	Saving rate as a percent of income Y
δ	Rate of depreciation of physical capital
ΔK	Change of K ($= K_{t+1} - K_t$)
K_{ss}	Steady-state capital stock
$(K/Y)_{ss}$	Steady-state capital-output ratio
k	Capital per worker, or capital-labor ratio ($= K/L$)
g_y	Discretely-compounded growth rate of Y
g_l	Discretely-compounded growth rate of L
g_a	Discretely-compounded growth rate of A
d	Government purchases as a share of output (G/Y)

5
Sources of Economic Growth

Tools: Cobb-Douglas production function; level and growth accounting; continuously-compounded growth rates.

Big Ideas:

- Level and growth accounting allow us to *quantify* the sources of growth: the contributions of capital, labor, and total factor productivity (TFP) to growth in real GDP.

- TFP accounts for most of the cross-country differences in output per worker and in differences in the growth rate of output per worker.

If saving rates aren't responsible for the enormous differences we see in living standards, what is? The answer is productivity, but our purpose here is to develop a tool that will give us the answer, whatever it might be. Our ingredients are data (always a good thing) and a little bit of theory (the production function). The combination allows us to attribute differences in output and its growth rate to differences in inputs (capital and labor) and total factor productivity (everything else). The answer, as noted, is mostly productivity: Rich countries are rich because they're productive, and countries that are growing quickly typically have rapid productivity growth, as well. Robert Solow gets credit for this line of thought, too.

5.1 Cross-country differences in output per worker

The production function gives us some insight into cross-country differences in GDP per worker. You'll recall that the production function connects an economy's output (real GDP) to the quantity of inputs used in production (capital and labor) and the efficiency with which those inputs are used (productivity). In equation form:

$$Y = AF(K, L) = AK^\alpha L^{1-\alpha}, \tag{5.1}$$

where (as before) Y is real GDP or output, A is total factor productivity (TFP), K is the capital stock, and L is the quantity of labor (typically employment). More commonly, we divide both sides by L and express output per worker as

$$Y/L = A(K/L)^\alpha, \tag{5.2}$$

so that output per worker depends on total factor productivity (A) and capital per worker (K/L). For most countries, we have reasonably good data for GDP, employment, and the capital stock, and productivity can be found as a residual:

$$A = Y/(K^\alpha L^{1-\alpha}). \tag{5.3}$$

We'll continue to use $\alpha = 1/3$, so there is nothing about equations (5.1) and (5.2) that we don't know. In this sense, the production function is no longer an abstract idea, but a practical tool of analysis.

Table 5.1: Data for Mexico and the US.

	Employment	Education	Capital	GDP
Mexico	46.94	7.61	4,278	1,293
US	155.45	12.27	42,238	12,619

Aggregate data for 2009 (education for 2007). Employment is expressed in millions, education in years, and capital and GDP in billions of 2005 US dollars.

The production function allows us to make explicit comparisons across countries. If we apply equation (5.2) to two countries and take the ratio, we get

$$\frac{(Y/L)_1}{(Y/L)_2} = \left[\frac{A_1}{A_2}\right] \left[\frac{(K/L)_1}{(K/L)_2}\right]^\alpha, \tag{5.4}$$

where the subscripts 1 and 2 refer to the two countries. The ratio of output per worker is, thus, attributed to some combination of the ratios of TFP and capital per worker. Exercises based on (5.4) are referred to as *level comparisons*. If we have data, we can say which of these factors is most important.

If we did this in logarithms, the components would add rather than multiply. As a result, the contribution of each component can be expressed as a fraction of the total. We were tempted to do this, but worried it would unduly try your patience.

Example (Mexico and US). You occasionally hear people in the US say that Mexican workers are paid so much less that they pose a threat to American jobs. (In Mexico, you hear the same thing about Chinese workers.) We can't address that issue (yet) but we can say something about the source of differences in output per worker, which is closely related to differences in wages. The data in Table 5.1 imply that output per worker is 2.95 times higher in the US, but why? We'll use the data in Table 5.1 to come up with an answer.

Let's start with TFP. For Mexico, the data in the table imply that

$$A_M \;=\; 1293/[4278^{1/3}46.94^{2/3}] \;=\; 6.12.$$

A similar calculation for the US gives us $A_{US} = 12.53$. Thus, TFP is 2.05 ($= 12.53/6.12$) times higher in the US. Similarly, the capital-labor ratio is 2.98 times higher in the US. The impact on output per worker is summarized by

$$\begin{aligned}
\frac{(Y/L)_{US}}{(Y/L)_M} &= \frac{A_{US}}{A_M}\left[\frac{(K/L)_{US}}{(K/L)_M}\right]^{1/3} \\
&= (2.05)(2.98)^{1/3} \\
&= (2.05)(1.44) \;=\; 2.95.
\end{aligned}$$

It seems, therefore, that both TFP and capital per worker play a role in accounting for the 2.95-to-1 ratio of US to Mexican output per worker. So the reason why output per worker is higher in the US is a combination of higher productivity and higher capital per worker.

This is your chance for speculation: Why do you think the capital-labor ratio is lower in Mexico? Why do you think productivity is lower?

5.2   Cross-country differences in growth rates

Our next task is to apply similar methods to account for cross-country differences in *growth rates* rather than levels.

Warning, growth rates ahead: Before you continue, you might want to go back and review continuously-compounded growth rates in the Mathematics Review, Chapter 1.

As before, the starting point is the production function. If we take the natural logarithm of both sides of the production function (5.1), we find that

$$\ln Y_t \;=\; \ln A_t + \alpha \ln K_t + (1 - \alpha)\ln L_t$$

for any date t. This follows from two properties of logarithms: $\ln(xy) = \ln x + \ln y$ and $\ln x^a = a \ln x$. If we take the difference between two adjacent periods t and $t-1$ we get

$$\ln Y_t - \ln Y_{t-1} \;=\; (\ln A_t - \ln A_{t-1}) + \alpha(\ln K_t - \ln K_{t-1}) + (1-\alpha)(\ln L_t - \ln L_{t-1}).$$

Notice that each of the components should be recognizable as continuously-compounded growth rates discussed in the growth-rate discussion.

If we consider differences over n periods, we can divide each term by the number of periods to get

$$\left(\frac{\ln Y_t - \ln Y_{t-n}}{n}\right) \;=\; \left(\frac{\ln A_t - \ln A_{t-n}}{n}\right) + \alpha\left(\frac{\ln K_t - \ln K_{t-n}}{n}\right)$$
$$+ (1-\alpha)\left(\frac{\ln L_t - \ln L_{t-n}}{n}\right).$$

Notice that we have expressed the average, continuously-compounded growth rate of GDP into the average, continuously-compounded growth rate of each component of the production function (i.e., TFP, capital, and labor). Using our notation convention that continuously-compounded growth rates are represented by γ, we can express the formula above more succinctly as

$$\gamma_Y \;=\; \gamma_A + \alpha\gamma_K + (1 - \alpha)\gamma_L. \tag{5.5}$$

In words, this equation says that the growth rate of output can be attributed to growth in TFP, capital, and labor. Moreover, the terms add up because of our use of logarithms and continuously compounded growth rates. Additivity is nice, as it allows us to make statements about the contributions of each component to the growth of GDP.

As with levels, we can do the same for the growth rate of output per worker:

$$\begin{aligned}\gamma_{Y/L} \;&=\; \gamma_Y - \gamma_L \\ &=\; \gamma_A + \alpha(\gamma_K - \gamma_L) \\ &=\; \gamma_A + \alpha\gamma_{K/L}. \end{aligned} \tag{5.6}$$

Exercises based on (5.5) and (5.6) are referred to as *growth accounting*, which allows us to make statements about the contributions of each component in accounting for the growth of GDP (5.5) or GDP per worker (5.6).

Both versions of growth accounting give us some insight into the sources of economic growth, as the example below shows.

Example (Chile between 1965 and 2009). GDP increased by almost a factor of five between 1965 and 2009. Can we say why? The relevant data are reported in Table 5.2.

Table 5.2: Chilean aggregate data for 1965 and 2009.

	Employment	Education	Capital	GDP
1965	2.71	4.77	65.63	33.62
2009	7.52	7.97	819.81	199.2

The first step is to compute growth rates. Over this period, the average annual growth rate of real GDP was

$$\gamma_Y = \frac{\ln Y_{2009} - \ln Y_{1965}}{44} = (5.29 - 3.52)/44 = 0.0404,$$

or 4.04 percent. Using the same method, we find that the growth rates of the other variables we need are $\gamma_K = 5.74$ percent and $\gamma_L = 2.32$ percent. The growth rate of total factor productivity is the residual in equation (5.5):

$$\gamma_A = \gamma_Y - [\alpha\gamma_K + (1-\alpha)\gamma_L] = 0.58\%.$$

(You could also compute A for each period and calculate the growth rate directly.) So why did output grow? Our numbers indicate that of the 4.04 percent growth in output, 0.58 percent was due to TFP; 1.91 percent $[= 5.74 \times \frac{1}{3}]$ was due to increases in capital; and 1.55 percent $[= 2.32 \times (2/3)]$ was due to increases in employment.

What about output per worker? That seems to be the more interesting comparison, because it's closer to an average living standard. The growth rate of output per worker is $\gamma_{Y/L} = 1.72$ percent. Its components are

$$\gamma_{Y/L} = \gamma_A + \alpha\gamma_{K/L}$$
$$1.72 = 0.58 + (1/3)3.42.$$

In this case, most of the growth in output per worker came from capital per worker, rather than TFP.

5.3   Extensions

We will sometimes use modifications of these tools. Two of the more common ones are based on (i) more-refined measures of labor and/or (ii) GDP per capita rather than GDP per worker. The logic is the same as before, but we gain an extra term or two.

Labor measures. Consider a measure of labor that includes adjustments for hours worked h and human capital H. If the labor input is hHL (with L the number of people employed), the production function becomes

$$Y = AF(K, hHL) = AK^\alpha(hHL)^{1-\alpha}. \tag{5.7}$$

How does this change our analysis of levels and growth rates? In a level comparison, this leads to

$$\frac{Y_1}{Y_2} = \left[\frac{A_1}{A_2}\right]\left[\frac{K_1}{K_2}\right]^\alpha\left[\frac{L_1}{L_2}\right]^{1-\alpha}\left[\frac{h_1}{h_2}\right]^{1-\alpha}\left[\frac{H_1}{H_2}\right]^{1-\alpha}.$$

The subscripts 1 and 2 again represent countries. You can derive further modifications for output per worker (Y/L) and output per hour worked (Y/hL). In a growth-rate analysis, the augmented production function (5.7) leads to

$$\gamma_Y = \gamma_A + \alpha\gamma_K + (1-\alpha)(\gamma_h + \gamma_H + \gamma_L)$$

for output and

$$\gamma_{Y/L} = \gamma_A + \alpha\gamma_{K/L} + (1-\alpha)(\gamma_h + \gamma_H)$$
$$\gamma_{Y/hL} = \gamma_A + \alpha\gamma_{K/hL} + (1-\alpha)\gamma_H$$

for output per worker and output per hour, respectively. If this sounds complicated, remember that the choice of tool depends on the question we're trying to answer.

We have some choices when it comes to measuring human capital capital. One simple choice is to equate human capital capital with years of school: $H = S$ if we want to give it mathematical form. A more sophisticated choice is to give education a rate of return, so that

$$H = \exp(\sigma S), \tag{5.8}$$

where σ is kind of a rate of return on school, as each year raises human capital capital proportionately. Estimates of σ are in the range of 0.07, so that each year of school raises human capital capital by about 7 percent.

Per capita GDP. The analysis above concerned GDP per worker (rather than per capita). How can we adapt our analysis to account for GDP per capita? Here's a trick: start with equation (5.2) and multiply both sides by the ratio of employment to population:

$$Y/POP = (L/POP)(Y/L) = (L/POP)A(K/L)^\alpha.$$

In a level comparison, this gives us an extra term: the ratio of L/POP across countries. In growth rates, we'd add an extra term for the growth rate of the employment ratio:

$$\gamma_{Y/POP} \;=\; \gamma_{L/POP} + \gamma_A + \alpha\gamma_{K/L}.$$

And if you want to get fancy, you can add hours and human-capital terms, as we did above.

Example (Mexico and US, revisited). How does our analysis of the US and Mexico change if we incorporate differences in human capital? We set human capital H equal to years of school and redo our earlier analysis. TFP is now

$$A_M \;=\; 1293/[4278^{1/3}(7.61 \times 46.94)^{2/3}] \;-\; 1.58$$

for Mexico and $A_{US} = 2.36$ for the US. Note that the ratio has fallen from 2.05 to 1.49. Why? Because part of the previous difference now shows up in human capital. [Reminder: A is a residual, so any change in the analysis changes our measure of it.] We now attribute some of the difference in output per worker to a difference in education:

$$
\begin{aligned}
\frac{(Y/L)_{US}}{(Y/L)_M} &= \frac{A_{US}}{A_M}\left[\frac{(K/L)_{US}}{(K/L)_M}\right]^{1/3}\left[\frac{H_{US}}{H_M}\right]^{2/3} \\
&= (1.49)(2.98)^{1/3}(1.61)^{2/3} \\
&= (1.49)(1.44)(1.38) \;=\; 2.95.
\end{aligned}
$$

It appears that more than half of our earlier difference in TFP stems from differences in education. We amend our previous analysis to add: A substantial part of the difference between output per worker in the US and Mexico stems from differences in education.

An alternative is to measure human capital using our rate-of-return formula, equation (5.8). If we do this, the ratio of human capital is 1.39, which is less than we had before. This choice makes an even bigger difference with countries like India, which have low average education. If years of school go from two to three, is that a 50-percent increase in human capital or a seven-percent increase? You be the judge. Of course, it may depend on what they learn in school, too.

Executive summary

1. Recall that a production function links output to inputs and productivity.

2. Therefore, differences in output and growth rates across countries stem from differences in the levels and growth rates of inputs and productivity (TFP).

3. Level accounting and growth accounting allows us to quantify the differences in output and growth arising from differences in inputs and total factor productivity.

Review questions

1. Growth rates. Take the following data:

	Output Y	Employment L
1950	10	2
2000	50	3

   (a) What are the average annual continuously-compounded growth rates of Y and L?

   (b) What is the analogous growth rate of Y/L?

   Answer.

   (a) The growth rate of output is

$$\gamma_Y = [\ln(50) - \ln(10)]/(2000 - 1950) = 0.0322,$$

   or 3.22% per year. A similar calculation gives us $\gamma_L = 0.0081 = 0.81\%$ per year.

   (b) We can do this two ways. The easiest is

$$\gamma_{Y/L} = \gamma_Y - \gamma_L = 0.0241.$$

   You can also compute it by dividing Y by L and applying the same method we used in (a).

2. France and the UK. In 2007, the data were:

	Employment	Education	Capital	GDP
France	29.51	8.48	6,478	1,986
UK	31.79	9.88	5,243	2,070

   Which country had higher output per worker? Why? You should assume that human capital is equal to years of school.

Answer. Ratios were as follows:

$$\left(\frac{(Y/L)_F}{(Y/L)_{UK}} \right) = \left(\frac{A_F}{A_{UK}} \right) \left(\frac{(K/L)_F}{(K/L)_{UK}} \right)^{1/3} \left(\frac{H_F}{H_{UK}} \right)^{2/3}$$

$$1.03 = (1.04)(1.33)^{1/3}(0.86)^{2/3}.$$

That is, France had slightly higher TFP and more capital per worker, but a lower level of education than the UK.

3. US and Japan. Explain why output grew faster in Japan between 1970 and 1985. Data:

	United States			Japan		
	1970	1985	Growth	1970	1985	Growth
GDP	2083	3103	2.66	620	1253	4.69
Capital	8535	13039	2.83	1287	3967	7.50
Labor	78.6	104.2	1.88	35.4	45.1	1.61

Employment is measured in millions of workers, GDP and capital in billions of 1980 US dollars. Growth rates are continuously-compounded average annual percentages.

Answer. In levels (as opposed to growth rates), we see that the US had much greater output per worker in 1970: 26.5 (thousand 1980 dollars per worker) vs 17.5. Where did this differential come from? One difference is that American workers in 1970 had three times more capital to work with: K/L was 108.6 in the US, 36.4 in Japan. If we use our production function, we find that total factor productivity A was also slightly higher in the US in 1970: 5.55 v. 5.29. Thus, the major difference between the countries in 1970 appears to have been in the amount of capital: American workers had more capital and, therefore, produced more output, on average.

By 1985, much of the difference had disappeared. For the US, the output growth rate of 2.66 percent per year can be divided into 0.94 percent due to capital and 1.26 percent due to employment growth. That leaves 0.47 percent for growth in total factor productivity. For Japan, the numbers are 2.48 percent for capital, 1.08 percent for labor, and 1.13 percent for productivity. Evidently, the largest difference between the two countries was in the rate of capital formation: Japan's capital stock grew much faster, raising its capital-labor ratio from 36.4 in 1970 to 88.0 in 1985.

If you're looking for more

Our calculations are based on various editions of the Penn World Table,

http://www.rug.nl/research/ggdc/data/penn-world-table,

which includes data on GDP per worker and related variables constructed on a consistent basis for most countries in the world. We typically post a spreadsheet of the latest version for our classes, but this is the source.

The tools of growth accounting are widely used by industry analysts. Some of the most interesting applications have been done by McKinsey, whose studies have connected cross-country differences in TFP to government regulation, management practices, and the competitive environment. Some of this work is summarized in William Lewis's *The Power of Productivity* (University of Chicago Press, 2004). Other examples are available on McKinsey's web site; search "mckinsey productivity."

Symbols used in this chapter

Table 5.3: Symbol table.

Symbol	Definition
Y	Output (real GDP)
POP	Population
A	Total factor productivity (TFP)
K	Stock of physical capital (plant and equipment)
L	Quantity of labor (number of people employed)
$F(K, L)$	Function of inputs K and L in production function
α	Exponent of K in Cobb-Douglas production function (= capital share of income)
γ_x	continuously-compounded growth rate of variable x
g_x	Discretely-compounded growth rate of variable x
$\ln$	Natural logarithm (inverse operation of exp)
$\exp$	Exponential function (inverse operation of ln)
h	Hours worked per worker
H	human capital
σ	Value of an extra year of schooling (= rate of return on schooling)
Y/POP	Output per capita
L/POP	Ratio of employment to population

6
Institutions and Policies

Key Words: Institutions; governance; time consistency; property rights; markets.

Big Ideas:

- Cross-country differences in productivity (TFP) are connected to differences in institutions that shape productivity and policy.

- Good institutions include good governance; time consistency; rule of law; property rights; open and competitive markets.

The enormous international differences in GDP per person reflect, in large part, enormous differences in productivity. But where do these differences in productivity come from? It's tempting to attribute them to the ability and dedication of the people who live there, but (on second thought) there are smart, dedicated people everywhere. We now believe that productivity reflects the quality of local institutions and policies. Stated more concretely: it's not Steve Jobs who makes an economy productive; it's the institutions and policies that allow and encourage someone like Jobs to operate effectively. Some countries have environments that encourage productive activity, and others do not. What's striking is not that this is true, but how big a difference it seems to make.

6.1 Good institutions

So what do we mean by good institutions? The world's a complicated place, and it doesn't come with any simple recipes. But countries with good economic performance share some features. We would say good institutions are social mechanisms that facilitate good economic performance. Here's a short list.

Good governance. It's essential that the government be strong enough to guarantee the security and safety of the country and people, but not so strong that those in power abuse others for their own benefit. It's a delicate balance, but most productive economies have both strong governments and clear limits to the government's power.

Time consistency. Policy consistency over time reduces uncertainty and supports economic growth. Institutions that allow governments to commit credibly to good long-run policies (low inflation, fiscal prudence, etc.) help reduce risks and allow businesses to plan with confidence.

If governments can easily renege on promises (say, to keep inflation and taxes low) when it suits them, economic performance suffers. Finn Kydland and Edward Prescott shared the 2004 Nobel prize partly for their analysis of this "time consistency" problem, which arises not just in economics but in many walks of life, from child-rearing to diplomacy, to military strategy.

In formal research, the lack of time consistency is known as the "dynamic inconsistency of intertemporal plans," which arises when a future policymaker is likely to be motivated to break a current policy promise. Institutions and practices that help governments pre-commit to future policies in a credible way — such as the announcement of inflation targets by independent central banks or the constitutional prioritization of debt payments by state governments — help overcome the time-consistency problem.

Such pre-commitments typically involve the introduction of rules that limit *policy discretion.* You might think that allowing future policymakers complete discretion would result in the best possible policies. However, in these notes you will find numerous examples in which the ability to pre-commit results in better economic outcomes (such as keeping inflation low or fostering greater investment). The reason is that a commitment to prudent policies has a favorable influence on the expectations and behavior of households and businesses today. When economists incorporate the analysis of time consistency into their assessment of various policy approaches, the age-old choice between policy rules and policy discretion usually tips in favor of rules.

Rule of law. It's also important that the legal system enforce the law: that the police and judiciary are honest and enforce the laws of the land.

Property rights. We sometimes take this for granted, but the laws should be clear about who owns what. Without that, effective economic activity is impossible. How can you sell something you don't own? Imaginative people may be able to do just that, but it's not a sound basis for a productive economy. How can you get a mortgage if you can't establish that you own real estate? Why would anyone lend on those terms?

Open and competitive markets. You often hear about "free markets," but what seems to work best are honest, open, flexible, competitive markets for products as well as capital and labor. That's different from what you might term business-friendly governments, those who protect sellers from competition or fraud. The idea is not to protect producers, but to allow them to compete honestly.

We'll give examples of each in class, but you might try to think of your own.

6.2   Institutions or policies?

Institutions bring to mind the difference between North and South Korea. The two countries have the same culture — and the same history until 1950. At that time, living standards were similar, probably a little higher in the North. Today, best estimates indicate that GDP per capita in the South is more than 15 times that of the North. The huge difference in performance surely reflects the huge difference in institutions between the countries: the form of government and the nature of economic activity.

In other cases, policies may play an important role. We think of policies as less fundamental aspects of the economic environment than institutions. An honest judicial system is an institution, but tax rates and government spending are policies. There's a fuzzy line between the two, but the idea is that policies are more easily changed than institutions.

Peter Henry (our dean) and Conrad Miller illustrate the role of policies in a comparison of Barbados and Jamaica. We'll draw liberally from their paper. They note that the two countries have similar backgrounds and institutions:

> Both [are] former British colonies, small island economies, and predominantly inhabited by the descendants of Africans.... As former British colonies, Barbados and Jamaica inherited almost identical political, economic, and legal institutions: Westminster Parliamentary democracy, constitutional protection of property rights, and legal systems rooted in English common law.

Nevertheless, Barbados grew 1.3 percent a year faster between 1960 and 2002, giving it a substantially higher standard of living. (This difference is larger than it looks — the power of compound interest and all that.)

One clear difference between the two countries was their macroeconomic policies. In the 1970s, Jamaica increased government spending on job creation programs, housing, food subsidies, and many other things. When tax revenue failed to keep up, the government found itself with large, persistent budget deficits, which they financed by borrowing from the central bank. This, in turn, led to inflation rates of 20 percent and higher. A fixed exchange rate raised the price of Jamaican goods relative to imports, which led to restrictions on imports and wage and price controls.

Barbados also had a fixed exchange rate, but combined it with fiscal discipline, monetary restraint, and openness to trade. The result was a very different macroeconomic outcome. It's possible other factors played a role, too, but in this case policies were arguably as important as institutions.

Executive summary

1. Good institutions are the primary source of good economic performance.

2. A short list would include: governance, rule of law, property rights, and open competitive markets.

3. Stable and predictable macroeconomic policies matter, too.

Review questions

1. Foxconn's next frontier. Hon Hai Precision Industry Co. Ltd. ("Foxconn") is a Taiwan-based manufacturer that makes products for Apple, Intel, Sony, and others. Known for its plants in China, including one in Shenzhen that makes iPads, it also has operations in Brazil, Malaysia, Mexico, and other locations.

   With wages rising rapidly in China, Foxconn is exploring other locations. As a private consultant, you have been asked to write a short report outlining the advantages and disadvantages of locating in Thailand and Vietnam and to compare both to China. You collect the information in Table 6.1 and begin your report.

   (a) Which of these indicators are most important to your venture? How do the two countries compare on them?

   (b) Which country or countries would you recommend to your clients? What are the primary challenges they would face?

   Answer. This is a qualitative question, but here's an outline of what an answer might look like. A good answer should put some structure on the analysis, not simply list what's in the table.

Indicator	China	Thailand	Vietnam
General			
GDP per capita (2005 USD)	8400	9200	3500
Doing Business overall (percentile)	50.8	90.3	46.5
World Economic Forum overall (percentile)	80.0	73.6	47.9
Governance			
Political stability (percentile)	25.0	16.5	52.8
Govt effectiveness (percentile)	60.7	59.7	45.0
Regulatory quality	45.5	56.4	29.4
Rule of law	41.8	48.8	39.9
Control of corruption (percentile)	30.3	43.6	33.6
Labor			
Minimum wage (USD per month)	204	118	65
Severance after 10 years (weeks of pay)	43	50	43
Labor market efficiency (percentile)	71.5	47.2	64.6
Literacy (percent of adults)	94	94	93
Years of school (adults)	8.2	7.5	6.4
Infrastructure and trade			
Infrastructure quality (percentile)	66.7	68.1	34.0
Export documents required (number)	8	5	6
Export delay (days)	21	14	21
Export cost (USD per container)	580	585	610

Table 6.1: Institutional indicators for China, Thailand, and Vietnam. Percentiles range from 0 (worst) to 100 (best). Sources: Penn World Table, World Economic Forum, World Bank, Governance Indicators, Doing Business.

(a) If you build a plant in another country, you'll be concerned with overall institutional quality, property rights (whether the government might steal the plant), labor cost and quality, labor market institutions, and the challenges of exporting your product. There's no clean link to the indicators, but you might guess that property rights would be related to the governance indicators, esp political stability and the rule of law. The labor indicators obviously address concerns with labor. Infrastructure and trade address the challenges of exporting.

As a rough guide:

- Overall: It's interesting that Doing Business rates Thailand highest, but the World Economic Forum rates China highest. And the differences are large. In the real world, this would call for a closer look. Ditto the source of political instability in Thailand.

- Property rights and overall: Thailand looks a bit better than the others on Control of Corruption and Rule of Law, Vietnam looks better on Political Stability.

- Labor cost and quality: Vietnam is considerably cheaper than the other two, if we use GDP per capita or the minimum wage as rough guides to wages. Literacy is similar in the three countries, China is highest, and Vietnam lowest, on education.

- Labor institutions: The World Economic Forum ranks China highest, and Thailand lowest, on overall labor market efficiency. Another thing that's worth a closer look. Severance looks similar.

- Exporting: cost and delay look similar, but Vietnam has the worst infrastructure. You'll want to look into this, see what aspects of the infrastructure are likely to affect you.

(b) They both look like reasonable candidates. For Thailand, we would look closer at political stability, see what that represents and think about how it would affect us. (And that's an understatement!) For Vietnam, we would look closer at infrastructure.

2. Business analytics in the EU. As a graduating MBA at the prestigious ecole des Hautes Etudes Commerciales (HEC) de Paris, you face a daunting job market. Together with two classmates, you start developing plans for a business analytics startup. The idea is to provide data insights to a broad range of businesses located throughout the European Union. The beauty of the plan, you think, is that you can do it anywhere. The three of you have begun to compare the pros and cons of Paris, Barcelona, and Stockholm, your respective home bases. You collect the data in Table 6.2 and begin to sketch out a plan.

   (a) What features do you need in a city to make it attractive to you and your business?

   (b) What are the pros and cons of each city along these dimensions?

   (c) Which city do you think best fits your plans?

   Answer. This question is less than black and white, here is one possible answer.

   (a) You need, among other things: an environment friendly to startups, access to the internet and related infrastructure, and possibly a pool of well-educated talent. There are other things, but these seem like the important ones.

   (b) How do they stack up?

      - Paris: looks good on ease of starting a business, as well as ease of doing business in general; ditto education; questions/concerns

Country Indicators	France	Spain	Sweden
Ease of doing business (rank)	38	52	14
Ease of starting a business (rank)	41	142	61
Protecting investors (rank)	80	98	34
Getting electricity (rank)	42	62	9
Resolving insolvency (rank)	46	22	20
Minimum wage (USD/month)	778	1009	none
Mandatory severance (weeks of pay)	4	14	none
Unemployment rate	10.5	24.4	7.4
Employment rate	64.3	55.8	74.7
Difficulty of dismissals (index, 1-6)	2.6	2.0	2.5
Education of workers (years)	12.6	11.5	12.5
Internet quality (Ookla, index)	81.3	84.0	86.9
City Indicators	Paris	Barcelona	Stockholm
Quality of life (rank, Mercer)	34	44	20
Cost of living (index)	226	223	157

Table 6.2: Business indicators for three cities and countries.

about getting electricity and internet quality; the same for cost of living.

- Barcelona: huge red flag over ease of starting a business; concerns with getting electricity.

- Stockholm: looks good on overall ease of doing business, getting electricity; solid on ease of starting a business; highest internet quality of the three; and lowest cost of living.

(c) Stockholm looks like the clear choice. It would take a good argument to suggest otherwise. Also highly rated for quality of life, which is something you definitely want to consider.

The World Economic Forum has a similar take: "Sweden has managed to create the right conditions for innovation and the knowledge-based economy. The education system is of high quality and seems to deliver the right skills. But it should address its labor market regulations and high tax rate, which are considered the two most problematic factors for doing business."

Update. Since using this as an exam question, we're learned two things. One is that rent control in Stockholm makes it virtually impossible to find a place to live — unless you have enough money to buy. The other is that Berlin might be better than all of these places. A friend in the business tells us that rents are low and there's a huge amount of technical talent available from central Europe at modest cost.

If you're looking for more

The comparison of Barbados and Jamaica comes from Peter Henry and Conrad Miller, "A tale of two islands."

Here are some other good reads, in order of increasing length:

- Ben Bernanke, "Lessons from emerging markets." Nice short summary of what good institutions and policies look like.

- Nicholas Bloom and John Van Reenan, "Management practices across firms and countries." They connect productivity to management practices, including monitoring, targets, and incentives. Some find this obvious, but we find it reassuring that good management has a measurable difference on performance.

- Bill Easterly, *The Elusive Quest for Growth*. Essentially a collection of essays on topics related to helping poor countries, unusually witty for an economist.

- David Landes, *The Wealth and Poverty of Nations*. Less witty than Easterly, but he gives us an interesting historical perspective on the major countries of the world: Europe, India, China, etc.

The idea of good institutions has been around forever, or close to it, but we now have better measures of institutional quality than we used to. One of the leading sources is the World Bank's Doing Business, available at

http://www.doingbusiness.org/.

The reports of the Economist Intelligence Unit are thoughtful aggregators of this kind of information.

7
Labor Markets

Tools: Labor supply and labor demand diagrams; simple model of unemployment dynamics.

Key Words: Labor force; employment; unemployment; vacancies; accessions and separations.

Big Ideas:

- Employment and unemployment rates summarize the labor market status of the adult population.

- Labor market institutions and policies affect employment, unemployment, and job creation.

- Unemployment and vacancy rates tell us about excess supply and demand in labor markets. Unemployment arises from the time it takes to match a worker and with an appropriate job and firm.

Some of the most important markets for aggregate economic performance are those for labor and (financial) capital, which affect every industry and product. Countries differ markedly in their treatment of both markets, with (evidently) different outcomes as a result.

Our focus here is on labor markets. We describe in broad terms what well-functioning markets might look like and compare them to the kinds of institutions and regulations we see around the world.

7.1 Indicators of labor-market "status"

Most countries collect extensive labor-market data. This includes measures of employment, unemployment, and, sometimes, detailed information about flows of workers in and out of jobs.

We'll start with what are called indicators of labor-market status: whether an individual is working, unemployed, or something else. The first such indicator is the *population*, a count of the total number of people in a given geographic area. Strangely enough, numbers like this are estimates: We don't know exactly how many people there are in the US, Canada, or China, but statistical agencies come up with estimates by a number of methods, typically based on surveys. For most labor-market statistics, the starting point is the *adult population*. Countries differ in their definitions of an adult. The US counts anyone 16 or over, the OECD counts people between the ages of 16 and 64 ("working age").

The next step is to identify the labor-market status of everyone in the adult population: (i) employed (has a job), (ii) unemployed (not working but would like to), and (iii) inactive or not in the labor force (everyone else). Category (ii) is a little fuzzy: How do we know whether or not someone wants to work? In some countries, the answer comes from a survey in which the person is asked whether he or she is actively looking for a job. In others, only people claiming unemployment benefits are classified as such.

Information on the labor-market status of individuals leads to statistics on the *labor force*, the *employment rate*, the *participation rate* , and the *unemployment rate*. The employment rate is the ratio of employment to the adult population. The labor force is the number of people in categories (i) and (ii): either working or unemployed. The participation rate is the ratio of the labor force to the adult population. The unemployment rate is the ratio of the number of people who are unemployed to the labor force.

The details here are important. We see large differences, for example, in employment rates across countries. In Germany and Japan, for example, the employment rate has averaged about 71 percent over the last decade, and in Italy about 57 percent, according to the OECD. The source of this difference lies primarily in the number of inactive people, not the number of unemployed. For that reason, and because it's easier to measure, many of the experts focus on employment rather than unemployment. Newspapers, of course, tend to do the opposite.

In the US, employment data are collected and reported monthly by the Bureau of Labor Statistics. The BLS releases its closely-watched monthly report, "The Employment Situation," at 8:30 am on the first Friday of the month. It includes such indicators as employment ("nonfarm payroll"), the unemployment rate, and the size of the labor force. This release is based on two surveys, the Current Employment Statistics (CES) survey of firms' payroll records and the Current Population Survey (CPS) of households. The CES covers 300,000+ businesses and provides detailed industry data on employment, hours, and earnings of workers on nonfarm payrolls. The most closely watched number in the US is probably the monthly estimate of the change in nonfarm employment, which comes from this survey. The CPS covers 60,000+ households and is conducted for the BLS by the Bureau of the Census. It provides a comprehensive body of data on labor-force status: employment, unemployment, and so on. Both sets of data are updated periodically as more information comes in. Since the two sources are radically different, they occasionally result in conflicting information about such basic indicators as the number of people employed.

Other countries collect similar data, but the sources and definitions vary.

7.2   Supply and demand for labor

Differences in the abilities and skills of individuals make labor markets incredibly complex, but we can get a sense of the impact of government regulation in a model in which there is a single market for a single kind of labor.

Demand for labor. The demand for labor comes from (typically) firms. The short version: The higher the wage, the fewer employees firms will hire.

A more complex version follows from thinking through a hypothetical firm's decision-making process. Let us say our firm produces output using the production function $Y = AF(K, L) = AK^\alpha L^{1-\alpha}$ ("Cobb-Douglas "). Let us say, for the sake of simplicity, that the capital stock is some fixed number K. How does the firm's profit depend on the choice of labor input L? If p is the price of one unit of output and w is the price (wage) of one unit of labor, the firm's profit is

$$
\begin{aligned}
\text{Profit} \quad &= \quad pY - wL - \text{Fixed Costs} \\
&= \quad pAF(K, L) - wL - \text{Fixed Costs.}
\end{aligned}
$$

How does profit vary with L? The fixed costs might be attributed to capital or other factors, but they do not vary with L. For this reason, they won't affect the demand for labor. What is affected by L is output (which, in turn, affects sales revenue) and cost (the wage bill).

If the firm maximizes its profit, it will add labor as long as the marginal benefit is greater than the marginal cost. We learned earlier that we can characterize the solution to the firm's maximization problem by computing the derivative of the profit function and setting it equal to zero. After arranging terms, we see that maximum profit occurs when the marginal benefit of an additional unit of labor (more revenue) equals its marginal cost (the wage):

$$pA \, \frac{\partial F(K, L)}{\partial L} \;=\; w.$$

This is an equation we can solve for L and represents the amount of labor the firm will hire (demand) for any given values of p, w, and K. In the Cobb-Douglas case, $Y = AK^{\alpha}L^{1-\alpha}$, the demand function follows from

$$p(1 - \alpha)AK^{\alpha}L^{-\alpha} \;=\; w,$$

which implies (solve for L)

$$L \;=\; K \left[\frac{p(1 - \alpha)A}{w} \right]^{1/\alpha}. \tag{7.1}$$

The aggregate (total) demand for labor is the sum of demands across all firms. Its important feature, for our purposes, is that it falls when the wage rises, just as we assume most demand functions do. (This property follows from the diminishing marginal product of labor, one of the conditions we imposed on the production function.)

Supply of labor. Now let's turn to the supply of labor. The short version: Supply increases with the wage.

A more complete version goes like this. When selling their labor services, individuals make two decisions: whether to work at all and, if so, how much. Obviously, many jobs offer limited flexibility on the second dimension. For this reason, and also because it simplifies the analysis, we will ignore the second choice and consider the decision of an individual deciding whether or not to work a given number of hours h. What is the gain from working? The monetary gain is wh. However, what matters for the individual is the increase in happiness, or satisfaction, that such pay induces. This may vary across individuals. For example, the same pay may be more valuable to a poor individual than to a rich one. What is the loss from working? Simple! He has less time to dedicate to other activities, including playing bridge or football, cooking, reading economics books, or spending time with family. The value of these activities is what economists call the *reservation wage*. For any wage less than this, the benefits of not working are greater than the benefits of working. For the economy as a whole, the higher the wage, the greater the number of people who decide to work. Thus, aggregate labor supply L^s increases with the wage rate w.

Labor-market equilibrium.   We represent labor demand and supply with straight lines in Figure 7.1. The equilibrium wage rate w^* is the value at which demand and supply are equal. The number of workers employed at this wage defines the level of employment L^*. This kind of analysis should be familiar to anyone who has taken an economics course.

Figure 7.1: Equilibrium in the labor market.

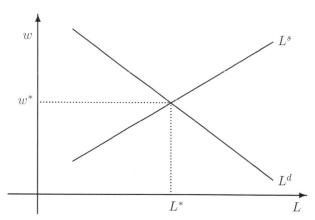

Where is unemployment in Figure 7.1? We might think of L^* as representing both employment (the number of people hired by firms, since the point is on their demand curve) and the labor force (the number of people who want to work at the going wage). Unemployment is the difference between these two numbers, so evidently there is none. There is an almost perfect analogy between this market and a dealer-type securities market such as the Nasdaq. At the Nasdaq, dealers post bid and ask prices and are committed to executing transactions at those prices. If you want to sell a given security, you just contact one of the dealers (or ask your broker to do this for you). If you'd like to sell at less than the bid, you have a deal. There are no "unemployed" securities.

7.3 Supply and demand with a minimum wage

There are many reasons that labor markets don't work quite like our frictionless market. Let's look at one: government policies and institutions. Examples include minimum wages, restrictions on wage adjustments, labor unions, limits on hiring and firing, and so on. We don't argue that these

Figure 7.2: The labor market with a minimum wage.

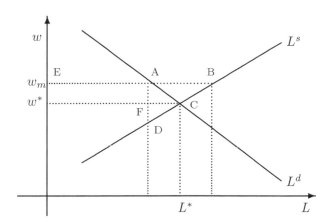

things are bad — they may very well have benefits — but they do have an impact on how the labor market works.

We'll look at the minimum wage since it's the simplest example. (Remember: Simple is a good thing.) If we prohibit purchases of labor services below a given wage, how does the market work? Figure 7.2 shows how the supply-and-demand analysis might be applied in this case. In the figure, the minimum wage (w_m) is higher than the equilibrium wage (w^*). At the minimum wage, the supply of labor (the line segment EB) is greater than the demand for labor (the line segment EA). Minimum wage laws don't force firms to hire, so employment is given by their demand function. The difference between supply and demand is unemployment (the line segment AB). In the figure, unemployment is represented by the line segment AB. The unemployment *rate* is the ratio of unemployment (AB) to the supply of labor (EB). As a practical matter, it's an open question whether the impact of the minimum wage on unemployment is large or small, but few economists doubt that it's there.

Who are the winners and losers from the minimum wage? The winners are the employed, who get a higher wage than they would otherwise. The losers are the unemployed (who would prefer to work) and firms (who must pay more for labor). Taken as a whole, the policy reduces welfare by an amount represented by the triangle ACD. This will seem clear if you recall how welfare triangles work, mysterious otherwise, but it's true in this setting that a minimum wage reduces overall welfare.

7.4   Labor-market institutions

The minimum wage is a useful illustration, but labor-market institutions and regulations differ dramatically across countries along many dimensions. Some of them have been collected and reported by the World Bank's Doing Business. They report, for most countries in the world, the flexibility an employer has over the terms of employment, including the employer's ability to vary hours, the cost and difficulty of dismissal, and whether workers can be hired under fixed-term (as opposed to permanent) contracts. Some countries also limit hours (no more than 35 hours a week!) or give unions more power over the terms of employment contracts.

The evidence suggests that many kinds of labor-market regulation have the ultimate effect of reducing employment. There is, of course, a useful role for laws that enforce fair dealing. Paying workers for fewer hours than they worked, for example, is impossible to justify. But many labor-market regulations seem to discourage firms from hiring, although their stated purpose is to "protect jobs." Restrictions on layoffs and mandatory severance payments seem to do this since they raise the long-term cost of hiring workers. In many countries, we've seen growth in the number of part-time and unofficial workers, precisely to get around this kind of regulation.

7.5   Labor-market flow indicators

The supply and demand diagram is indicative, but it can't address one of the most striking features of modern economies: the huge amount of turnover we see in labor markets. Economies create and destroy jobs at truly amazing rates. Even MBA graduates often find themselves changing jobs frequently, either by choice (they find jobs they like better) or by misfortune (economic downturns, mergers, and so on).

In the aggregate, we see this in data from both firms and households. At firms, new positions are created either because existing firms expand their operations or because new firms hire workers. We refer to this phenomenon as *job creation*. At the same time, existing firms sometimes eliminate positions. We refer to this process as *job destruction*. An establishment (a production unit, such as a factory or store) is said to create jobs if it increases the number of positions between one period and the next. The economy's overall job creation is the sum of the increases in positions across all the establishments that created jobs. Similarly, an establishment is said to destroy jobs if it decreases its number of positions from one period to the next. The economy's overall job destruction is the sum of the decreases in jobs across all establishments that destroyed jobs. The sum of job creation and job destruction is referred to as *job reallocation* or *job turnover*. Job creation, destruction, and reallocation *rates* are ratios of job creation, destruction, and reallocation, respectively, to the total number of jobs in the economy. These rates vary greatly across countries, but their magnitudes are impressive everywhere.

We see similar turnover in household data, with individuals reporting frequent changes in jobs or employment status. An employed individual can stay in her job, move to another job, become unemployed (leave one job but look for another), or leave the labor force (leave one job without seeking another). Similarly, an unemployed person can become employed (get a job), stay unemployed (look for a job without taking one), or leave the labor force (stop looking for a job). Someone out of the labor force can become employed (take a job), become unemployed (look for a job without taking one), or remain out of the labor force. We have information from surveys on each of these possible changes.

Some summary measures will give you a sense of how this looks for a typical individual. *Accessions* occur when individuals take new jobs, regardless of their current status. *Separations* occur when individuals leave jobs, regardless of their reason. The accession and separation *rates* are ratios of accessions and separations, respectively, to total jobs. The sum of the two rates is referred to as the *worker reallocation rate*. In the late 1980s, the annual accession rate in the US was 45.2 percent and the annual separation rate was 46.0 percent. The worker reallocation rate was a staggering 91.2 percent! These numbers do not say why workers change jobs, merely that they do. Worker reallocation rates are generally lower in other countries, including France (59.6 percent) and Italy (68.1%). Apparently, it is more common in the US both to leave a job and to take a new job. You might ask yourself whether the factors that make the separation rate high also make the accession rate high, or whether they are influenced by different factors.

7.6   Virtues of flexible input markets

There's a big picture point hidden here somewhere. In a modern economy, the mix of products is changing constantly. Many of the products and services we use today simply weren't available twenty years ago: high-speed internet access, iPods, databases, and so on. A successful economy needs a mechanism to shift capital and labor to these new uses and away from others. The evidence suggests that countries with labor and capital markets that do this well tend to perform well in the aggregate. The ability of an economy to reallocate jobs across firms, industries, and geographical areas is, perhaps, even more important than capital. Sometimes, labor-market institutions are an obstacle to this reallocation process, reducing aggregate productivity and output.

Most developed economies have gone through at least one major reallocation in their history, as most people shifted from agriculture to industry. In the US, there's been a further shift from manufacturing to services. Services seem less vivid than physical goods to most of us, but the fact is that goods represent a smaller part of modern developed economies than services do. You might ask yourself what sector you're likely to go into. Past experience suggests that few of our students are targeting jobs in manufacturing, much less agriculture.

If reallocation is important, then labor-market institutions are central to aggregate performance. If people cannot be shifted quickly to more-productive sectors and firms, aggregate productivity will be lower. Consider the impact of an increase in productivity in a single industry. What is the impact on employment? The immediate effect is probably to throw some people out of work, since a smaller number of people can produce the same output. The employment impact depends on the elasticity of demand: If the elasticity is low, the increase in productivity reduces employment. The long-term effect is to reallocate these workers to other sectors. We would argue that this is good for the economy as a whole, even if it's painful for the people who had reallocation forced on them. Nevertheless, there's a long history of concern about reallocation, dating back at least to the machine-smashing "Luddites."

Deregulation is similar, in the sense that it often leads to reallocation of capital and labor. Consider an example from Europe. In recent years, the European airline market has gone through a deregulation process resembling that of the US in the 1980s. Before deregulation, every European country had its own national airline. The airline was typically a monopolist on internal routes and a (collusive) duopolist (with the other country's airline) on international routes. Like many monopolists, these airlines charged high prices and operated inefficiently. Now, any company can fly any route in the European Union. The entry of new carriers has meant big trouble for many of the incumbents. Sabena and Swissair went bust. Others (Alitalia?) may follow suit. It is clear that at the end of the reorganization of the industry, fares will be much lower (they are already, as a matter of fact). As a result, people will fly more often, and there may even be more jobs in the industry. Along the way, job destruction by the incumbents will be accompanied by job creation by the new entrants.

Who gains? Consumers and workers in new firms. Who loses? The workers and shareholders of incumbent firms. Traditional welfare analysis tells us that the gains are greater than the losses, but the political process does not necessarily weight them equally. In fact, the costs are often concentrated, while the benefits are thinly spread over many individual consumers and firms, so the political process will tend to give greater weight to the former. Nevertheless, it's likely that such a reallocation is a net benefit to the society as a whole.

7.7 A model of unemployment dynamics

These flows suggest a more dynamic labor market than our supply-and-demand analysis. Where do they come from? You might consider your own case: What factors might cause you to leave a job? take a new one? A simple model can help us understand the overall impact of individual decisions like this on economy-wide employment and unemployment rates. To keep things simple, we will ignore transitions in and out of the labor force and focus on employment and unemployment.

To start, individuals may be either unemployed, U, or employed, E, with $U + E = L$ and L a fixed number. The unemployment and employment rates are then $u = U/L$ and $e = E/L$. Since the only states are U and E, the employment and unemployment rates sum to one: $u + e = 1$.

The unemployment rate can change over time if individuals change their labor-market status. Let us say that a constant fraction $0 < s < 1$ (s for separation) of employed people lose their jobs and become unemployed. Why might this be? Perhaps because their firms are doing poorly, and either shrink or go out of business altogether. Let us also say that a constant fraction $0 < a < 1$ (a for accession) of unemployed people find new jobs, as they find employers who need their skills. We've seen that this kind of reallocation is the norm for modern economies. With these two ingredients, the unemployment rate changes like this from one period to the next:

$$u_{t+1} = u_t + se_t - au_t$$

or

$$\Delta u_{t+1} = se_t - au_t.$$

Unemployment rises over time if more employed people lose their jobs than unemployed people find new jobs, and it falls over time if the reverse is true. (Formally, this should remind you of the dynamics of capital accumulation in the Solow model). Since $u_t + e_t = 1$, we can write this as

$$\Delta u_{t+1} = s(1 - u_t) - au_t. \tag{7.2}$$

This is useful because we have summarized the dynamics of unemployment in a single equation. If you were told that the unemployment rate was now (say) u_0, then repeated application of (7.2) would enable you to calculate the unemployment rate in future periods. It would be a very simple matter to do these calculations in Excel.

Using equation (7.2), we can compute both the period-by-period dynamics and the steady-state unemployment rate. We find steady-state unemployment ($\overline{u}$, say) by setting $\Delta u_{t+1} = 0$ so that

$$0 = s(1 - \overline{u}) - a\overline{u}.$$

Solving for $\overline{u}$ gives

$$\overline{u} = \frac{s}{s + a},$$

a number between zero and one. Over time, the unemployment rate "gravitates" to this value, so we might also refer to it as the "long run" or "natural" unemployment rate. The idea is that we want a measure of the underlying unemployment rate that would prevail if it were not for temporary shocks that make $u_0 \neq \overline{u}$. Clearly, steady-state unemployment is higher when s, the separation rate, is higher and is lower when a, the accession rate, is higher. That is, if people lose jobs easily and have difficulty finding them, then the unemployment rate will be higher.

You should think of the parameters of this model, a and s, as standing in for various country-specific labor-market policies and institutional arrangements that affect the willingness of firms to hire and fire workers, the willingness of workers to take and quit jobs, and so on. Examples of such policies include: minimum wages; taxes on labor income; regulations that control the length of the working week (such as the 35-hour week in France); the size of severance payments for layoffs; the size of unemployment benefits; and so on. Which of these policies decrease a? Which of these policies decrease s?

Here is a different way to look at the steady-state calculation. With a little bit of statistics, one can show that an individual's average duration of unemployment in this model is $1/a$, and an individual's average duration of employment is $1/s$. Steady-state unemployment is given by

$$\overline{u} = \frac{s}{s + a} = \frac{\frac{1}{a}}{\frac{1}{a} + \frac{1}{s}} = \frac{\text{duration of } U}{\text{duration of } U + \text{duration of } E}.$$

So, to think about why European unemployment is relatively high compared to that of the US, we might begin with factors that either increase the duration of unemployment or reduce the duration of employment. Which of these factors do you think is more important for European unemployment?

7.8   Institutions and labor-market dynamics

We can get a sense of the dynamics of labor-market reallocation by putting our earlier labor-market analysis to work. In our model, the accession and separation rates also govern the response of the unemployment rate to a shock that pushes unemployment above (or below) its steady-state value. In particular, these rates govern the *speed of adjustment* back to the steady state. To see this, write the equation governing the dynamics of the unemployment rate as

$$u_{t+1} \;\; = \;\; s + [1 - (s + a)]u_t.$$

In order for the model to be empirically realistic, we need a worker reallocation rate, $s + a$, that satisfies

$$0 < s + a < 1.$$

With a little bit of algebra, the unemployment rate can be written in terms of deviations from its steady-state value

$$u_{t+1} - \overline{u} \;\; = \;\; \lambda(u_t - \overline{u}),$$

where $\lambda = 1 - (s + a)$ is the speed of adjustment of the unemployment rate to its steady-state value. The reason for this is that with a little bit more algebra one can show that if the unemployment rate is hit by a temporary shock (that does not affect a or s) that takes on the value u_0, the adjustment back to steady state is given by the formula

$$u_t - \overline{u} \;\; = \;\; \lambda^t(u_0 - \overline{u})$$

or

$$u_t \;\; = \;\; (1 - \lambda^t)\overline{u} + \lambda^t u_0.$$

What's important is not the algebra but the idea: In economies with low values of s and a, worker reallocation is slow. Here, we see that this results in slow adjustment of the unemployment rate. But you can imagine, as well, slow reaction of producers to consumer preferences. The churning of the labor market implied by high values of s and a, thus, serves a purpose of shifting workers to jobs in which their value is the highest.

Numerical example. Suppose that in both Europe and the US, $s = 0.01$, and that accession is $a_{US} = 0.19$ in the US, but lower in Europe, $a_{EU} = 0.09$. Then, not only is European unemployment 10 percent as opposed to 5 percent in the US, but European unemployment also takes considerably longer to respond to shocks than does US unemployment ($\lambda_{EU} = 0.90, \lambda_{US} = 0.80$). Based on this example, can you imagine the economic consequences if, as recent evidence suggests, the US labor market has become less flexible?

Executive summary

1. Labor-market indicators include employment (the number of people working), unemployment (the number not working who would like to), the labor force (employment plus unemployment), and the unemployment rate (the ratio of unemployment to the labor force).

2. Measures to protect workers often have the opposite effect; that is, by making labor more expensive to firms, they may reduce employment.

3. Many developed economies are characterized by high rates of job and worker reallocation. People change jobs and firms change workers — frequently.

4. The efficiency of work reallocation affects the performance of the economy as a whole. In particular, flexible labor markets help an economy respond to the inevitable changes in products and industries that occur.

Review questions

1. Labor-market indicators. You are the mayor of a small village whose labor-market data are: adult population (100), employment (55), and unemployment (5).

   (a) Draw a circle on a piece of paper corresponding to the population of your village. Divide it into sections corresponding to employment, unemployment, labor force, and not in the labor force.

   (b) Compute the employment rate, the participation rate, and the unemployment rate.

   Answer.

   (a) For you to do.

   (b) The employment rate is 55 percent $[= 55/100]$. The participation rate is 60 percent $[= (55 + 5)/100]$. The unemployment rate is 8.3 percent $[= 5/60]$.

2. Supply and demand. Consider an economy with one firm (which is nevertheless a price taker). It produces widgets according to the production function $Y = AK^{1/2}L^{1/2}$ and sells them for two dollars each. [Yes, we know we said α would always be one-third, but apparently we lied. Sorry.] For simplicity, assume that $A = K = 1$. The supply of labor in this economy is $L^s = w^{3/2}$.

   (a) What is the demand for labor? How does it depend on the wage?

   (b) What are the equilibrium values for the labor force, the wage, and employment? What is the unemployment rate?

(c) Suppose the government imposes a minimum wage of \$1.1. What are the equilibrium values for the labor force, the wage, and employment? What is the unemployment rate?

Answer.

(a) The demand for labor is given by $L^d(w) = 1[2 \times (1/2)]/w]^2 = w^{-2}$. This follows from the labor demand function, equation (7.1).

(b) Equating demand and supply yields $L^* = w^* = 1$. The labor force is one and the unemployment rate is zero.

(c) With a minimum wage of \$1.1, the supply of labor (the labor force) is $1.1^{3/2} = 1.15$. The demand for labor is $1.1^{-2} = 0.826$. Therefore, employment is 0.826 and the unemployment rate is $(1.15 - 0.826)/1.15 = .2817$ or 28.17 percent.

3. Minimum wage. Milton Friedman once suggested that the minimum wage discriminated against people with low skills. To see what he had in mind, consider an environment with two kinds of workers, high-skilled and low-skilled. Suppose each group has its own separate labor market, each subject to the same minimum wage.

   (a) Which kind of worker is most likely to be affected by a minimum wage? Why?

   (b) Who gains or loses from a minimum wage? Does this explain Friedman's comment?

Answer.

   (a) You might imagine that high-skilled workers will not be affected by a minimum wage, since their skill demands a wage well above it. But workers with low skill might find that no one is willing to hire them at the minimum: their skills don't justify it.

   (b) The winners are those with low skill who happen to find jobs. The losers are the firms that hire them and, more to the point, the low-skilled who can't find work. The might get jobs if we allowed the wage to fall. So they bear much of the cost of the system.

4. Taxing labor. Suppose we put a tax on labor, paid by firms. Use a supply and demand diagram in which the vertical axis is the pretax wage and the horizontal axis is the quantity of labor.

   (a) Draw a supply and demand diagram. What happens to the curves when you add the tax?

   (b) What is the impact on the pretax wage and quantity of labor?

   (a) Draw something like Figure 7.1. When you add the tax, the demand curve falls by the amount of the tax. The amount of the fall equals the tax per unit. [If you put the after-tax wage on the vertical axis, the supply curve would shift, but that's another story. The point is to be careful about the pre- and post-tax wage.]

(b) Since demand has fallen, so does the pretax wage and the quantity of labor. Put simply: if you tax labor, you would expect firms to buy less.

5. Layoffs. From the *New York Times*, March 6, 2009 (rough paraphrase): The WARN Act requires employers to give 60 days' notice if a plant is closed or 500 or more people are laid off at one location. Some wonder whether notice should be required for other job losses. A Berkeley professor says it's a matter of "transparency and decency." An IBM executive disagrees, noting that it's routine for the company to lay off some employees while hiring others. "This business is in a constant state of transformation." If you were asked to advise the government, how would you describe the costs and benefits of wider application of the WARN Act?

Answer. This is another cost of firing workers, and we know that higher firing costs tend to discourage firms from hiring workers in the first place. The question is how high the cost is. If we figure workers will keep producing, it may be small; if not, it's larger, especially if there's a chance of sabotage or other damaging behavior.

We asked two of our favorite management professors the same question. Professor Wiesenfeld said: "I think giving people advanced notice (not 60 days, but not escorting them to the door immediately) is generally beneficial, because it helps to retain the commitment and motivation of the person's former colleagues." Professor Freedman said: "It depends on the situation. I have encountered situations where people who are given notice act in a very destructive manner."

6. Income support systems. In the US and UK, flexible labor markets are accompanied by income support systems in which (for example) people with low incomes pay negative income tax; that is, they receive money. In the US, this is referred to as the Earned Income Tax Credit. In what ways is this better than direct intervention in labor markets? Worse?

Answer. Many see this as an effective way to reconcile the benefits of a flexible labor market with a safety net that protects workers from some of the challenges of losing one's job. Restrictions on firing, for example, help people with jobs keep them, but discourage firms from hiring more people. An income support system avoids the latter.

7. Labor-market dynamics. In our model of unemployment dynamics, suppose that the accession rate is $a = 0.2$ and the separation rate is $s = 0.01$.

(a) Compute the steady-state unemployment rate and the speed of adjustment parameter.

(b) Suppose that a restriction on firing makes workers less attractive to firms. What effects might this have on long-run unemployment and the response of the economy to an increase in the unemployment rate?

Answer.

(a) The steady-state unemployment rate is $\bar{u} = s/(s+a) = 0.048$ or 4.8 percent. The speed of adjustment parameter is $\lambda = 1-(s+a) = 0.79$.

(b) This restriction is likely to lower the accession rate a, thereby increasing long-run unemployment and making periods of high unemployment last longer (i.e., making λ closer to one).

If you're looking for more

Labor data are less standardized across countries than national income and product accounts. The US Bureau of Labor Statistics has a nice collection (unfortunately being phased out) of international data constructed in roughly comparable ways across countries:

http://www.bls.gov/fls/.

Ditto the OECD:

http://www.oecd.org/std/labourstatistics/
http://www.oecd.org/els/emp/keyemploymentstatistics.htm.

Yes, two links! The second includes data on labor market policies and employment protection. The World Bank's Doing Business also has an extensive collection of indicators of labor-market institutions.

Finally, Denmark is a fascinating example when it comes to labor markets since it combines flexibility (it's easy to fire people, for example) with generous social support (unemployment insurance and training, for example). A nice overview is Jianping Zhou, IMF working paper, "Danish for All? Balancing Flexibility with Security."

Symbols and data and used in this chapter

Table 7.1: Symbol table.

Symbol	Definition
p	Price of output
w	Wage of one unit of labor (say, one hour)
Y	Output
K	Stock of physical capital
L	Quantity of labor
A	Total factor productivity (TFP)
α	Exponent of K in Cobb-Douglas production function (= capital share of income)
$F(K, L)$	Production function of K and L
L^*	Equilibrium level of employment
w^*	Equilibrium wage
w_m	Minimum wage
L^s	Labor supply
L^d	Labor demand
U	Unemployed persons
E	Employed persons
u	Unemployment rate $(= U/L)$
e	Employment rate $(= E/L)$
s	Separation rate (share of people who lose a job)
a	accession rate (share of people who find a job)
Δx_{t+1}	Change of x_{t+1} $(= x_{t+1} - x_t)$
$\overline{u}$	Steady-state unemployment rate
u_0	Unemployment rate in start-period zero
λ	speed of adjustment of unemployment rate to steady state

Table 7.2: Data table.

Variable	Source
Nonfarm employment	PAYEMS
Unemployment rate	UNRATE
Employment ratio	EMRATIO
Nonfarm openings rate	JTSJOR
Duration of unemployment	UEMPMEAN
U6 unemployment rate	U6RATE
Civilian labor force	CLF16OV
Civilian participation rate	CIVPART

To retrieve the data online, add the identifier from the source column to http://research.stlouisfed.org/fred2/series/. For example, to retrieve nonfarm employment, point your browser to http://research. stlouisfed.org/fred2/series/PAYEMS

8
Financial Markets

Key Words: Time consistency; information asymmetry.

Big Ideas:

- Effective financial markets require strong institutional support.

- Good institutions deal with information asymmetries and time consistency issues.

Some of the most important markets for aggregate economic performance are those for labor and (financial) capital, which affect every industry and product. Countries differ markedly in their treatment of both markets, with (evidently) different outcomes as a result.

Our focus here is on financial markets, which are, perhaps, the most difficult markets to manage effectively.

8.1   Features of effective financial markets

Financial markets are central to economic performance, because they facilitate (if they work well) the allocation of resources to the most-productive firms. In the US today, some firms borrow from banks, others issue bonds and equity in capital markets, and still others raise money through venture capitalists. Countries differ widely in how they do this, but they all have ways of channeling funds from households (savers) to firms (borrowers).

The primary issue with financial markets is information, and we know that markets sometimes handle information poorly. Here, investors need to understand the risks faced by borrowers, but borrowers typically know more about themselves than others do. A bank, for example, needs to know enough about its borrowers to assess the risk of default, and its depositors need to know enough about the bank's ability to do this well to assess the risk to their deposits. A bank (or other financial institution) is, therefore, in the information business: Its goal is to process information efficiently so that it can assess and manage risk.

None of this is easy to do. All of these financial arrangements require institutional support. An effective financial system requires some version of:

- **Creditor protection.** If A lends money to B, it's essential that A's claim be honored. That requires a legal system that makes the creditor's rights clear and enforces them if necessary. (You might think about "property rights" and the "rule of law" about now.) Without this, people will either not make loans or will make loans only to friends and relatives. Weak, ineffective financial systems follow naturally when creditors are not protected, and economic performance suffers as a result.

- **Corporate governance.** The laws of most countries give creditors some say over the management of firms. Equity investors, for example, are represented (in principle) by boards of directors. There's endless debate about how best to do this, but there's no question that doing it well is important.

- **Disclosure.** When people invest in securities, they need to understand what they're buying. In most countries with active securities markets, the law dictates disclosure of relevant financial information. Again, some countries do this better than others.

- **Central banks.** Most countries have central banks. If run well, they play an important role in the economy, particularly as lenders of last resort during financial crises.

Measures of these things are available from a number of sources, including the World Bank's Doing Business website, particularly the categories Getting Credit and Protecting Investors.

8.2   Financial regulation and crises

From the perspective of a country, one of the challenges of managing financial markets is that they can cause enormous collateral damage if something goes wrong. If a farmer goes bankrupt, you buy milk from someone else. But if a large financial institution goes under, it can slow down the whole economy. The question is how to manage financial markets to get the benefits of a thriving financial system with the least risk.

No one yet has come up with a perfect answer. An unregulated financial system may work well most of the time, but will experience occasional crises. A more tightly regulated system may (it's not a sure thing) have lower crisis risk, but the regulation may distort the allocation of capital. Most approaches to financial regulation face a tradeoff of this sort.

Consider deposit insurance. In the US, bank panics were a common occurrence up through the 1930s. During the Depression, thousands of banks went under. Some of them were insolvent. Others closed because depositors demanded their money back for fear that the bank would go under: what we call bank runs. It's a consequence, in part, of people having imperfect information about the bank's soundness.

The solution — or, rather, one solution — was to provide deposit insurance. Milton Friedman and Anna Schwartz called federal deposit insurance "the most important structural change" made in the 1930s to deal with bank runs. And it worked — bank runs pretty much ended.

But like many solutions, it raised new problems. The problem with deposit insurance is what economists call "moral hazard" and others might call the "other people's money" problem. Since depositors don't face the risk of losing their money, banks don't face the risk of withdrawal, and they have less reason to control the risk of their investments. Or to put it differently, their borrowing costs don't reflect the risk of their loan portfolios. So they take excessive risk, which is hardly what we're looking for. Therefore, we add to deposit insurance some regulatory oversight intended to limit banks' ability to take risks. We know from bitter experience that it's hard to get this right, and we're still trying.

A related challenge is the "too big to fail" dilemma, a classic version of the time-consistency problem discussed in Chapter 6. Policymakers insist that they will never bail out failing banks, but everyone knows in advance that a failed behemoth can topple the financial system (think Lehman or AIG). So the promise lacks credibility: a future policymaker is likely to bail them out anyway. Investors know this, and reward the largest intermediaries with low funding costs, thereby subsidizing excessive risk taking.

Executive summary

1. Financial markets work best when based on effective institutions.

2. It's hard to get that exactly right.

If you're looking for more

The logic and operation of financial institutions is a huge subject in its own right. Among the courses we have on the topic are Professor Schoenholtz's "Money and Banking," course ECON-GB.2333, and "Financial Crisis and Policy," course ECON-GB.2343. Or see his book: Stephen Cecchetti and Kermit Schoenholtz, *Money, Banking and Financial Markets*; or visit their blog at http://www.moneyandbanking.com. Ben Bernanke's testimony to Congress (search "Bernanke testimony") is a wonderful overview of financial regulation and the 2008 crisis. He also did a series of lectures that are posted on the Fed's website.

Beyond that, financial crises make good reading, and there's no shortage of good books on the subject. One of the best reads is Edward Chancellor's *Devil Take the Hindmost*, a history of financial speculation. On the most recent crisis, we enjoyed David Wessel's *In Fed We Trust* and Andrew Ross Sorkin's *Too Big to Fail*.

9
International Trade

Tools: Ricardo's model of trade; consumption and production possibility frontiers.

Key Words: Absolute advantage; comparative advantage; autarky.

Big Ideas:

- Trade is a positive-sum game: both countries benefit.

- Gains from trade are similar to increases in TFP: trade increases aggregate consumption opportunities.

- Trade creates winners and losers, but the winners win more than the losers lose. Trade affects the kind of jobs that are available, not the number of jobs.

Virtually all economists, liberal or conservative, believe that free (or "free-er") trade is a good thing: good for consumers, good for workers, good for all countries involved. Why? Because consumers are able to buy products from the cheapest vendor, which forces production to the highest productivity firms, which, in turn, supports the highest wages for workers.

No one else seems to believe that. Most are convinced that one side of trade is unfair, that one country is gaining at the other's expense. The purpose of this chapter is to outline the logic for trade. The logic is mathematical, by which we mean it's clear and precise, if a little abstract. You can decide for yourself whether you find it persuasive.

9.1   Ricardo's theory of trade

David Ricardo was one of the most influential economists of the early nine-
teenth century, but he came to economics by accident. Born to a Jewish
family in Amsterdam, he left the Netherlands and broke off relations with
his family (and they with him) to avoid an arranged marriage, and married
a Quaker instead. He set himself up in London as a government securities
dealer and became, in his words, "sufficiently rich to satisfy all my desires
and the reasonable desires of all those about me." Looking for something to
occupy his time, he developed the modern theory of international trade.

Many people in Ricardo's day (and ours) regarded trade as a zero-sum activity: If you gain from trade, then I must lose. His insight was that both
sides typically benefit, even if it appears that one has an *absolute productivity advantage* over the other. In his words, each country has a *comparative
advantage*.

We develop Ricardo's theory in a particularly simple setting: Two countries produce and consume two products, and both products are produced
with labor alone. In many respects, this version of the theory is unrealis-
tic, but the lack of realism is exactly what makes the analysis simple and
understandable. None of the simplifications are essential to the argument.

To be specific, let us call the countries the US (country 1) and Mexico
(country 2) and the products apples and bananas. (Yes, we know neither
the US nor Mexico produces many bananas, but we like the letters a and
b.) We start by specifying the productivity levels: the quantities of product
(either a or b) in country i (either 1 or 2) produced with one unit of labor.
We'll use specific numbers, which we report in Table 9.1. Let us say, also
in the interest of simplicity, that the labor force is the same in the two
countries: $L_1 = L_2 = 100$.

Table 9.1: Productivities for trade example.

	Apples	Bananas
US (country 1)	$\alpha_1 = 20$	$\beta_1 = 10$
Mexico (country 2)	$\alpha_2 = 5$	$\beta_2 = 5$

The productivities mirror the discussion you hear about trade between a
rich country (the US here) and a poor one (Mexico). For example, one
unit of labor produces more in the US whether it's used to produce apples
or bananas. We would say the US has an absolute advantage in producing
both goods. A number of factors might play a role here. Perhaps the weather

is better, labor is better educated, the distribution system is more efficient, or the institutions are better.

The question is: Would Mexico and the US both benefit from completely free trade, relative to a position of *autarky* (no trade at all)? The answer is yes, but let's run through the argument. Suppose Mexico had high enough tariffs or other barriers to kill off trade altogether. Then Mexico would likely produce both products. How much of each? It could produce apples in quantity $a = L_2\alpha_2 = 100 \times 5 = 500$ or bananas in quantity $b = L_2\beta_2 = 100 \times 5 = 500$. It could also produce any combination in between, as shown in Figure 9.1 (the solid line). We call the solid line the production possibility frontier for Mexico, since every point on the line represents a possible production/consumption combination. In this example, the line has a one-for-one tradeoff between apples and bananas, implying a relative price of $q = p_b/p_a = \alpha_2/\beta_2 = 1$.

What happens if Mexico and the US allow trade? It depends on the relative price q. Suppose that Mexico can export bananas at a relative price of $q > 1$ apples for each banana. Then Mexico will produce only bananas. Why? Because it can produce each at the same cost ($1/5 = 0.2$ units of labor), but bananas sell for more on the world market. As a country, it faces strictly better possibilities if it trades rather than producing both goods itself. If it produces only bananas ($b = 500$) and then trades some for apples at a rate of q apples for every banana, it does better than the one-for-one tradeoff it got from producing apples itself. (See the dashed line in Figure 9.1, which is above the solid line.) [As a check on your understanding: How would this work if $q < 1$? What would Mexico produce? What would its possibility frontier look like? Would Mexico still benefit from trade?]

In short, trade benefits Mexico, even though it is less productive than the US for both products. Similar reasoning shows that the US would benefit from trade, too. [Another check: What is the possibility frontier for the US if there's no trade? Trade with $q > 1$? Trade with $q < 1$?]

Ricardo had a rationale for these gains from trade: Even though Mexico is less productive absolutely ($\alpha_1 > \alpha_2$ and $\beta_1 > \beta_2$), it is comparatively more productive in bananas than the US ($\beta_2/\alpha_2 > \beta_1/\alpha_1$). Conversely, the US is comparatively more productive in apples ($\alpha_1/\beta_1 > \alpha_2/\beta_2$). If each country produces the good for which it is comparatively more productive, then world productivity rises and both countries benefit. For this reason, Ricardo referred to this as the theory of comparative advantage.

Figure 9.1: Gains from trade in Mexico.

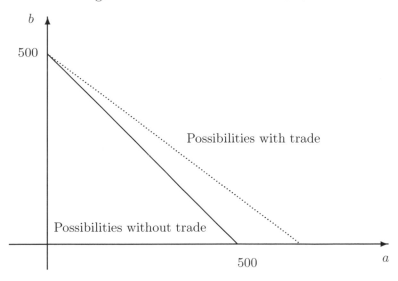

9.2   Digging a little deeper

Moving to free trade is similar to an increase in productivity because when you shift production to high productivity products, aggregate productivity rises. The impact is similar to our discussion of labor and financial markets. Countries with good labor and financial markets allocate inputs more effectively and increase aggregate productivity as a result. This is a natural feature of trade models, but it takes some effort to work out the details, even in a setting as simple as our ·example. If you're averse to math, you might skip to the next section the first time through.

Our goal is to compare production and consumption in two cases: one with no trade, and one with completely free trade (no tariffs or transportation costs). The comparison is somewhat extreme, but the hope is that it will give us the flavor of less-extreme moves toward freer trade. In each case, we need to find the competitive equilibrium. Competitive means that consumers and producers take prices as given. (No monopolies allowed here!) Formally, a competitive equilibrium is a set of prices and quantities that satisfies three conditions:

1. Consumers are on their demand curves; they buy what they want at the given prices.

2. Producers make zero profits (the effect of competition).

3. Total production equals total consumption for each product.

Finding an equilibrium can be difficult, particularly if you have a low threshold for algebra, but we can readily verify a proposed equilibrium by checking the three conditions.

Consumers. The citizens of each country consume apples and bananas. They also work for the firms, getting a wage w for each unit of labor. Each consumer (we can index them by i) earns an income $y_i = wl_i$ (for simplicity, we assume that l_i is given). Obviously, $L = \sum_i l_i$. How do consumers spend their income? Like any of us, they receive satisfaction (or *utility*) from consuming both apples and bananas. Let us say that their utility from consumption is given by the following function:

$$U(a, b) = a^s b^{1-s}.$$

Given her income and prices for apples and bananas, each consumer will make spending decisions that maximize her utility. Simple calculations show that a consumer will spend a fraction s of her income on apples and the complementary fraction $1 - s$ on bananas. Summing across all consumers, we find that a fraction s of national income Y ($Y = \sum_i y_i = w \sum_i l_i = wL$) is spent on apples, and the remainder is spent on bananas:

$$p_a a = sY$$
$$p_b b = (1 - s)Y.$$

These are (effectively) the demand functions for the two products. We'll assume below that $s = 0.75$ in both countries.

Producers. Consider producers in a specific country. Let's say that labor sells for w per unit, with w potentially differing across countries. A producer of apples (say) will hire labor at cost w per unit and sell apples, getting a profit of

$$\text{Profit} = a(p_a - w/\alpha),$$

where α is apple productivity in the country we're examining. If $p_a < w/\alpha$, the price is too low and no apples will be produced. If $p_a > w/\alpha$, competition among apple producers will drive the price down until $p_a = w/\alpha$. In short, if apples are produced, their price will be $p_a = w/\alpha$. Similarly, if bananas are produced, their price will be $p_b = w/\beta$. If both apples and bananas are produced (and they need not be), their relative price will be $q = p_b/p_a = \alpha/\beta$.

Equilibrium without trade. If there's no trade, then each country will produce both products. Let us say that the wage rate is $w = 1$ in both countries (but not comparable, because they may be measured in different units). Since the total labor input is 100 in either country, national income is $Y = wL = 1 \times 100 = 100$ in both Mexico and the US (again, the units are not comparable). In the US, prices will be

$$
\begin{aligned}
p_a &= w/\alpha = 1/20 = 0.05 \\
p_b &= w/\beta = 1/10 = 0.10 \\
q &= p_b/p_a = 2.
\end{aligned}
$$

At these prices, the demands for apples and bananas are, respectively,

$$
\begin{aligned}
a &= sY/p_a = 0.75 \times 100/0.05 = 1500 \\
b &= (1-s)Y/p_b = 0.25 \times 100/0.1 = 250.
\end{aligned}
$$

Total utility is, therefore, $U = a^{0.75}b^{0.25} = 958$.

What about Mexico? Using similar methods, we find that prices are

$$
\begin{aligned}
p_a &= w/\alpha = 1/5 = 0.20 \\
p_b &= w/\beta = 1/5 = 0.20 \\
q &= p_b/p_a = 1.
\end{aligned}
$$

Demands are $a = 375$, $b = 125$. Utility is $U = 285$. The numbers are summarized in Table 9.2 for future reference.

Equilibrium with trade.

The complete solution is reported in Table 9.2, but let's see where it comes from. It's moderately complicated, so skip directly to the next section unless you're incredibly curious. The objective is to find prices and wages that equate supply and demand for apples, bananas, and labor in both countries. We'll focus on bananas; if the banana market clears, so do the others.

Let's guess (we made up the example, so our guesses are pretty good) that the US produces only apples and Mexico produces only bananas. In this way, the two countries specialize in the production of the good in which they have a comparative advantage. We'll verify this guess later. Let's think about how the banana market works. Supply is whatever Mexico produces given its available labor L_2 and productivity β_2:

$$\text{Supply of Bananas} = L_2\beta_2.$$

What about demand? This is more complicated. Since each country spends a fraction $1 - s$ on bananas, total demand is

$$\text{Demand for Bananas} = (1-s)Y_1/p_b + (1-s)Y_2/p_b,$$

Table 9.2: Prices and quantities with and without trade.

	Free Trade	No Trade
	US	
Price of apples p_a	0.05	0.05
Price of bananas p_b	0.0667	0.10
Wage w	1	1 (dollar)
Consumption of apples a	1,500	1,500
Consumption of bananas b	375	250
Utility	1,061	958
	Mexico	
Price of apples p_a	0.05	0.2
Price of bananas p_b	0.0667	0.2
Wage w	0.3333	1 (peso)
Consumption of apples a	500	375
Consumption of bananas b	125	125
Utility	354	285

In the no-trade case, the wages are normalizations; they're in different units and are not comparable across countries.

where Y_1 and Y_2 are incomes in the US and Mexico, respectively. Competition in labor and output markets will equate income paid to workers to the value of output they produce:

$$Y_1 = L_1 \alpha_1 p_a$$
$$Y_2 = L_2 \beta_2 p_b.$$

Why? Because competition drives profits to zero. That gives us

$$\text{Demand for Bananas} = (1-s)L_1 \alpha_1 p_a/p_b + (1-s)L_2 \beta_2.$$

Equating supply and demand and doing some algebra gives us

$$p_b/p_a = \frac{(1-s)L_1 \alpha_1}{s L_2 \beta_2}. \tag{9.1}$$

Plugging in numbers, we find $p_b/p_a = 4/3$. If you're unusually curious, you can show (using the same approach) that supply and demand are equal for apples at the same price.

We can now get a sense where the relative price of bananas comes from: supply and demand! On the supply side, higher productivity for bananas (higher β_2) drives the price down. This is the usual shift out of the supply curve. Similarly, higher apple productivity (higher α_1) makes apples relatively less expensive. On the demand side, lower s indicates a lower desire for apples and a higher desire for bananas and, thus, drives the price of bananas up. This is essentially a rightward shift of the demand curve.

Finally, we verify that the US produces only apples, Mexico only bananas. How do we show this? At these prices and wages, US banana producers lose money — so they don't produce any. Ditto Mexican apple producers — the wage rate supported by banana production is too high for apple producers to break even, so they won't produce either. This is really a good thing for Mexican workers, as producing bananas supports a higher standard of living.

9.3 Wages and productivity

In the US you sometimes hear: "US workers can't compete with Mexican workers, because their wages are so low." In Mexico, you sometimes hear: "Mexican workers can't compete with US workers, because their productivity is so much higher." Who is right? The answer, of course, is neither. In our model, wages reflect productivity. Mexican wages are lower because Mexican workers are less productive. Their wage is low enough to (just) make up for their lower productivity. Ditto American workers: Firms hire them despite their higher wage because their productivity is higher. The value of labor to a firm is a balance between the two forces: price and productivity.

We can be more specific about the connection between productivity and wages. As a rule, the wage ratio will be somewhere between the productivity ratios for the two products. In this case, the ratio of the US to the Mexican wage will be between 2 (= 10/5, the ratio of banana productivities) and 4 (= 20/5, the ratio of apple productivities):

$$2 = \beta_1/\beta_2 < w_1/w_2 < \alpha_1/\alpha_2 = 4.$$

If we were to (somehow) force up the Mexican wage above the upper bound, we would simply make Mexican bananas more expensive to Americans than producing them locally would. Demand for Mexican labor would dry up. Similarly, if we were to force down the Mexican wage below the lower bound, Mexico would find it profitable to produce both goods. However, demand for Mexican labor would exceed supply, which you'd expect to increase its price.

Overall, wages are connected to productivities. Between the two bounds, demand plays a role, as we've seen. If people have a stronger desire for bananas, that tends to benefit the Mexican workers who produce them by increasing the price of bananas, as we see in equation (9.1).

9.4   Bottom line

Let's think about the calculations summarized in Table 9.2 from a non-technical perspective. The numbers make several points that extend to more-general settings:

- **Trade makes consumers (=workers) better off.** In the US, consumption of apples stays the same and consumption of bananas increases. As a result, utility rises from 958 to 1061. In Mexico, consumption of bananas does not change, but consumption of apples is larger. Therefore, utility rises from 285 to 354. In more-realistic models, the impact of trade is typically small, but both countries gain, as they do here. It's a byproduct of Adam Smith's invisible hand (aka the first theorem of welfare economics), which you might recall from microeconomics.

- **Trade changes production.** In this case, Mexico shifted out of apples into bananas, and the US did the reverse. In other models, the change in production may not be so extreme, but it's generally true that they predict that every country will stop producing some products and import them instead. The result is a more efficient system of production, as each country produces those goods for which its relative productivity is the highest.

- **Trade raises productivity.** Both effects show up in macroeconomic data as increases in productivity. If we were NIPA people, we might compute GDP this way: sum production of apples and bananas, valued at a consistent set of prices. In this case, we'll use the free-trade prices, which is similar to PPP adjustment (apply the same prices in every country). GDP at world prices is

	Free Trade	No Trade
US	100.0	91.7
Mexico	33.3	27.1

Once trade shows up in GDP, it shows up in aggregate productivity, too. We don't have capital in this model, so the production function is $Y = AL$. Since L is unchanged across trade regimes, the change in Y reflects an increase in TFP.

- **No jobs are lost — or found.** In our example, every unit of labor is used whether trade was possible or not. This is only a little extreme: No trade models suggest that trade will have much impact on employment. Any effect there might be comes from the impact on labor supply of an increase in the wage. So when you read the newspaper, especially in an election year, remember that trade has an impact on what the jobs are, not on how many there are.

9.5   Winners and losers

From what we've seen, trade is a wonderful thing. Who could be against it? In fact, lots of people seem to have a passionately held view that trade and globalization are a plague on the world. What could they be thinking? What follows is a short list of their arguments. In practice, our experience is that most arguments against trade are simply self-interest in disguise.

Differences among residents of a country. Our example also had the built-in feature that all citizens of a country have the same tastes and the same productivity in the workplace. In practice, this is not true, and trade will affect each person differently. One example that shows up regularly in the popular debate about trade: people who lose their jobs when production adjusts to trade. In this case, suppose that you worked for an apple producer and lost your job. The long-term answer is: Get a job working for a banana producer, since their productivity is higher. But in the short run, there's no question that you suffer a loss from losing your job. Also, if working for a banana producer requires skills that you do not have, you might have to retrain yourself. In short, there can be losers. What the theory says, however, is that the winners win a lot more than the losers lose — Mexicans gain, on average. In principle, you might want to take some of the winners' gains and give them to the losers, but in practice this isn't that easy to do. People lose jobs all the time for lots of reasons, and trade is unlikely to be a major factor in most cases.

Another illustration: in the example summarized in Figure 9.1, all Mexican consumers are better off. Now suppose that Mexicans differ in how much they like apples and bananas (i.e., the parameter s is not the same across individuals). In this case, the ones who like apples less and bananas more may be worse off since the relative price of bananas has gone up with free trade. Again, the winners should be able to compensate the losers and still be better off, but in practice it rarely happens.

Externalities. This is a classic "failure" of markets, the (unpriced) impact of one person's decision on another's utility. For example, a polluting producer may inflict bad air on you and reduce your welfare. When talking about trade, people often refer to positive external effects on productivity. Are there advantages to having a local industry beyond the profit and loss? Could it help others to increase their efficiency? This is a legitimate argument, but probably not a good one in most cases. Moreover, it's typically used by firms and industries looking for special deals from their governments. For example, European car makers used this argument when seeking government protection from Japanese and Korean imports. Their argument was that the domestic producers generated technology spillovers that benefited related industries.

Concentrated and dispersed interests. One of the political challenges is that the losses from trade are often concentrated in a small group of firms or people. That makes them a natural political force. Suppose, for example, that five people lose $1 million each from unrestricted trade and one million people gain $10 each. The gains ($10m) outweigh the losses ($5m), but the one million people who benefit are less likely to change their votes or otherwise express an opinion on the issue than the five people who lose a million each.

Executive summary

1. International trade allows consumers to buy products more cheaply and workers to take jobs where their productivity is highest.

2. There can be both winners and losers from trade, but, in theory at least, the winners gain more than the losers lose.

Review questions

1. Gains from trade. In Mexico, how does consumption of apples and bananas change when we move from No Trade to Free Trade? Are Mexican worker better off? Who in Mexico loses?

   Answer. We read from Table 9.2. Consumption of apples rises from 375 to 500, and consumption of bananas stays the same at 125. So Mexicans (who are both workers and consumers) are better off. No Mexicans lose here, but you might imagine in a different world that the former Mexican producers of apples suffer. What we know in general is that the gains outweigh any such losses.

2. Trade politics. Although the logic for trade is clear, politicians all over the world complain about "unfair" competition from abroad. Why?

   Answer. It's hard to see this as anything but protection of their supporters. In addition, people don't vote in other countries' elections. In our example, you can imagine Mexican apple producers asking their government to protect them from US competition. What they should do here is switch to bananas, but the the political process often favors the well-connected over the average worker or consumer.

3. Changing demand. In the example, show that an increase in s to 0.78 is good for US workers and bad for Mexican workers. Why might that be?

   Answer. This increases the price of the product produced by US workers, which improves their situation. The opposite is true for Mexican workers. We say that the "terms of trade" (relative price of their export good) have moved against them. Think of an oil-exporting country: An increase in the price of oil is good for them, bad for importers. [Duh!]

4. Could there be losers? If trade eliminates apple-producing jobs in Mexico, could apple producers and workers be worse off?

   Answer. Yes! But the gains for others are typically larger than these losses, so we should be able to compensate the losers and leave everyone better off. This is trickier than it sounds, though.

5. Food prices and trade. When food prices rose sharply in 2008, India restricted food exports to keep prices down. Who would you expect to benefit from this policy? Lose? Is the overall impact on the Indian economy likely to be positive or negative?

   Answer. You might expect this to keep prices down in the short run because we've reduced the demand for locally produced food. (You could also express this as an increase in supply to the domestic market, but it's cleaner this way.) Who gains? Domestic food buyers and foreign producers. Who loses? Domestic sellers/producers and foreign buyers. Generally, any market intervention like this is a net loss. You could show this formally using a supply and demand diagram.

If you're looking for more

Doug Irwin's "History of trade policy" is a nice overview of two centuries of thought on trade issues.

Part III
Short-Term Economic Performance

Short-Term Overview

This outline covers key concepts from the second part of the course: short-term economic performance. It is not exhaustive, but is meant to help you (i) anticipate what is coming and (ii) organize your thoughts later on.

Business Cycle Properties

Tools: Basic statistics: standard deviation, correlation.

Key Words: Volatility; procyclical and countercyclical.

Big Ideas:

- Economies do not grow smoothly or regularly. We refer to the fluctuations in economic activity as business cycles.

- Growth rates of expenditure components move up and down with GDP over the business cycle, but they move by different amounts. Spending on investment and consumer durables moves more than output; we say it is more volatile. Spending on services and nondurable goods is less volatile than output. Labor and capital markets move with the cycle as well.

Business-Cycle Indicators

Tools: Basic statistics (standard deviation, correlation); cross-correlation function.

Key Words: Volatility; procyclical and countercyclical; leading, lagging, and coincident.

- Business cycle indicators are characterized by several properties: procyclical and countercyclical, leading and lagging.

- Cross-correlation functions identify these properties.

Aggregate supply and Demand

Tools: Aggregate supply and demand (AS/AD) graph.

Key Words: Short- and long-run aggregate supply; sticky wages; aggregate demand; supply and demand shocks; Keynesian.

Big Ideas:

- The AS/AD model relates output and prices in the short and long runs. The model is composed of (i) an upward-sloping short-run aggregate supply curve, which inherits its shape from sticky wages; (ii) a vertical long-run aggregate supply curve; and (iii) a downward-sloping aggregate demand curve.

- Shocks to the aggregate supply and demand curves have different effects on inflation and output.

Policy in the AS/AD model

Tools: Aggregate supply and demand (AS/AD) graph.

Key Words: Policy objectives; potential output; output gap.

Big Ideas:

- The objectives of macroeconomic policy are generally thought to be (i) stable prices and (ii) output near its long-run equilibrium level.

- A direct consequence is that monetary policy should respond differently to demand and supply shocks. As a general rule, policy should resist/offset changes in output triggered by shifts in demand and accommodate/reinforce changes triggered by shifts in supply.

- We can identify supply or demand shocks from whether output and prices move together or in opposite directions.

Money and Inflation

Tools: The quantity theory of money.

Key Words: Money; medium of exchange; liquidity; store of value; unit of account; money supply; hyperinflation; quantity theory; velocity; fiscal dominance, deflation.

Big Ideas:

- Money is the medium of exchange – whatever people generally use to complete transactions. It is also a unit of account and a store of value.

- The quantity theory of money links the money supply with the price level and output.

- Inflation is the growth rate of the price level, which is typically measured by a price index.

- Hyperinflation refers to an inflation rate of 100 percent or more per year. High rates of money growth are the proximate cause of hyperinflations. High rates of money growth in turn are usually caused by ongoing government budget deficits that are financed by printing money. We call this *fiscal dominance* over monetary policy.

Monetary Policy

Tools: Central bank balance sheet; Taylor rule.

Key Words: Nominal interest rate, real interest rate, expected inflation rate, expectations hypothesis, term premium, open market operations, discount rate, reserve requirement ratio, quantitative easing (large scale asset purchases), forward guidance, interest on bank deposits at the Fed, overnight reverse repurchase agreements, federal funds rate, monetary base, bank reserves, effective lower bound.

Big Ideas:

- Central banks conduct monetary policy by translating their overall macroeconomic objectives into operating targets. In the US, the traditional operating target for the Fed is the overnight interest rate on uncollateralized borrowing by banks from other banks and financial institutions, called the fed funds rate.

- The Taylor rule provides guidance on what the target interest rate should be as a function of observed data on inflation and real GDP.

- Traditionally, the Fed used open market operations – altering the size of its balance sheet by buying and selling Treasury securities – to influence the fed funds rate. When this policy rate approached the effective lower bound in the aftermath of the financial crisis, the Fed began using unconventional instruments (including quantitative easing and forward guidance) to conduct policy.

- Since 2015, the Fed used the overnight interest rates it pays on bank deposits at the Fed and reverse repurchase agreements to raise short-term interest rates without altering the size of its balance sheet.

10
Business-Cycle Properties

Tools: Basic statistics: standard deviation, correlation.

Key Words: Volatility; procyclical and countercyclical.

Big Ideas:

- Economies do not grow smoothly or regularly. We refer to the fluctuations in economic activity as business cycles.

- Growth rates of expenditure components move up and down with GDP over the business cycle, but they move by different amounts. Spending on investment and consumer durables moves more than output; we say it is more volatile. Spending on services and nondurable goods is less volatile than output. Labor and capital markets move with the cycle as well.

Over the last two centuries, US real GDP has grown at an average rate between 3 and 3.5 percent a year, but this growth has been anything but smooth. Annual growth rates over the last fifty years have ranged from −2 percent or less (in 1975, 1982, and 2008) to 8 percent (in 1966 and 1984). These short-term "fluctuations" or "business cycles" (we'll use the terms interchangeably) are the subject of intense interest by businesses and play an important role in their decisions to hire, produce, and invest. And it's not just the US; although we will use US data, other countries exhibit similar volatility. Emerging markets, including the US in the 19th century, differ primarily in having greater volatility. The bottom line: Fluctuations in economic growth are a fact of life.

Our mission is to outline some of the basic features of these fluctuations, which point to ways of dealing with the inevitable risk and uncertainty they bring to our lives.

10.1   Cycles and volatility

Arthur Burns and Wesley Mitchell, two of the pioneers of business-cycle research, noted:

> business cycles are a type of fluctuation found in the aggregate
> economic activity of nations. ... A cycle consists of expansions
> occurring at about the same time in many economic activities,
> followed by similarly general recessions, contractions and revivals
> which merge into the expansion phases of the next cycle; this
> sequence of changes is recurrent but not periodic; in duration
> business cycles vary from more than one year to ten or twelve
> years.

(From: *Measuring business cycles*, NBER, 1946.)

You can get a sense of these economy-wide fluctuations from Figure 10.1, where we plot real GDP and its year-on-year growth rate — the rate of growth of quarterly GDP over the same quarter a year earlier. As someone once said: The variance is so large that you hardly notice the mean. The figure also suggests that volatility was lower between 1985 and 2007. People used to refer to this as the "great moderation," but that seems less appropriate now.

Figure 10.1: Level and fluctuations of US real GDP.

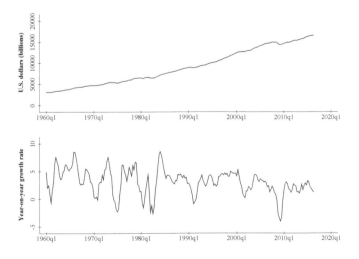

The National Bureau of Economic Research, which dates business cycles in the US, defines a recession as "a significant decline in economic activity spread across the economy, lasting more than a few months, normally visible in real GDP, real income, employment, industrial production, and wholesale-retail sales." Using subjective methods, they identify dates of peaks and troughs. Less formally, many people use the rule of thumb that a recession consists of two consecutive quarters in which GDP has fallen. The year-on-year growth rates in the figure don't coincide exactly with this definition, but you can see the eight official NBER recessions since 1960 as sharp downward spikes in GDP growth.

10.2   Expenditure components

Burns and Mitchell refer to fluctuations in "many economic activities." Among these activities are the expenditure components of GDP. Are their fluctuations similar to those of GDP? On the whole, the components, particularly consumption and investment, move up and down together, but the magnitudes differ enormously. Consumption currently accounts for nearly 70 percent of US GDP; as you might expect, its fluctuations are similar (see Figure 10.2). The correlation of year-on-year growth rates in consumption (total) and GDP is 0.84.

Table 10.1 shows us that consumption's components — services, nondurable goods, and durable goods — also vary with GDP, but their correlations and (especially) volatilities differ somewhat. Consumption of nondurables and services is less volatile than GDP, in the sense that the standard deviation of its growth rate is smaller. Consumption of durables is far more volatile than consumption of nondurables and services. You might think of specific products and industries that reflect the same phenomenon. Why do you think cars and refrigerators are more volatile than haircuts and medical care?

Investment also moves up and down with output and is substantially more volatile (see Figure 10.2). As a rule of thumb, a one-percent increase in GDP is associated with about a three-percent increase in total investment. (We're looking at the ratio of standard deviations here, and the high correlation of the two series.) Table 10.1 shows that the major components of investment — structures, equipment, and residential housing — are highly correlated with, and more volatile than, GDP.

When we turn to business-cycle indicators, we'll see that many of them are more detailed measures of some aspect of consumption or investment. Consumption is important because it accounts for most of GDP. Investment is important because it is highly responsive to changes in economic conditions.

Table 10.1: Properties of business cycles.

	Std Dev (%)	Corr w/ GDP
GDP	2.19	1.00
Consumption: total	1.75	0.84
Consumption: services	1.22	0.63
Consumption: nondurable	1.65	0.75
Consumption: durables	6.29	0.76
Investment: total	6.64	0.86
Investment: structures	7.85	0.46
Investment: equipment	7.35	0.81
Investment: housing	13.05	0.60
Employment	1.77	0.76
S&P 500 Index	14.98	0.36

Numbers refer to year-on-year growth rates computed from quarterly US data.

Figure 10.2: Fluctuations in consumption, investment, and GDP.

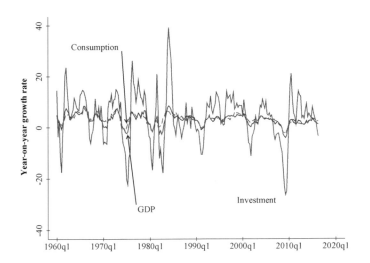

10.3   Labor and capital markets move with the cycle

Labor markets also move with the business cycle; indeed, it's the way in which business cycles make themselves known to us most directly. Figure 10.3 shows us how fluctuations in employment covary with GDP. Note that employment growth is generally less than GDP growth; the difference reflects an increase in output per worker — a good thing, to be sure! You can see in the figure that the ups and downs in employment typically lag those in GDP by a little — a quarter or two. The current expansion is an extreme case, with GDP rebounding well before employment, but the general pattern is not unusual.

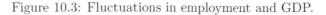

Figure 10.3: Fluctuations in employment and GDP.

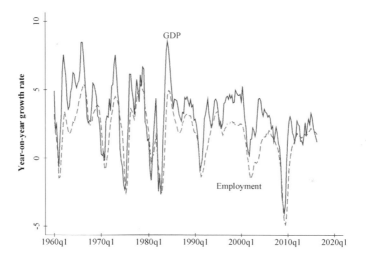

Figure 10.4: Fluctuations in asset prices and GDP.

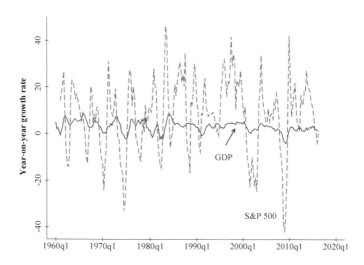

Financial (capital) markets move with the business cycle, as well. Figure 10.4 plots the growth rate of real GDP against versus the yearly growth rate of the S&P 500 index. Notice that aggregate stock prices are extremely volatile, with a standard deviation about eight times larger than GDP. Moreover, aggregate stock prices and GDP are positively correlated (0.36). This suggests that good news about the economy is good news for stock prices. It's hard to see in Figure 10.4, but we'll see later that stock prices lead GDP; the correlation of stock prices with GDP two quarters later is above 0.5. Financial measures often lead economic activity. Another example is the yield curve (the difference between long-term and short-term interest rates), which tends to flatten or invert ahead of business downturns. We'll look at this more closely when we turn to indicators.

Labor markets and asset prices are both sources of useful indicators of economic activity. We'll see more of each shortly.

Executive summary

1. Economies do not grow smoothly; they exhibit lots of short-term volatility.

2. Spending on investment goods (by firms) and consumer durables (by households) are more volatile than output as a whole. Household spending on nondurable goods and services is less volatile than output.

3. Most variables are procyclical; that is, they move up and down with GDP. Examples include consumption, investment, employment, and the stock market.

Review questions

1. Statistics. What statistic would you use to show that two economic series move up and down together?

   Answer. The correlation between them. Table 10.1, for example, includes the correlations of year-on-year growth rates of GDP and several expenditure components. The correlations in most cases are above 0.8, indicating they do indeed mostly move up and down together.

2. More statistics. What statistic would you use to show that one series is more "volatile" than another.

   Answer. The standard deviation. In the same table, we saw that investment is more volatile than consumption in the sense that its standard deviation is about three times higher.

3. Do it yourself. Reproduce Figure 10.3 in FRED. The variables are real GDP (FRED code GDPC1) and nonfarm employment (PAYEMS).

If you're looking for more

These basic features of business cycles are covered in most macroeconomics textbooks. A reasonably good overview is Finn Kydland and Edward Prescott, "Real facts and a monetary myth."

Data used in this chapter

Table 10.2: Data table.

Variable	Source
GDP	GDPC1
Consumption	PCECC96
Services	PCESVC96
Durables	PCDGCC96
Nondurables	PCNDGC96
Investment	GPDIC96
Nonresidential	PNFIC96
Equipment	NRIPDC96
Housing	PRFIC96
Employment	PAYEMS
S&P500	SP500
10yr Treasury yield	GS10
2yr Treasury yield	GS2
Federal funds rate	FEDFUNDS

To retrieve the data online, add the identifier from the source column to http://research.stlouisfed.org/fred2/series/. For example, to retrieve nonfarm employment, point your browser to http://research.stlouisfed.org/fred2/series/PAYEMS

11
Business-Cycle Indicators

Tools: Basic statistics (standard deviation, correlation); cross-correlation function.

Key Words: Volatility; procyclical and countercyclical; leading, lagging, and coincident.

- Business cycle indicators are characterized by several properties: procyclical and countercyclical, leading and lagging.

- Cross-correlation functions identify these properties.

Probably the leading use of macroeconomic data (and macroeconomists) is forecasting: predicting future movements in economic variables so that businesses can decide how much to produce, investors can decide how to allocate their assets, and households can decide how much to spend. The good news is that forecasting is possible; we're not simply throwing darts at a board. The bad news is that it's not easy; even the best forecasters are far from perfect.

This chapter is devoted to short-term business-cycle indicators — variables that indicate changes in near-term economic conditions — and how to use them. In principle, we could be interested in many features of the economy: output, inflation, interest rates, exchange rates, and so on. We'll focus on output, but the methods can easily be applied to other variables. We look at the US, but similar ideas and methods apply to any country with reliable data.

11.1   Terminology

We refer to the properties of economic indicators with two related sets of terms. One set of terms describes whether an indicator's movements tend to come before or after movements in output. We say an indicator *leads* output if its ups and downs typically precede those of output, and *lags* output if they come after. An indicator whose movements are contemporaneous with those of output is referred to as *coincident*. Thus, the adjectives leading, lagging, and coincident describe the timing of an indicator's movements relative to those of output. Looking ahead, you might guess that leading indicators are most useful in forecasting. The stock market, for example, is a common leading indicator; it leads output by six to eight months, as we'll see shortly.

A second set of terms refers to whether an indicator's movements are positively or negatively correlated with output. If the correlation is positive, we say it is *procyclical*; if the correlation is negative, we say it is *countercyclical* . Most indicators are procyclical: employment, stock prices, housing starts, and so on. The most common countercyclical indicators have to do with unemployment: Both the unemployment rate and new claims for unemployment insurance rise during recessions.

11.2   Forecasting

The classic forecasting problem goes something like this: What do we expect the value of [some economic variable] to be k periods in the future? Here, k is any period of time you like, but we're usually interested in anything from next week to a few years in the future.

If we're forecasting GDP, there's an extra difficulty because we don't know the present or the recent past, much less the future. We've seen, for example, that fourth-quarter GDP is first reported near the end of the following January, and even that number is a preliminary estimate. From the perspective of mid-January, then, we need to "forecast" the previous quarter.

We're going to shortcut this difficulty (somewhat) by using the monthly Industrial Production (IP) index as a substitute for real GDP, but the issue is a general one, in that the time lag in getting data is both an issue in its own right and a constraint on forecasting the future. IP measures output in manufacturing, mining, and utilities. More important, its fluctuations are strongly correlated with those in GDP. You can see that in Figure 11.1, which compares year-on-year growth rates in GDP and IP (aggregated to a quarterly frequency). You will notice that IP is more volatile than GDP but otherwise follows its ups and downs reasonably well. You may also

Figure 11.1: US GDP and industrial production.

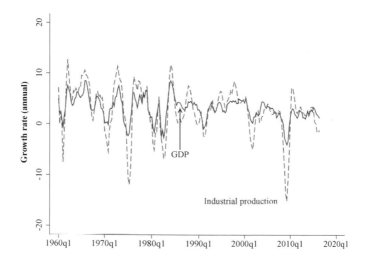

notice some differences between them in the recent past, which have been traced to the rising importance of services in the US economy. In the US, IP is reported by the Federal Reserve in the middle of the following month. Data for December, for example, are available in mid-January. Using IP, therefore, gives us a shorter information lag than GDP. In addition, the monthly frequency gives us a finer time interval for near-term forecasting. For both reasons, we will focus our discussion of forecasting on IP rather than, GDP, although the same principles apply to both, as well as to other macroeconomic and financial variables.

11.3   Good indicators

Good forecasts require good inputs. One way to forecast a variable is with its own past. Future growth rates of IP, for example, might be related to current and past growth rates. We can usually do better than that by adding other indicators to our analysis. Speaking generally, a good indicator should have one or more of these properties:

- **Correlation.** A good indicator is correlated with the variable we are forecasting.

- **Lead.** A good indicator leads the variable we are forecasting.

- **Timeliness.** A good indicator is available quickly.

- **Stability.** A good indicator does not undergo major revisions subsequent to its initial release, and its relationship with the variable we are forecasting doesn't change over time.

On the whole, measures of economic activity (employment, for example) tend to be strong on correlation and weak on timeliness (see the discussion of GDP above) and stability (many economic series are revised frequently). The best ones lead the business cycle. In contrast, financial indicators (equity prices, interest rates) are weaker on correlation but stronger on the other three properties: They're typically available immediately, often lead the cycle, and are not revised. Various indexes of leading indicators combine multiple series with the hope of getting the best from each. The Conference Board's quasi-official index of leading indicators is the most common example.

11.4   Identifying good indicators

How do we identify indicators with high potential? We'll use another bit of terminology that leads to an extremely useful graphical representation of the dynamic relation between two variables: the *cross-correlation function* (ccf).

You may recall that the correlation between two variables (x and y, say) is a measure of how closely they are related in a statistical sense. If the correlation is (say) 0.8, then observations with large values of x tend also to have large values of y. If the correlation is 0.4, this association is weaker. And if the correlation is –0.8, observations with large values of x tend to have small values of y — and vice versa.

The cross-correlation function extends the concept of correlation to the timing of two indicators. Specifically, consider the correlation between x at date t and y at date $t - k$. If k is negative, then we're talking about the correlation between x now and y k periods in the future. If k is positive, we have the correlation between x now and y k periods in the past. By looking at the pattern of correlations, we can identify indicators x that tend to lead the variable y. We refer to k as the lag of y vs x, but if k is negative it refers to a lead. Mathematically, we write

$$\mathrm{ccf}(k) \ = \ corr(x_t, y_{t-k}).$$

Typically, we would graph this against k, with k starting with a negative number and moving to positive numbers. The pattern of correlations tells us whether an indicator x leads or lags (on average) a variable y.

Figure 11.2: Cross-correlations: the S&P 500 and industrial production.

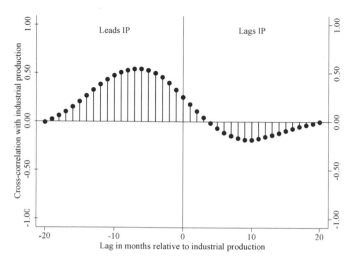

Both series are year-on-year growth rates for the period 1960-present.
The large correlations to the left tell us that the S&P 500 index is a
good indicator of future industrial production.

Let's move from the abstract to the concrete to make sure we understand
what the ccf represents. [You might want to work your way through this
paragraph slowly, it's important.]   We calculate the year-on-year growth
rates of the S&P 500 index and industrial production and compute their ccf
using the S&P 500 for x and industrial production for y. Figure 11.2 is a
plot of their correlations against the lag k. There's a lot of information here,
so let's go through it one dot at a time. The dot at $k = 0$ (on the vertical line
at the center of the figure) shows that the contemporaneous correlation is
about 0.2. Contemporaneous means that we're looking at the two variables
at the same time: March 2001 industrial production is lined up with March
2001 S&P 500, and so on. Next, consider the dot corresponding to $k = -10$
on the left side of the figure. The correlation of (roughly) 0.5 pictured in
the figure shows the growth rate of industrial production with the growth
rate of the S&P 500 index dated ten months earlier. Evidently high growth
in equity prices now is associated with high growth in IP 10 months later.
Finally, consider a dot on the right side of the figure. The dot at $k = +10$
suggests that the correlation of industrial production growth with equity
price growth ten months later is about −0.2.

This pattern of correlations tells us a lot about the timing of movements in
the two variables. In general, negative values of k (the left side of the figure)
indicate correlations of the S&P 500 with future industrial production; we

would say that they reflect the tendency of stock prices to lead output. Positive values of k (the right side of the figure) indicate correlations of the S&P 500 with past industrial production; they reflect the tendency of stock prices to lag output. What we see in the figure is a strong correlation of the S&P 500 index with industrial production seven to eight months later. Evidently, the stock-price index is a leading indicator of industrial production.

We'll use the cross-correlation function to identify whether an indicator is leading or lagging, procyclical or countercyclical.

To do this, we find the largest correlation in absolute value. If it occurs to the left of the figure, we say it's a leading indicator; if on the right, lagging. Similarly, if the (largest) correlation is positive, we say the indicator is procyclical; if negative, countercyclical. In principle an indicator could be both leading and lagging, or both pro- and counter-cyclical, but we'll deal with that if and when it happens.

Digression. We snuck something in here that we should mention again, although it's not particularly important for our purposes. We used year-on-year growth rates instead of monthly growth rates. We could use either, but the year-on-year pictures are smoother and, in our view, more attractive. We'd see a similar pattern with monthly growth rates, but the correlations would be both smaller and choppier.

Let's look at some other indicators and see which ones lead IP. Some of the most common indicators are labor-market variables, constructed by the Bureau of Labor Statistics. Cross-correlation functions for four of them are pictured in Figure 11.3. Nonfarm payroll employment (a measure of employment constructed from a survey of firm payrolls) is a slightly lagging indicator since the ccf peaks with a lag of one to two months. It is, nevertheless, useful because the correlation (over 0.8) is unusually strong. And even a two-month lag is more timely than the GDP numbers. The unemployment rate is countercyclical (note the negative correlations) and lags IP in the sense that the largest correlation comes at a lag of three to four months. It seems that a rise (fall) in output is associated with a fall (rise) in the unemployment rate three to four months later. New applications ("claims") for unemployment insurance are also countercyclical, but the correlation is stronger than for the overall unemployment rate, and it leads industrial production by two to three months. Another popular indicator is average hours worked per week in manufacturing. This indicator is strongly procyclical and leads industrial production by two to four months. The labor market, in short, provides a good overall picture of the economy and, in some cases, supplies indications of future movements in industrial production. The leading variables ("new claims" and "average weekly hours") are more highly

Figure 11.3: Cross-correlation functions: labor market indicators.

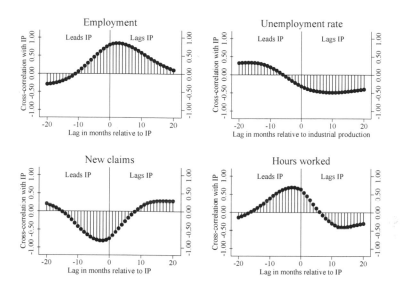

correlated with industrial production than the S&P 500 index, but the leads are shorter.

Other sources of useful information are various measures and surveys of economic activity conducted by the Bureau of the Census and private organizations. Cross-correlation functions for four common ones are pictured in Figure 11.4. The first two are building permits and housing starts, two indicators of new home construction reported by the Census. Two ideas lie behind their use: that construction of new capital is more volatile than other sectors of the economy and that decisions to build new homes reflect optimism about the future. The cross-correlation functions suggest that they work; while the correlations are smaller than with (say) employment, the leads are substantial (ten months or so). The next two are popular private surveys. Consumer sentiment, based on a survey of consumers collected by the University of Michigan, reflects consumers' optimism about current and future economic conditions. The purchasing managers index is what we call a "diffusion index." It's based on a survey of purchasing managers who report whether they see economic activity increasing or decreasing. Each is used as is. We see in the figure that both are procyclical leading indicators.

We could go on. There are hundreds of indicators, more all the time. The most common one we've skipped is the slope of the yield curve: Flat or downward-sloping yield curves are associated with slower-than-usual future

Figure 11.4: Cross-correlation functions: surveys of economic activity.

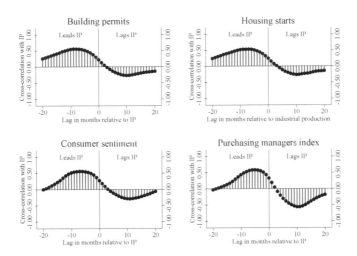

growth in output. More on this in the Appendix.

11.5   The business-cycle scorecard

Now that we understand how to identify good indicators, how do we put them to work? The central question here is how to combine the inputs of multiple indicators. One way to do that is to summarize them informally, which is what we do here. Another is to use multivariate regression, which is the next topic, but not one we'll spend much time on in this course.

The business-cycle scorecard is a summary of what selected indicators tell us about near-term economic conditions. We'll use the four monthly indicators pictured in Figures 11.5 and 11.6. In the first figure, we see the monthly growth rate of IP (top panel) and the change in (nonfarm) employment for the period 1960 to the present. They show similar patterns, with the major postwar downturns evident in each. Evidently, employment is procyclical, rising in good times and falling in bad times. Industrial production is a "noisier" series, which is one reason that many analysts prefer employment as a measure of current economic conditions. The lines show us the mean value (the solid line) and plus and minus one standard deviation (the dashed lines). The lines are useful benchmarks for telling how strong the current value of an indicator is relative to past experience.

In the second figure (Figure 11.6), we see similar data for new claims for unemployment insurance and housing starts. New claims are reported weekly;

Figure 11.5: Industrial production and employment.

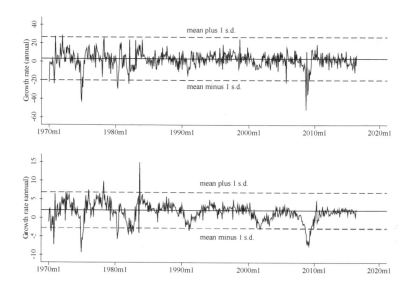

The two panels show, respectively, the annual growth rate of industrial production and the year-over-year change in the number of people employed.

the figure is based on the four-week moving average. Remember, they are
countercyclical: they rise when the economy weakens. The second panel is
housing starts. You can see in the figure that housing starts don't always
go up and down with the economy. In the 2001 recession, housing starts fell
only slightly. In 2008, we made up for that, with housing starts falling to
their lowest point since (at least) 1960. None of that will come as a surprise
to you. These four indicators come from the Federal Reserve (industrial
production), the Bureau of Labor Statistics (employment, new claims), and
the Bureau of the Census (housing starts). These government agencies are
the primary sources of economic indicators in the US. There are private indicators also, but the government indicators are widely used and publicly
available.

In the business-cycle scorecard, we rate each pro-cyclical indicator as strong
positive if the current value of the indicator is above the "mean plus one
standard deviation" line, weak positive if it's between the mean line and
the one above it, weak negative if it's below the mean line but above the
"mean minus one standard deviation" line, and strong negative if it's below
the bottom line. For countercyclical indicators we reverse the direction:
for example, strong positive means below the "mean minus one standard
deviation" line.

Figure 11.6: New claims and housing starts.

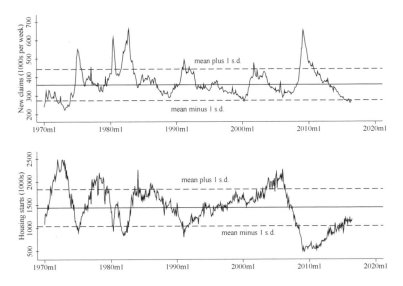

The two panels show, respectively, new claims for unemployment insurance
and housing starts, two popular indicators of economic conditions.

This is a rough cut, to be sure, but a useful one. It leads to this summary
of economic conditions as of August 2016 based on the four indicators we
have seen so far:

- Industrial production: Growth has recently been close to the mean. Assessment: weak positive.

- Employment growth: The most recent numbers show steady moderate
  growth. Assessment: weak positive.

- New claims: They are the only countercyclical indicator in our list. They
  have fallen dramatically over the last two years, and are now well below
  the long-run average. Assessment: strong positive.

- Housing starts: They remain low by historical standards, although there
  has been improvement since 2009. Assessment: weak negative.

These assessments are collected in Table 11.1. Overall, we see one strong
positive, two weak positives, and one weak negative, a mixed set of signals
that's not unusual. A more extensive analysis would use more indicators,
decide how much weight to give each one, assess how far into the future they
point, and so on.

Table 11.1: Business-cycle scorecard in action

Indicator	Strong Negative	Weak Negative	Weak Positive	Strong Positive
Industrial production			x	
Employment			x	
New Claims				x
Housing starts		x		
Summary	0	1	2	1

11.6   Regression-based forecasting

A more formal statistical approach is to include as many indicators as we like in a multivariate regression. We estimate the regression by some appropriate method and use it to forecast the future. Here are the steps we might follow in constructing a forecast of (say) industrial production k months in the future.

The first step is to construct the variable we're forecasting. Let us say that we're interested in the growth rate of industrial production between now and k months in the future. You can do what you want, but we compute the (annualized) growth rate this way:

$$\gamma_{t,t+k} = \ln(IP_{t+k}/IP_t) \times (12/k).$$

We refer to k (here measured in months) as the *forecast horizon*. The adjustment factor "12/k" converts the growth rate to annual units. For a one-year forecast, then, we would set $k = 12$ and compute the year-on-year growth rate.

The second step is to find some variables you think would be useful in forecasting. The previous section might give you some ideas. There's a half-step that sneaks in about here, too: what form of the indicator to use. In most cases, we use growth rates of the indicators, too, either over one period or a year, whichever you think works best. But some variables are used as is. In Figure 11.3, for example, the cross-correlation for the unemployment rate is for the rate, period — not its growth rate, change, or other transformation.

Third, you put all the ingredients into a statistical package and run a regression. For example, to forecast IP growth, we would estimate the regression

$$\gamma_{t,t+k} = a + bx_t + \text{residual},$$

where x_t is the value of the indicator we have chosen. We use a sample of data to estimate the parameters a and b. Note well: The growth rate is between now (date t) and a future date $(t + k)$, but the indicator is observed now (at t). This is central to the exercise: We use what we know now to predict the future. It's not kosher to use future variables to predict the future because we don't know the future when we make the forecast (duh!).

Fourth and last: Once we have estimates of the regression parameters ($\widehat{a}$ and $\widehat{b}$, say), we use them and the current value(s) of the indicator(s) (x, say) to compute the forecast:

$$\widehat{\gamma}_{t,t+k} = \widehat{a} + \widehat{b}\, x_t.$$

The "hats" remind us that we are using estimates; $\widehat{\gamma}_{t,t+k}$ is our forecast of future growth. There are lots of variants of this approach — you can add multiple indicators, lags of the indicators ($x_{t-1}, x_{t-2}, ...$), and even past values of the growth rate of industrial production. We recommend all of the above.

The result of such an exercise is generally a useful forecast — useful in the sense that it tells us something about the future. Something, but not everything! Over periods of a year or two, forecast accuracy is usually modest. Even in-sample, the regressions rarely have R^2s above 0.25, which tells us that most of the variation (at least 75 percent) in our forecast variable is unexplained. Some people see a lesson in this: It might be more important to know how to respond when the unexpected occurs than to have better forecasts. In practice, both are useful: knowing something about the future, and having backup plans to deal with the inevitable forecasting errors. It pays to carry an umbrella when the forecast calls for rain.

11.7   Aggregation and prediction markets

There's another appealing approach to forecasting: Let markets do the work. Most of the best forecasts aggregate information from multiple indicators and sources. Indexes of leading indicators do this one way by combining multiple indicators to produce an index, which is then used to forecast the future. Or we could use multiple indicators in regression-based forecasts, as we suggested above.

Another approach is to aggregate the forecasts themselves — that is take several forecasts, perhaps based on different indicators, and average them. The business-cycle scorecard is a simple version of this. The so-called "Blue Chip" forecast is an average of forecasts generated by experts, and it performs better than any single forecaster. Some statistical forecasters do the same sort of thing on their own. They generate multiple forecasts with methods like our forecasting regression, and then average them to generate a final aggregate forecast. Again, the aggregate tends to do better than the individual forecasts.

A related idea is to rely on markets, which aggregate information from the people using them. Presidential futures markets, for example, have predicted the popular vote in the last four elections more accurately than any of the major polls. In the economic arena, there are a growing number of markets in which you can trade futures contracts whose payoffs are tied to the value of specific economic numbers: the consumer price index, the fed funds rate, and so on. These markets are increasingly used as forecasts themselves, with one wrinkle. The simplest interpretation is that the futures price is a market forecast of the relevant economic number. For example, if we are interested in the value of an economic number y to be released in 6 months (y_{t+6}, say), we might use its current futures price (f_t, say):

$$f_t = \text{Market's Current Forecast of } y_{t+6}.$$

Experience (and possibly some insight) tells us that we may want to make a correction for the risk of the contract:

$$f_t = \text{Market's Current Forecast of } y_{t+6} + \text{Risk Premium}.$$

There's no limit to the amount of sophistication we can bring to bear on the last term, but for now, you can simply note that we probably want to address it in some way. Once you do, markets are an extremely useful source of information about the future.

Executive summary

1. Fluctuations in economic activity can be (partially) predicted by a number of indicators.

2. The cross-correlation function is a tool for describing the timing of the relation between two indicators: for example, whether one indicator leads another.

3. Markets are useful aggregators of information — and increasingly popular sources of economic forecasts.

Review questions

1. Terminology. Consider economic indicators in general.

(a) What is a procyclical indicator? A countercyclical indicator?

(b) Give an example of each.

(c) What is a leading indicator? A lagging indicator?

(d) Give an example of each.

Answer.

(a) A procyclical indicator moves up and down with GDP. A counter-cyclical indicators goes up when GDP moves down. We typically identify this feature with the sign of the correlation.

(b) Most indicators are procyclical : employment, the S&P 500, and so on. The unemployment rate is the classic countercyclical indicator.

(c) A leading indicator is correlated with future GDP growth, a lagging indicator is correlated with past GDP growth.

(d) The stock market is a leading indicator, the unemployment is a lagging indicator. We typically identify this feature with the cross-correlation function.

2. Housing starts. We mentioned housing starts as an indicator of future economic activity. In what ways do you think it's a good indicator? A bad one? (For further information, see the US Census Bureau's web site.)

Answer. Good: connected to housing, which, as a durable good, should be cyclically sensitive and volatile; available quickly; it leads the cycle (as you can see from its ccf). Bad: based on a sample, which leads to short-term noise; revised periodically; strong seasonality; possibly misleading now that we have a glut of housing to work off.

3. Unemployment. The unemployment rate is widely reported in the press, but professionals rarely use it. Why do you think that is?

Answer. One reason is that the unemployment rate understates the change in employment in a downturn. Some people who lose jobs leave the labor force, so they're not included in the unemployment rate. Another reason is that the unemployment rate is a lagging indicator. It falls slowly, well after the economy turns around. Employment (the number of people actually working) is the preferred indicator for both reasons.

4. Terrorism futures. In 2002, a government agency recommended that we establish a futures market in terrorist attacks, on the grounds that it would give us a useful public indicator of their likelihood. The idea was widely criticized. Do you think it was a good idea or a bad one? What would you need to do to implement it?

Answer. Another case of a good idea thrown out because it sounded bad to politicians. It's not clear that such attacks are predictable, but if they are, we'd expect futures markets to do as well as any other method.

To implement the idea, you'd need to define (and possibly quantify) a terrorist event.

If you're looking for more

There are many sources of leading indicators around the world and almost as many guides to them. Among them:

- The best book we've seen on the subject is Bernard Baumohl, *The Secrets of Economic Indicators*. If you use economic indicators in your job, you should buy this book.

- The Bloomberg Economic Calendar gives release dates and short summaries of a wide range of indicators. Ditto the WSJ, Yahoo, etc.

- The CME has a nice report, "Impact of economic indicators," on the information content of common indicators for futures prices.

Most statistical software packages have one-line commands to compute cross-correlation functions. You can also do it in a spreadsheet, but it's a lot more cumbersome.

To do more with this topic, you need some knowledge of time series statistics. If you'd like to learn more about forecasting economic and financial variables specifically, we recommend "Forecasting Times Series Data," course STAT-GB.2302, taught in alternate years by Professors Deo and Hurvich, two of our best statisticians.

Symbols and data used in this chapter

Table 11.2: Symbol table.

Symbol	Definition
ccf	Cross-correlation function
$ccf(k)$	Correlation of (x_t, y_{t-k}) at lag k
$\gamma_{t,t+k}$	Continuously compounded growth rate from t to $t + k$
$\widehat{x}$	Estimate of x
f_t	Futures price at time t

Table 11.3: Data table.

Variable	Source
Industrial production	INDPRO
Real GDP	GDPC1
S&P 500	SP500
Employment	PAYEMS
Unemployment rate	UNRATE
New claims	IC4WSA
Hours worked	AWHMAN
Building permits	PERMIT
Housing starts	HOUST
consumer sentiment	UMCSENT
Purchasing managers' index	NAPM
10-year Treasury yield	GS10
2-year Treasury yield	GS2
Federal funds rate	FEDFUNDS

To retrieve the data online, add the identifier from the source column to http://research.stlouisfed.org/fred2/series/. For example, to retrieve nonfarm employment, point your browser to http://research.stlouisfed.org/fred2/series/PAYEMS

12

Aggregate Supply and Demand

Tools: Aggregate supply and demand (AS/AD) graph.

Key Words: Short- and long-run aggregate supply; sticky wages; aggregate demand; supply and demand shocks; Keynesian.

Big Ideas:

- The AS/AD model relates output and prices in the short and long runs. The model is composed of (i) an upward-sloping short-run aggregate supply curve, which inherits its shape from sticky wages; (ii) a vertical long-run aggregate supply curve; and (iii) a downward-sloping aggregate demand curve.

- Shocks to the aggregate supply and demand curves have different effects on inflation and output.

We've seen that economic fluctuations follow regular patterns and that these patterns can be used to forecast the future. For some purposes, that's enough. But if we want to make sense of analysts' discussions of business conditions, of monetary policy, or of situations that don't fit historical patterns, we need a theoretical framework. The aggregate supply and demand model is the analyst's standard, the implicit model behind most popular macroeconomic analysis. It's not the answer to all questions, but it's a useful tool for organizing our thoughts. Think of these notes as the executive summary; textbooks devote hundreds of pages to the same topic. If you'd like to go deeper, see the references at the end of this chapter.

We take one common shortcut. In our theory, the variables are real output and the price level. In practice, we refer to output growth and inflation.

There's a modest disconnect here between theory and practice, but it's something that can be worked out. You can thank us later for saving you the trouble of doing it explicitly.

12.1 Aggregate supply

The standard business-cycle model used by analysts is an adaptation of the supply and demand diagram. We refer to the curves as aggregate supply and aggregate demand to emphasize that we're talking about the whole economy rather than a single market — and to remind ourselves that the analogy with supply and demand in a single market is imperfect. Figure 12.1 is an example. The aggregate supply (AS) curve represents combinations of output (real GDP, which we denote by Y) and the price level (an index P such as the GDP deflator) consistent with the decisions of producers and sellers ("supply"). The aggregate demand (AD) curve represents combinations of output and the price level consistent with the decisions of buyers ("demand").

Here's how aggregate supply works. We start with the production function,

$$Y \;=\; AK^\alpha L^{1-\alpha}, \tag{12.1}$$

where (as usual) Y is output, A is total factor productivity, K is the stock of physical capital (plant and equipment), L is labor, and $\alpha = 1/3$.

In the simplest "classical" theory, Y is fixed because nothing on the right-hand side of (12.1) changes in the short run. Although current productivity A and capital K can change over time, we often assume that their current values are set — that is they can't be changed by current decisions. Capital, for example, takes time to produce: We can increase next year's capital stock by investing today, but today's capital stock is whatever we happen to have. Labor L is determined by supply and demand in the labor market, which gives us a level of work that reconciles firms' demand with individuals' supply. The result is a vertical aggregate supply curve, such as AS* in the figure, in which output does not depend on the price level P.

A vertical aggregate supply curve was the state of the art until the 1930s, when John Maynard Keynes (pronounced "canes") decided that the Depression demanded a new theory. He and his followers (the "Keynesians") argued that the aggregate supply curve should be upward-sloping. Why? The most popular argument is that wages or prices are "sticky": They do not adjust quickly enough to equate supply and demand for labor or goods. One version of this story is that wages are sticky downward (that is, wages generally don't fall when demand for labor declines). The sticky wage analysis goes

Figure 12.1: Aggregate supply and demand.

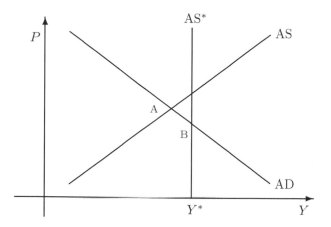

The horizontal axis is real GDP; the vertical axis is the price
level. The lines represent aggregate supply (two versions, AS
and AS*) and demand (AD).

something like this: If the nominal wage W is fixed (i.e., very sticky), then
an increase in the price level reduces the real wage W/P, making labor more
attractive to firms, who hire more workers, which raises output. (That is,
we continue to use the labor demand curve.)

The Keynesian sticky wage/price story leads to an aggregate supply curve
that is upward-sloping, since an increase in the price level leads to a lower
real wage and, therefore, more people hired by firms. We refer to it as the
short-run aggregate supply curve, because wages and prices are not thought
to be sticky forever. Eventually they adjust, putting us on the vertical
aggregate supply curve AS*, which we refer to as long-run aggregate supply.

That's what aggregate supply looks like, but what kinds of things make it
shift over time? Here's a list:

- Productivity: An increase in A shifts AS to the right. You can see why
  from the production function (12.1) — an increase in productivity A raises
  output Y.

- Capital: ditto an increase in K.

- Price of imported oil: This is a more subtle one, but an increase in the
  price of oil works like a negative productivity shock in an oil-importing
  country like the US and shifts AS to the left. Why? Because production

involves energy, as well as capital and labor, as an input. In our measurement system, GDP consists only of value added by capital and labor. If the price of oil rises, then a larger fraction of total production is paid to oil producers, leaving less for capital and labor and, therefore, reducing GDP. There's very little question that this is what happens in practice: An increase in the price of oil leads to larger payments to oil producers and smaller payments to capital and labor. Oil producers benefit; oil consumers do not.

To simplify matters, we'll assume that these factors shift both AS and AS* left or right by the same amount.

12.2 Aggregate demand

The primary role of the Keynesian aggregate supply curve is to allow demand to influence output; if supply is vertical, then changes in demand affect the price level, but not output. That's what we assumed when we discussed the quantity theory — that changes in the money supply affect prices, but not output. But if aggregate supply is flatter, shifts in demand affect both prices and output.

But what is the aggregate demand curve and where does it come from? Recall that aggregate demand refers to the purchase of goods and services. The aggregate demand curve tells us how much demand for output there is at each price level.

The simplest version follows from the *quantity theory of money*,

$$M^S V \;=\; PY, \tag{12.2}$$

where M^S is the money supply, V is the velocity of money (the number of times each dollar of money is used for transactions during the year), P is the price level, and Y is real GDP. The product PY is the money value of GDP (or nominal GDP), and is a proxy for the total value of transactions. We will discuss the quantity theory in more depth in Chapter 14.

The aggregate demand curve is the relation between P and Y for a given supply of money M^S, presumably controlled by the country's monetary authority. For simplicity, assume that velocity V, is constant. Then, equation (12.2) gives us an inverse relation between P and Y, shown as AD in Figure 12.1. Changes in M^S lead to shifts in AD. If the monetary authority increases M^S, then for each possible value of P, we need a larger value of Y in order to satisfy (12.2), so AD shifts to the right.

There's a more complex version in which monetary policy operates through other instruments (e.g. by controlling interest rates). The idea is that a fall in the interest rate stimulates interest-sensitive components of demand, such as business investment and housing.

Other shifts in AD come from the expenditure components: demand by consumers (C); firms (I); government (G); and the rest of the world (NX). You often read, for example, that high demand by consumers leads to higher output — more on this shortly. Ditto increases in government purchases (wars are the biggest examples historically) and investment by firms (remember, investment is the most volatile expenditure component). Keynes thought investment fluctuations stemmed, in part, from the "animal spirits" of business people, which you might think of as shifts in investment demand driven by psychological factors.

Let's summarize. The aggregate demand curve is downward-sloping, reflecting the decline in the real money supply as the price level increases. The following factors ("shocks") shift the aggregate demand curve to the right:

- An increase in the supply of money.

- An increase in government purchases.

- An increase in consumer demand: For given levels of income, consumers decide to spend more.

- An increase in investment demand: For given levels of interest rates and output, firms decide to invest more (animal spirits).

- An increase in net exports (a rise in foreign demand for domestic goods or a reduction in domestic demand for foreign goods or some combination).

12.3 Aggregate supply and demand together

Now let's put supply and demand together. Equilibrium is where supply and demand cross. The only difference in this respect from the traditional supply and demand analysis is that we have two supply curves. The short-run equilibrium is where AD and AS cross. The long-run equilibrium is where AD and AS* cross.

Here's how that works. The short-run equilibrium is where aggregate supply AS and aggregate demand AD cross: the point labeled A in Figure 12.1. In this example, the economy's output is below its long-run value Y^*, indicated by AS*. The reason is that the real wage is too high, leading firms to demand less work than individuals would like to offer at the going real wage.

The long-run equilibrium is where aggregate demand AD crosses long-run aggregate supply AS*: point B in the figure. How do we get there? Eventually, the real wage falls, shifting the AS curve down, until we get to the point where AD crosses the long-run aggregate supply.

Figure 12.2: The impact of an increase in the money supply.

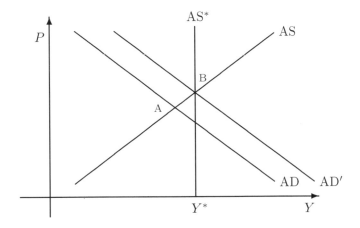

Aggregate demand AD shifts right to AD', moving the short-run equilibrium from A to B.

Let's put our theory to work:

What is the impact of an increase in the supply of money? Consider a short-run equilibrium at a point like A in Figure 12.2. Could the monetary authority do something to raise output to its long-run level? An increase in the money supply will shift AD to the right, as in the new aggregate demand curve AD'. If we increase the money supply by the right amount, we can establish a new equilibrium at B, where output is exactly its long-run value. [We recommend that you work through all these shifts of curves on your own to make sure you follow the argument.] How was this accomplished? The increase in the supply of money increased the price level. Since the nominal wage is fixed, the real wage falls, making labor more attractive to firms and thereby increasing employment and output.

Alternatively, suppose that we're at the long-run equilibrium. What are the short- and long-run effects of increasing the money supply? The short-run impact is to raise prices and output, as we move up the aggregate supply curve. [You should work this out yourself in a diagram.] But the long-run effect is to increase prices, with no impact on output. Why? Because monetary policy doesn't affect the economy's long-term ability to produce. That's what we saw with the quantity theory.

What is the impact of an increase in government purchases? You might recognize this as an example of a stimulus program. Suppose that we start, as we did above, with output below its long-term value, such as point A in Figure 12.2. Then, an increase in government purchases shifts aggregate demand to the right, as illustrated in the same figure.

What is the impact of an increase in the price of oil? Consider an initial short-run and long-run equilibrium, such as point A in Figure 12.3. An increase in the price of oil shifts the aggregate supply curve to the left. Remember: we shift both supply curves horizontally by the same amount. The new short-run equilibrium is at point B, where AD and AS$'$ cross. Eventually the short-run aggregate supply curve shifts until it crosses AD at AS$^{*'}$, giving us long-run equilibrium at C.

Figure 12.3: The impact of an increase in the price of oil.

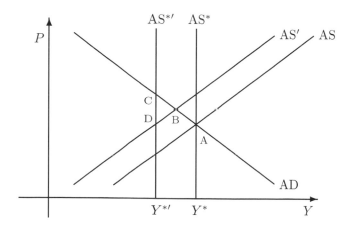

Aggregate supply curves shift left from AS/AS* to AS$'$/AS$^{*'}$, moving the short-run equilibrium from A to B.

Note that this adverse supply shock reduces output but raises the price level. People sometimes refer to this combination as "stagflation," a term coined to describe what seemed to be a surprising or implausible outcome. In fact, it's a natural result of leftward shifts in the aggregate supply curve. Note that adverse supply shocks are inflationary, in the sense that they raise the price level unless something is done to aggregate demand to offset them.

Where do business cycles come from? It's obvious that we can generate economic fluctuations by shifting the aggregate supply and demand curves around. Less obvious is what kinds of shifts are most common, or how they lead to the patterns we see in the data. As a rule, shifts in AD move price and output in the same direction, while shifts in AS move price and output in opposite directions. By looking at the statistical relation between prices and output, we can get a sense of whether supply or demand shifts are more prevalent.

12.4　Beyond supply and demand

This is a nice model, relatively easy to use, and applicable to lots of things. But it's theory, not the real world. Eliza Doolittle notwithstanding, it's often a mistake to fall in love with your own creation. Economists have learned to be humble; some might say that we have a lot to be humble about.

The aggregate supply and demand framework can be developed further, but it has two weaknesses that are hard to overcome. The first is what we might term general equilibrium: Many things affect both supply and demand, so it seems artificial to separate them as we have. The second is dynamics: The impact of many shocks depends not only on what happens now, but also on what we expect to happen in the future. That's a hard thing to model explicitly, more so in a single diagram.

Consider the interaction of supply and demand. If productivity rises, is that a shift of supply or demand? Obviously it shifts supply: The production function shifts, which directly affects producers. But consumers are also producers. An increase in productivity raises wages, which gives them more income, perhaps leading them to consume more. It also raises the demand for capital goods, since capital is now more productive. Are these shifts in demand? In the sense that they change consumption and investment decisions, the answer is yes. The closer you look, the harder it is to separate supply from demand.

Another example is the financial crisis. Did it shift supply or demand? Think about it and let us know what you come up with.

Or consider dynamics. One issue is causality. Think about popular comments to the effect that consumer demand is driving the economy. A journalist might say: "High consumer demand led to an economic boom." The logic is perfectly consistent with our AS/AD analysis, but is that really what's going on? If we think about consumption, one of our first thoughts should be to think about our future income. If we expect to have much higher income in the future (that MBA is really paying off!), we might consume more now. But think about what that does to causality. For the economy as a whole, has output gone up because we consumed more, or did we consume more because we expected output to go up? It's not easy to tell the difference between the two mechanisms.

Investment is similar. Firms make investment decisions based on their assessment (i.e., guess) of market conditions years down the road. That's why "institutions" are so important. Good institutions give firms some assurance that the rules won't change in ways that make the investment less attractive. With respect to business cycles, we could ask the same question we asked of consumption: Did high investment lead to a booming economy, or did expectations of a booming economy lead to high investment? If we're forecasting, we may not care, as long as the two go together. But if we want to understand what's going on, we need to address this issue one way or the other. Fed minutes and analysts' reports are filled with conjectures over exactly this kind of issue.

A related issue is what we might call context: the set of assumptions people use to think about the connection between current and future events. Monetary policy is a good example. In most developed countries, central banks have worked hard to convince people that if they increase the money supply now, it does not signal future increases in the money supply. If it did, people might immediately demand higher wages, which would lead to higher prices and inflation. But if they regard a current increase in the money supply as temporary, they might very well be content with wages and prices where they are. That's one of the reasons that monetary policy is different in the US and Argentina. The contexts for understanding current events are different. It's also an important practical issue for monetary policy: central banks must signal not only their current policies, but their likely future policies. That's exactly what the Fed is struggling with right now — how to do that effectively.

Executive summary

1. In the long run, output is determined by the production function: the productivity of the economy and the behavior and institutions that determine investment and employment.

2. In the short run, output may respond to changes in aggregate demand (e.g., the money supply) because of sticky wages or prices or possibly other market frictions.

3. This is theory, not reality. There's no substitute for adding some common sense.

Review questions

1. AS/AD review. Get out a piece of paper and do the following without looking at the text:

   (a) Draw the aggregate demand curve on a piece of paper. Why does it slope downward?

   (b) Draw the short-run aggregate supply curve on a piece of paper. Why does it slope upward?

   (c) Draw the long-run aggregate supply curve where the two cross. Why is it vertical?

   (d) What happens in the short run if we increase the money supply? In the long run?

   Answer. You may refer to Figure 12.2.

   (a) The AD curve slopes down because a given quantity of money can support a high price level P or high real output Y, but not both. See the quantity theory equation (12.2).

   (b) The idea is that a higher price level leads, at a fixed wage rate, to lower real wages, leading firms to hire more workers and expand output.

   (c) In the long run, wages adjust, and output and employment do not depend on the price level.

   (d) If we increase the money supply, aggregate demand shifts to the right. The immediate impact is to raise output and prices as we move along the short-run aggregate supply curve. In the long run wages adjust, leading output to revert to its long-run equilibrium level and prices to rise.

2. Supply or demand? Suppose exports increase sharply. Is this a shift in supply or demand?

   Answer. The question is whether this has to do with the production (supply) or purchase (demand) of goods and services. Exports are sales, so it's a purchase, hence demand. We would approach it the same way we approached the increase in the money supply in the previous question.

3. France. We've seen that the employment ratio is lower in France than in the US. Should France increase its money supply in an attempt to increase employment and output?

   Answer. Good question, but the answer is no: One suspects that the level of employment associated with the long-run aggregate supply curve is lower than markets would produce on their own.

4. Causality. Do increases in consumption cause increases in output, or the other way around? That is, could the correlation between consumption and output be because high output leads consumers to spend more, rather than the reverse?

Answer. We observe data, not causality, and we may not be able to distinguish between alternative causal interpretations of the same events. That's what makes economic analysis so much fun. In some cases, we might be able to tell the difference, and these cases might lead to more general insights. For example, winning the lottery generates an increase in consumption, and we can say confidently that the causality runs from higher income to higher consumption. Why? Because the reverse argument is absurd: High consumption didn't cause the person to win the lottery. In most cases, however, we can have multiple plausible causal interpretations of events, and there's not much we can do about it.

If you're looking for more

Similar material is covered in greater depth in most macroeconomics textbooks.

Symbols used in this chapter

Table 12.1: Symbol table.

Symbol	Definition
Y	Real output (=real GDP)
A	Total factor productivity (TFP)
K	stock of physical capital (plant and equipment)
L	quantity of labor (number of people employed)
α	Exponent of K in Cobb-Douglas production function (= capital share of income)
P	Price level
Y^*	Long-run equilibrium (or potential) output
AS	Short-run aggregate supply
AS*	Long-run aggregate supply (AS)
AD	aggregate demand (AD)
AD′	aggregate demand (AD) after a shock
AS*′	Long-run aggregate supply after a shock
AS′	Short run aggregate supply after a shock
M^S	Money supply
V	Velocity of money
C	Private consumption
I	Private investment (residential and business investment)
G	Government purchases of goods and services (not transfers)
X	Exports
M	Imports
NX	Net exports ($= X - M$)

13
Policy in the AS/AD model

Tools: Aggregate supply and demand (AS/AD) graph.

Key Words: Policy objectives; potential output; output gap.

Big Ideas:

- The objectives of macroeconomic policy are generally thought to be (i) stable prices and (ii) output near its long-run equilibrium level.

- A direct consequence is that monetary policy should respond differently to demand and supply shocks. As a general rule, policy should resist/offset changes in output triggered by shifts in demand and accommodate/reinforce changes triggered by shifts in supply.

- We can identify supply or demand shocks from whether output and prices move together or in opposite directions.

We've seen that aggregate demand and supply can shift on their own or, sometimes, as a result of changes in policy, including monetary policy. But what policy changes are called for? Should we always shift the aggregate demand curve to maintain low inflation? High output? Are these two objectives in conflict? The short answer is that we should respond differently to changes in supply and demand. A somewhat longer answer follows.

13.1 Objectives of policy

The traditional guide to economic policy is the invisible hand. If markets work well, then we simply leave them to do their job. If not, we may act to facilitate their operation. In the aggregate demand and supply framework, the idea is that the long-run aggregate supply curve is where the uninhibited operation of markets would lead us. In the short run, sticky wages (or other market imperfections) may delay the adjustment, but that's where the invisible hand ultimately would direct us. One consequence is that there's no compelling reason to change aggregate demand to increase output beyond its long-run equilibrium value. We might be able to do it, but it won't make us better off. In a sense, we will have tricked people into working more than they want, typically by reducing their real wages through unexpected inflation.

The first objective of policy, then, is to get output as near as possible to the level associated with the long-run aggregate supply curve AS*. This is important enough a concept that people have given it lots of names: potential output, full employment output, and so on. We'll call it *potential output*, with the understanding that it's the long-run equilibrium, not an upper bound. The *output gap* is a related concept: the difference between actual and potential output. In practice, potential output is a little slippery, because the long-run aggregate supply curve isn't something we observe. We have a variety of ways of estimating potential output, ranging from the complex to the pragmatic (a smooth trend line drawn through actual output). We give some examples (and links) at the end of the chapter.

The second objective of policy is price stability. That's not an obvious implication of the invisible hand, but experience has taught us that low and (especially) stable rates of inflation are associated with good macroeconomic performance. You might ask whether we'd be better off with no inflation, low inflation (say, two or three percent a year), or even modest deflation (yes, there are theoretical arguments for that). However, experience suggests that it doesn't matter too much. Any stable target is better than the high and variable inflation that the US and many other countries experienced in the 1970s.

13.2   Policy responses to supply and demand shocks

With potential output and stable prices as our objectives, how should policy respond to changes in aggregate supply or demand? Curiously, the answer depends on whether we face supply shocks or demand shocks.

How should we respond to demand shocks? Consider a negative demand shock, illustrated by Figure 13.1. The long-run equilibrium is point A, where aggregate supply AS* and aggregate demand AD cross. Suppose that consumer pessimism shifts the aggregate demand curve to AD', leaving us

Figure 13.1: The impact of an adverse demand shock.

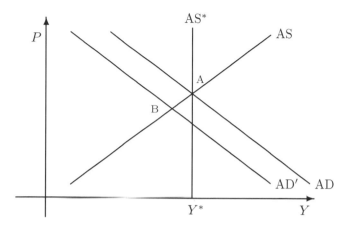

Aggregate demand AD shifts left to AD′, moving the short-run
equilibrium from A to B.

at point B. What should we do? If we do nothing, we fail on both of our
objectives because output is below potential and prices have fallen. The
appropriate policy, then, is to shift the demand curve back to AD, perhaps
by expanding the money supply.

That's a general rule: Policy should offset demand shocks. In this case,
there is no conflict between our two goals of hitting potential output and
maintaining stable prices. The policy lesson: We should resist or offset
demand shocks.

How should we respond to supply shocks? Consider the situation depicted
in Figure 13.2: an adverse supply shock that moves us from A to B. Should
policy try to offset the decline in output? If we follow our logic, the answer
is no; we want to move output as close to the long-run aggregate supply
curve AS*′ as possible. We do this by moving the aggregate demand curve
left (left!) until it intersects both aggregate supply curves at point D. At
this point, the price level is the same as it was at A, so we have delivered
stable prices. Output has fallen more than if we had not acted, but that's
what the invisible hand suggests. The policy lesson: We should acquiesce
to or accommodate supply shocks.

The basic lesson, then, is that we want to react differently to changes in
output that result from supply and demand shocks. We should resist demand shocks and accommodate supply shocks. The difficulty, in practice,

Figure 13.2: The impact of an increase in the price of oil.

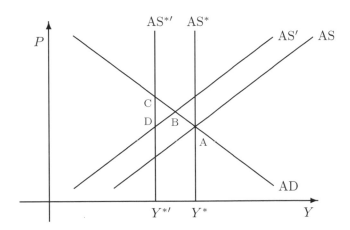

Aggregate supply curves shift left from AS/AS* to AS'/AS*',
moving the short-run equilibrium from A to B.

is knowing which is which. If we guess wrong, we can make things worse,
perhaps a lot worse.

By some interpretations, the Fed made exactly this mistake in the 1970s.
With output falling and inflation rising, the Fed increased the money supply
to keep output up. With hindsight, the OPEC oil price increase is under-
stood to be an adverse supply shock. It reduced output, but there was little
we could do about it. When we increased the money supply, the consequence was that low output was accompanied by even higher inflation than
before. Having failed to understand the problem, we decided to give it a
name: stagflation.

Executive summary

1. We typically think of the goals of macroeconomic policy as keeping inflation low and output near the long-run supply curve.

2. As a general rule, policy should resist changes in output triggered by
   shifts in demand and accommodate/acquiesce to changes triggered by
   shifts in supply.

Review questions

1. Consider the situation in Figure 13.1, where an adverse demand shock moves us from A to B.

    (a) What is your welfare analysis of the change? In what ways is B better than A? Worse?

    (b) How would your answer change if AD shifted to the right, rather than the left?

    Answer.

    (a) Recall the objectives of policy: (i) stable prices and (ii) output at its long-run equilibrium value Y^*. In this case prices fall, so we fail on (i), and output moves away from Y^*, so we fail on (ii).

    (b) In this case output and prices both rise, but both are bad from a welfare point of view. Note specifically that it's not true that more output is better.

2. Current economic conditions.

    (a) What have inflation and GDP growth been over the past year?

    (b) Would you say demand has shifted or supply relative to the year before?

    (c) Using this information and anything else you think is appropriate, where is the economy relative to the long-run equilibrium level of output Y^*?

    Answer.

    (a,b) The idea is to look at the numbers and decide whether we seem to be experiencing a shift in supply or demand — or perhaps neither. If inflation and output growth have moved together, we'd say demand. If they've moved in opposite directions, we'd say supply.

    (c) Good question. What would you suggest?

3. Stimulus in China. In 2009, China responded to the financial crisis by implementing a massive program of government spending on infrastructure. Your mission is to outline the argument for or against such a program using the aggregate supply and demand (AS/AD) framework.

    (a) Over the last year, output growth and inflation have both fallen in China. Would you say this comes from a shift in supply or demand? Illustrate your answer with the appropriate diagram.

    (b) Describe the impact of a large increase in government spending on infrastructure projects. What is the likely impact on output? On inflation?

(c) What are the traditional goals of macroeconomic policy, expressed in terms of aggregate supply and demand? Does the Chinese spending program move them closer to these goals?

Answer.

(a) Shifts in demand move output and prices in the same direction, shifts in supply move them in opposite directions. (By longstanding tradition, we interpret output as output growth and prices and inflation.) Since they both fell, we would interpret this as a shift left in demand.

(b) This is a *purchase* of goods; therefore, it affects demand. A shift right in demand increases both output growth and inflation.

(c) The goals are (i) output equal to the long-run aggregate supply curve AS* and (ii) stable prices. The answer depends where you start: Are we to the left of AS* prior to the stimulus? If so, then the stimulus program moves output in the right direction. Ditto with inflation: If we start with stable prices, the stimulus generates inflation.

4. Aggregate implications of employer-provided health insurance. By an accident of history, health insurance in the US is generally provided by employers. Suppose a sharp rise in healthcare costs leads firms to hire fewer workers.

(a) How would you represent this in an aggregate supply and demand diagram? Which curve shifts? In which direction?

(b) What is the new short-run equilibrium? Long-run equilibrium? What happens to inflation and output?

(c) How should the central bank respond? Be specific about its goals and how it would accomplish them.

Answer.

(a) Since we're talking about firms and production, this must involve the supply side of the model. We shift AS and AS* to the left, both by the same amount. See the figure below.

(b) We started at A. After the shift, we move to a new short-run equilibrium at B, where the new AS crosses AD. Evidently output falls and prices rise.

Eventually we move to a new long-run equilibrium at C, where AD crosses the new AS*. At this point, output has fallen more and prices have risen more.

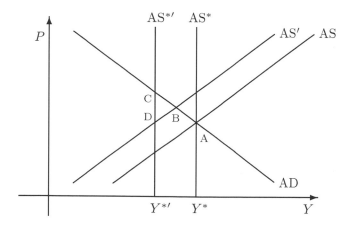

(c) The central bank has two goals: stable prices and output at its long-run equilibrium. Here we've moved from A to C. We're ok at C on the second goal: output fell, but that's the long-run equilibrium so there's nothing monetary policy can do about that. (We could consider other policies, but they're not the job of the central bank.)

Where C is bad is with respect to price stability: prices are higher. So the central bank could shift AD to the left, giving us the same long-run output but lower prices. The central bank would accomplish this by reducing the money supply, which it might do by targeting a higher interest rate.

5. The supply and demand of Abenomics. Shinzo Abe was elected Prime Minister of Japan in December 2012 after two decades of slow growth and falling prices. He pledged dramatic policy changes to revive the Japanese economy, dubbed the "three arrows" of "Abenomics." We consult the Economist Intelligence Unit for specifics:

- Fiscal stimulus. A sizeable economic stimulus package was passed by parliament in February 2013, and a smaller one in October.

- Monetary stimulus. A plan to double Japan's money supply within two years was implemented in April 2013 to help to achieve the Bank of Japan's target of 2% inflation.

- Structural reform. This is less clearly articulated, but some observers hope for a range of micro-based reforms, including loosening product-market regulations that reduce productivity, tightening corporate requirements for funding pensions, creating a more flexible labor market, and reducing subsidies to an inefficient agricultural sector.

Your mission is to explore the impact of the three arrows using the aggregate supply and demand framework.

(a) Explain, for each "arrow," whether it affects supply or demand. Which way does each one shift the appropriate curve(s)?

(b) Compare the short- and long-term impact on output of the three policies. Which are likely to have the greatest impact in the short term? In the long term?

Answer.

(a) We have:

- Fiscal stimulus. This shifts aggregate demand to the right.

- Monetary stimulus. Same.

- Structural reform. This shifts both aggregate supply curves to the right.

(b) Fiscal and monetary stimulus raise output in the short run. They have no long-run impact on output.

Structural reform is likely the most important of the arrows for the long-term performance of the Japanese economy. It should raise output long term, in large part by increasing productivity, but short-term transition issues could go the other way. It's also the arrow that's been executed least aggressively.

If you're looking for more

The measurement of potential output has generated some interesting debate. The bottom line, in our view, is that there's usually some question where the long-run aggregate supply curve is. Here is a range of opinion on the subject:

- The Congressional Budget Office (CBO) reviews a number of approaches. Search: "cbo potential output."

- Former Fed Governor Frederic Mishkin's speech, "Estimating potential output," is another good overview. Search: "mishkin potential output."

- The Kansas City Fed's 2005 Jackson Hole Symposium has an interesting exchange between Robert Hall and Greg Mankiw. Hall argues that potential output may very well not be smooth, which would contradict most measures of it. As a practical matter, this would change our view of monetary policy dramatically since many of the movements we see in GDP would be the result of the invisible hand and, therefore, not something for policymakers to resist. Mankiw says maybe, maybe not. Search: "Jackson Hole Symposium 2005."

Symbols and data used in this chapter

Table 13.1: Symbol table.

Symbol	Definition
Y	Real output (=real GDP)
Y^*	Long-run equilibrium (or potential) output
$Y^{*\prime}$	New long-run equilibrium (or potential) output
AS	Short-run aggregate supply
AS*	Long-run aggregate supply
AD	Aggregate demand
AD$'$	Aggregate demand after a shock
AS*$'$	Long-run aggregate supply after a shock
AS$'$	Aggregate supply after a shock

Table 13.2: Data table.

Variable	Source
NBER recession indicator	USRECM
CBO real potential GDP	GDPPOT
Oil Price (WTI)	OILPRICE

To retrieve the data online, add the identifier from the source column to http://research.stlouisfed.org/fred2/series/. For example, to retrieve oil prices, point your browser to http://research.stlouisfed.org/fred2/series/OILPRICE

14
Money and Inflation

Tools: The quantity theory of money.

Key Words: Money; medium of exchange; liquidity; store of value; unit of account; money supply; hyperinflation; quantity theory; velocity; fiscal dominance, deflation.

Big Ideas:

- Money is the medium of exchange – whatever people generally use to complete transactions. It is also a unit of account and a store of value.

- The quantity theory of money links the money supply with the price level and output.

- Inflation is the growth rate of the price level, which is typically measured by a price index.

- Hyperinflation refers to an inflation rate of 100 percent or more per year. High rates of money growth are the proximate cause of hyperinflations. High rates of money growth in turn are usually caused by ongoing government budget deficits that are financed by printing money. We call this *fiscal dominance* over monetary policy.

In the preceding chapter, we looked at the role of policy in pursuit of better macroeconomic performance – keeping output close to its potential and the price level stable. In this chapter and the following one, we analyze monetary policy. We begin by taking a closer look at money. We then develop a simple theory which links changes in the stock of money in the economy to output growth and inflation. Finally, we apply this theory to hyperinflations, extreme situations where the economy moves very far from price stability.

14.1   What is money?

To economists, money is a special type of financial asset whose key characteristic is that it can readily be used for transactions. In other words, money is the *medium of exchange*. Currency is money, as are balances in checking accounts at banks. You can buy a latte at Starbucks with cash or with a debit card, and the transaction instantly is complete. (Credit cards can also be used for transactions, though they are not money. When you use your credit card it creates a loan. Sometime in the future you complete the transaction by paying your credit card bill with money.). Other financial assets (e.g. stock holdings) usually have to be converted into money before they can be used in transactions. The ease with which an asset can be converted into the medium of exchange is sometimes referred to as the asset's *liquidity*.

Money serves two other functions. First it acts as a *store of value*. It is a way to store purchasing power and use it at a future date. How well it performs this function depends on what is happening to prices. If prices are rising, then a given amount of money has less and less purchasing power over time. Finally, money acts as a *unit of account*. Transactions are quoted in terms of money, e.g. the prices of goods and services or loan obligations.

The *money supply* (M^S) is the total value of all money assets held by everyone in the economy. There are different measures of the money supply. We will discuss two of the most commonly used ones. The first, referred to as narrow money, and denoted by M1 in the United States, includes currency and coin held by the nonbanking public, checking and similar transactions accounts held at banks, and travelers checks. This corresponds directly to the definition of money given above.

The other measure, broad money or M2, also includes assets which are very liquid – i.e. they can be easily converted into spending money. In the United States, the broad money supply measure M2 includes M1 plus savings deposits, small-denomination time deposits, and retail money-market fund balances.

14.2   The quantity theory of money

Inflation is the rate of growth of the price level, typically measured by the annualized percentage change in a price index (e.g., the Consumer Price Index or GDP deflator) . Why do prices rise? Milton Friedman, recipient of the 1976 Nobel prize in economics, once said, "Inflation is always and everywhere a monetary phenomenon. To control inflation, you need to control the money supply."

Friedman's claim is based on a theory that is several centuries old: the *quantity theory of money*. The quantity theory is based on the role of money in executing transactions. Money is used for all kinds of transactions, from household purchases of goods and services, business-to-business purchases and sales, and financial transactions. We can posit that the total value of transactions in the economy during a period of time (e.g., a year) is approximately equal to nominal GDP during the year, where nominal GDP is PY (Y is real GDP and P is the price level). Of course, a unit of money (e.g., a dollar) can be used to execute several different transactions during the year. Putting these ideas together, we obtain the following relationship:

$$M^s V \;=\; PY, \tag{14.1}$$

where V is the *velocity* of money, the number of times a dollar is used execute transactions during the year.

Friedman's claim uses equation (14.1) and makes two additional assumptions. First, real GDP is not affected by changes in the supply of money. Second, velocity is constant. Then, the equation directly implies that a change in M^s leads to a proportionate change in P. As we will see, these assumptions do not always hold, but this is a natural place to start.

We can also use equation (14.1) to talk about inflation by expressing it in terms of growth rates. As with growth accounting, we focus on continuously compounded growth rates where the growth rate of a variable X is $\gamma_X = \ln X_t - \ln X_{t-1}$. In logs, equation (14.1) and its first differences are:

$$\ln M_t^S + \ln V_t \;=\; \ln P_t + \ln Y_t \,,$$
$$(\ln M_t^S - \ln M_{t-1}^S) + (\ln V_t - \ln V_{t-1}) \;=\; (\ln P_t - \ln P_{t-1}) + (\ln Y_t - \ln Y_{t-1}),$$

so,

$$\gamma_{M^s} + \gamma_V = \pi + \gamma_Y, \tag{14.2}$$

where $\pi = \gamma_P$ is the inflation rate (the rate of growth of the price level).

If we continue to assume that velocity is constant and real GDP growth is not influenced by money growth or inflation, then changes in the growth rate of money supply translate one-for-one to inflation.

14.3   Evidence

Is the constant velocity assumption a good one? We can check this by looking at the components of equation (14.1). If velocity is constant, movements in the price level P should mirror those in M^S/Y.

We check this in Figure 14.1, which graphs both variables for the United
States. (Money here is M2.) The figure suggests that the theory is a reasonable approximation of the data, at least over the last fifty years or so.
The two increasing lines (P and M^S/Y) show some differences, but their
long-run movements are similar. Overall, velocity has been largely flat, but
since the financial crisis of 2007-09 it has fallen amid record low interest
rates. Time will tell whether or not the change is temporary.

Figure 14.1: The quantity theory in the long run.

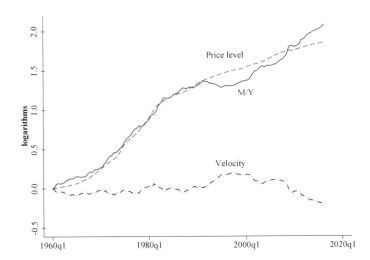

It is worth noting that the quantity theory is consistent with the long-run
premises of the aggregate demand-aggregate supply model presented in the
previous chapters: namely, that output and the price level are independent
in the long run, with output determined by the technology and factor inputs specified by the production function. The quantity theory adds that
monetary policy determines the price level in the long run. As we will see in
the next chapter, these long-run premises are largely shared by the Federal
Reserve.

The short-run evidence for the quantity theory is much weaker. When we
look at year-on-year growth rates, as we do in Figure 14.2, we see that velocity has as much short-run volatility as M^S/Y. As a consequence, movements
in prices are virtually unrelated to movements in money. To put it bluntly,
the quantity theory is a poor guide to short-run fluctuations in inflation in
the US. This turns out to be true more generally – the theory is not very
useful as a tool in situations with modest growth rates in money supply
and/or prices. As we will see in the next chapter, this implies that central

banks can use monetary policy to help stabilize the economy in the face of short-term fluctuations.

Figure 14.2: The quantity theory in the short run.

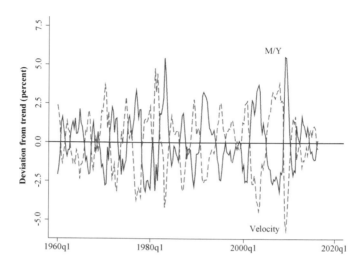

14.4   Hyperinflations

Another way to test the quantity theory is to look at situations where inflation rates are very high – a situation sometimes referred to as *hyperinflation*. (The exact numerical definition of hyperinflation is arbitrary. We are comfortable using an inflation rate of 100 percent per year or more. Another, even more extreme definition is at least 50 percent inflation per month, which is more than 12,000 percent per year.) People who live through such episodes describe them as traumatic. They spend much time and effort converting cash quickly into anything with stable value: food, cars, real estate, foreign assets. In severe hyperinflations, if they wait even a few hours, their purchasing power falls. The economy is usually a mess, but whether that is cause or effect is hard to say.

How can we use equation (14.2) to understand hyperinflation? The growth rate of real GDP is generally less than 10 percent per year. If we assume that the velocity is constant ($\gamma_V = 0$), then the driver of a very high inflation rate is a very high growth rate of the money supply.

Velocity is not constant, particularly when inflation is very high. During hyperinflations, people try to spend money as soon as they get it, because the value of the money is falling dramatically. As a result, velocity usually rises. This indirect effect on velocity V magnifies the direct effect of rapid money growth on inflation (in equation (14.2), γ_V is greater than zero and rises as the growth rate of the money supply increases).

If high rates of inflation are so painful, why do governments let them happen? The root of the problem usually lies with fiscal policy and large government budget deficits. A political impasse makes it nearly impossible to reduce the government budget deficit, and the government must issue debt. There is apparently no shortage of ready buyers of US government debt (ditto for other advanced economies), but the same cannot be said for every country. If no one will buy its debt, the only remaining option for the government is to finance the deficit with new money (read: oblige the central bank to purchase the government bonds). In short, when the government can't pay its bills in any other way, it pays them with new money, which is easy enough to print. The effect, of course, is inflation.

The impact here of fiscal policy (government deficits) on inflation is referred to as *fiscal dominance*, because fiscal policy dominates monetary policy. Nobel Prize-winner Thomas Sargent and his co-author, Neil Wallace, described a stark version of this. They showed that a central bank that aims for low inflation will fail if the government issues debt without end. Think of this as a version of the time-consistency problem problem discussed in Chapter 6. If everyone knows that the central bank eventually will be compelled to print money to avoid outright default by the government, people will expect high rates of inflation in the near future, despite the central bank's stated caution. The key is that the central bank cannot credibly commit to limit future money creation, while expectations of future inflation drive price setting today.

The conventional solution to ending a hyperinflation has two parts. The first is fiscal discipline: Balance the government budget. The second is monetary discipline: Separate the central bank from the treasury and tell the bank that its job is to maintain price stability. Though there are many fine points – how quickly must the deficit be eliminated? should the IMF supply short-term financing? – the outlines of the problem and its solution are clear. Going back to Friedman's quote: Inflation may be a monetary phenomenon, but the trouble often starts with fiscal policy and the political situation that led to it. When fiscal imperatives drive monetary policy – like the fiscal dominance in the Sargent and Wallace analysis – inflation eventually follows.

For someone operating an international business, the thing to remember is that episodes of high inflation rates are not unusual. What do you do if you're hit with one? You'll probably find that the most important thing you can do is streamline your cash management. If you can reduce the payment terms from (say) 60 days to 30 days, you increase your real revenue substantially. You may also find that big inflation leads to responses from policymakers – such as price controls and capital controls – that make your life and business more complicated. Finally, you may find that your local financial statements are highly misleading, since they measure performance in terms of the local currency, the value of which is changing rapidly. For a US subsidiary, high inflation triggers a change in the rules for translating financial entries into dollars for tax and reporting purposes.

14.5   Deflation

Another situation that is often a cause for concern is *deflation*: a decline in prices or negative inflation. There are two good reasons for this. The first relates to a couple of well-documented historical episodes in which sustained deflation was associated with very poor economic performance: the US in the Great Depression and Japan in the 2000s. The other reason is that deflation raises the real value of debt, which makes it more difficult for borrowers to repay their loans. Modest temporary deflation is unlikely to have much effect, but large sustained unexpected deflation, such as the US experienced in the early 1930s, likely has an adverse effect on the economy.

Whether that's the case or not, the issue comes up regularly in policy discussions, most recently in the US in the years following the global financial crisis in 2008 and in Europe in 2015-16.

Executive summary

1. The key characteristic of money is that it is a medium of exchange, i.e. it is used to complete transactions. Money is also a store of value and a unit of account.

2. Extremely high rates of inflation are invariably associated with high rates of money growth. High money growth is often the result of financing large fiscal deficits with money.

Review questions

1. Central bank independence. To reduce the risk of moving to hyperinflation, should a country make its central bank independent of the treasury?

    Answer. Hyperinflation usually results from the central bank monetizing (i.e. printing money to finance) large and sustained fiscal deficits. An independent central bank tasked with maintaining price stability is more likely to resist the fiscal pressures driven by the country's politics. If the government does not have assured access to new money from the central bank to finance excessive government spending, it will be forced to confront its fiscal deficit issues earlier or face the prospect of defaulting on its debt.

2. Zimbabwe. Zimbabwe ended its hyperinflation by abandoning its currency. Even official transactions were switched to either US dollars or South African rand. Does this seem like a good solution? Does it make sense for a country to abandon its currency?

Answer. There's a long tradition of each country having its own currency, but there's good reason to think at least some countries would be better off using someone else's. Zimbabwe's government showed no ability to manage its own currency effectively, so using another sounds like a move in the right direction. Essentially, Zimbabwe is outsourcing its monetary policy to another, more stable country, and thereby breaking the fiscal dominance. There are other examples – Panama and Ecuador use the US dollar – and perhaps there should be more.

If you're looking for more:

Steve Hanke and Nicholas Krus survey the history of hyperinflation in "World Hyperinflations." Search: "Hanke Krus hyperinflation." Wikipedia has a nice article on hyperinflation, including a list of the biggest ones of all time. Two really good (but more technical) pieces about specific episodes are Thomas Sargent, "The ends of four big inflations," and Thomas Sargent and Joseph Zeira, "Israel 1983."

Symbols and data used in this chapter

Table 14.1: Symbol table.

Symbol	Definition
M^S	Money stock
V	Velocity of money
P	Price level
Y	Real output or GDP
$\ln$	Natural log
γ_x	Continuously compounded growth rate of x
π	Inflation $(= \gamma_P)$

Table 14.2: Data table.

Variable	Source
Nominal GDP	GDP
M2 monetary aggregate	M2SL
M2 velocity	M2V
Consumer price index	CPIAUCSL

To retrieve the data online, add the identifier from the source column to http://research.stlouisfed.org/fred2/series/. For example, to retrieve nominal GDP, point your browser to http://research.stlouisfed.org/fred2/series/GDP

15
Monetary Policy

Tools: Central bank balance sheet; Taylor rule.

Key Words: Nominal interest rate, real interest rate, expected inflation rate, expectations hypothesis, term premium, open market operations, discount rate, reserve requirement ratio, quantitative easing (large scale asset purchases), forward guidance, interest on bank deposits at the Fed, overnight reverse repurchase agreements, federal funds rate, monetary base, bank reserves, effective lower bound.

Big Ideas:

- Central banks conduct monetary policy by translating their overall macroeconomic objectives into operating targets. In the US, the traditional operating target for the Fed is the overnight interest rate on uncollateralized borrowing by banks from other banks and financial institutions, called the fed funds rate.

- The Taylor rule provides guidance on what the target interest rate should be as a function of observed data on inflation and real GDP.

- Traditionally, the Fed used open market operations – altering the size of its balance sheet by buying and selling Treasury securities – to influence the fed funds rate. When this policy rate approached the effective lower bound in the aftermath of the financial crisis, the Fed began using unconventional instruments (including quantitative easing and forward guidance) to conduct policy.

- Since 2015, the Fed used the overnight interest rates it pays on bank deposits at the Fed and reverse repurchase agreements to raise short-term interest rates without altering the size of its balance sheet.

Where do interest rates come from? We doubt this was your first question
when you were growing up, but you probably have an opinion about it now.
Most people say they're set by the Fed — or the appropriate central bank
if you're in another country. There's some truth to that, but it can't be
that simple. We had interest rates before the Fed was established, and, if
anything, they varied more then than now. It's probably better to say that
the Fed "manages" market interest rates — towards levels that it thinks are
appropriate. Market interest rates reflect, after all, the behavior of private
borrowers and lenders, as well as the Fed.

We outline how this works, starting with a review of interest rates (there are
lots of them) and moving on to monetary policy as practiced in most developed countries these days. In many countries, monetary policy is probably
the most powerful and most nimble form of macroeconomic policy. (Fiscal
policy, which is concerned with taxes and government expenditures, is often
highly political, so decisions are often slow to arrive, and changes, especially
for government spending, are often slow to take effect.)

But, how does a central bank conduct monetary policy? This chapter examines the tools available to central banks, the operating targets that they
adopt, and how these elements are used in pursuit of their macroeconomic
goals. We begin with a review of different types of interest rates, and along
the way we will discuss how the global financial crisis and its aftermath have
changed central banking and monetary policy.

15.1   Interest rates

Interest rates are fundamental to the conduct of monetary policy. Before we
begin our discussion of monetary policy, it is useful to carefully distinguish
different types of interest rates: nominal and real, short and long, risk-free
and risky.

Nominal and real. The most common type of interest rates, the ones we
are all familiar with, represent an obligation of the borrower to pay (or the
right of the lender to receive) a certain amount of money as a percentage of
the principal value of the loan. Since these are denominated in money, we
refer to them as nominal interest rates.

As we discussed in Chapter 14, the purchasing power of money changes
over time due to inflation. One dollar of interest that we will receive one
year from now will have greater purchasing value if the inflation rate over

the next year is low (or, looked at the other way, a higher rate of inflation during the year will have eroded the purchasing power of that future dollar). If we adjust the nominal interest rate for the amount of inflation that we expect to occur during the next year, we arrive at the *real interest rate*. This represents the return measured in terms of purchasing power to lending or investment. That is, the nominal interest rate has two components:

$$i \;=\; r + \pi^e. \tag{15.1}$$

The nominal interest rate (approximately) equals the real interest rate plus the expected inflation rate. Changes in either component (the real interest rate or expected inflation) can change the nominal interest rate.

Short and long. Bonds differ, of course, by maturity: that's the idea behind the "term structure of interest rates," a popular topic in finance. If we consider a zero-coupon bond of maturity m years, the price and (nominal) interest rate or yield are related by

$$q_m \;=\; 100/(1 + i_m)^m.$$

The interest rate has been annualized — that's what the exponent does — so it applies to a bond whose maturity can be something besides one year.

The (annualized) interest rates on bonds of different maturities are usually different. This arises for a number of reasons. The first is due to expectations: the yield on a bond reflects investors' beliefs about the average return you could obtain by investing in a series of short bonds into the future (to the maturity date of the long bond). This is sometimes referred to as the *expectations hypothesis*. For example, if investors expect short-term interest rates to be higher in the future, then the interest rate of the long bond today will tend to be higher than the current interest rate on a short bond.

The long-term interest rate usually exceeds the average short term interest rate by more than would be implied by the expectations hypothesis. This difference is referred to as the *term premium*. One interpretation of this premium is that it reflects compensation for the fact that longer term bonds are riskier. This is because long bonds have greater exposure to the risk of changing interest rates – their market price changes by more than that of short term bonds if there is general upward or downward movement in all interest rates.

Another interpretation of the term premium is based on market segmentation. If the markets for bonds of different maturities are not perfectly integrated, then interest rates may also reflect relative supply and demand for long bonds and for short bonds.

Long-term interest rates have a similar distinction between real and nominal. The equation is the same with the appropriate maturities noted:

$$i_m = r_m + \pi_m^e.$$

The expected inflation rate in this case is the one that applies to the period from now until m years from now.

(Credit) risk-free and risky. There's another source of risk that comes up later in the course: the possibility that the borrower defaults. We tend to ignore this kind of risk (or think that it is very low) for US government bonds (Treasuries). For bonds issued by banks, corporations, and foreign "sovereigns" (governments), the default risk can be substantial. We might see that the interest rates on long-term dollar-denominated Brazilian government bonds are a couple of hundred basis points higher than US Treasuries of similar maturity, or that long-term euro-denominated Greek government bonds are several hundred basis points higher than German government bonds of similar maturity. (A basis point is one hundredth of a percent.)

15.2   Monetary policy: objectives, instruments, and targets

A useful framework for understanding monetary policy combines the ultimate objectives of the central bank, the specific instruments it uses to implement its policy, and the operating or intermediate targets that the central bank uses to judge whether the policy changes are beginning to have their intended effects. While monetary policy in most countries fits this general framework, the specifics often differ from one country to another. Here, we will use the general framework to examine the specifics of the US Federal Reserve (the Fed).

Objectives: We discussed the ultimate objectives or goals of macroeconomic policy in Chapter 13 – output equal to the economy's potential and price stability. When it comes to monetary policy, central banks are sometimes tasked with additional goals, including a sustainable composition of the country's balance of payments (see Chapter 18) or a financial system that is stable and less likely to experience a crisis (see Chapter 21).

In the United States, the 1977 Federal Reserve Reform Act directs the Fed to pursue "maximum employment, stable prices, and moderate long-term interest rates," with reference to "the economy's long-run potential to increase production." The Fed generally focuses on the first two objectives, leading to the common description of its goals as a "dual" mandate. The objective of maximum employment is closely linked to keeping actual output (i.e. real GDP) close to its potential (usually referred to as achieving an output gap of close to zero). On the price stability front, in 2012 the Fed explicitly stated that its target is an average rate of inflation of 2 percent per year over the medium term (a period of several years). For this purpose, the measure of inflation is the change in the personal consumption expenditure (PCE) price index. The PCE inflation rate is considered to be a more accurate measure of consumer inflation than the more well-known consumer price index (CPI) inflation rate.

In the United States, these two objectives are thought to have similar weights (as in the "dual" mandate). In a number of other countries, the central bank focuses primarily on price stability. Why do some countries place so much emphasis on price stability? One reason is that high inflation episodes in the past have been associated with poor macroeconomic performance (for instance, in the 1970s). A second reason has to do with that fact that, to keep prices stable today, the central bank must have significant credibility, i.e. consumers and firms must believe that it will not pursue policies that stimulate production and employment at the expense of future inflation. A central bank with a clear mandate for price stability is one way to reassure consumers and firms and bolster the central bank's credibility. Finally, predictability of future inflation rates is valuable, because many *current* decisions depend on *future* price developments (for example, interest rates, wages and salaries, long-term supply contracts between businesses are all usually denominated in units of currency, whose value fluctuates with future prices). Having monetary policy focus on price stability enhances this predictability. When we are far away from price stability (e.g. in hyperinflations, which we discussed in Chapter 14), day-to-day price changes tend to be not only large, but also wildly uncertain.

This desire for predictability is also the main reason why many advanced economies have made their central banks independent — in the sense that they can set their policy instrument (usually an interest rate) without being overridden by a legislature or a government for short-run political reasons. An independent, credible monetary authority lowers expectations of future inflation and helps improve performance on both the inflation and output fronts.

Instruments: What can a central bank like the Fed actually do to achieve its objective(s)? Here, we will introduce a number of instruments. Later in the chapter, we will examine in depth how they are used.

Traditionally (prior to late 2008), the Fed used three instruments. *Open market operations*, in which the Fed bought or sold previously issued US Treasuries in the secondary market, was the most important one. The Fed also directly set the rate at which banks can borrow from it (the *discount* rate). However, such borrowing was generally discouraged, and banks feared the stigma of borrowing from the Fed, so typically there were almost no discount loans. Finally, the Fed specified the *reserve requirement ratio*, the fraction of deposit liabilities at a bank that had to be held as reserves (deposits at the Federal Reserve or vault cash). For several decades now, the Fed has not used the reserve requirement ratio to change monetary policy.

During the global financial crisis in 2008 and in its aftermath, the Fed began using an unconventional set of instruments. It initiated a sequence of *large-scale asset purchase* programs, usually called *quantitative easing* (QE). In a sense, this is just a form of open market operations, but the scale and the assets traded are different, as are the effects on the economy, once the level of interest rates has declined close to the effective lower bound. The Fed also more actively used *forward guidance*, in which it describes the likely future path of its monetary policy.

Starting in late 2015, the Fed has also employed two additional instruments: the *interest rate on deposits that banks hold at the Fed* and the *interest rate on overnight reverse repurchase agreements* (which are a form of collateralized borrowing – financial institutions lend money to the Fed, against US Treasuries as collateral).

Central banks in other countries use many of these same types of instruments, and often have other instruments. For example, in some countries, the central bank directly sets interest rates on some types of deposits at banks or on bank loans. It can also sometimes set limits on the growth of outstanding bank loans or similar credit instruments.

Operating targets: Central banks conduct monetary policy by translating their overall macroeconomic objectives into *operating targets*, usually financial market variables (e.g. interest rates). This is easier said than done and requires a careful understanding of the connections between financial conditions and the real economy. The instruments listed above are then used to implement these operating targets.

In the United States, the Fed's standard operating target has been the *federal funds rate*, the rate at which banks borrow uncollateralized overnight from other banks and financial institutions through their balances with the Fed. The Federal Open Market Committee sets a target for this interest rate. The NY Fed, which is tasked with implementation, uses the instruments at its disposal to ensure that the federal funds rate stays close to the target.

Beginning in late 2008, with the federal funds rate at or near zero, the Fed also set balance-sheet targets regarding the size and composition its assets.

Central banks in most countries use some form of overnight or short-term interest rate target, and in recent years, several advanced-economy central banks used forms of QE to expand their balance sheets. In addition, central banks in other countries may have other operating targets. For example, some central banks have targets for the growth rate of the money supply, the growth rate of total bank loans, or the growth rate of total debt. Some central banks have targets for the exchange rate value of the country's currency.

15.3   The Fed's Balance Sheet

Before discussing how the Fed uses its instruments to achieve its objectives, it is helpful first to understand the balance sheet of a central bank. From the perspective of domestic monetary policy, here are the key items on the balance sheet of the central bank:

Central bank

Assets	Liabilities
Bonds and other securities	Currency
Loans to banks	Deposits from banks
	Deposits from financial institutions

The sum of currency and deposits from banks and from other financial institutions is referred to as the *monetary base* (M^B), and it is usually most of the central bank's liabilities.

Here are key items on the combined balance sheets of all the banks in the country:

Banking system

Assets	Liabilities
Loans to non-bank customers	Checkable deposits
Bonds and other securities	Time and savings deposits
Deposits at central bank	Loans from central bank
Currency	
Loans to banks/institutions (fed funds)	Loans from banks/institutions (fed funds)

When the banking system extends a new loan to a nonbank customer, it credits the deposit account of the borrower. Thus, both deposits from and loans to nonbank customers rise by the amount of the loan. This is essentially the process by which banks create money.

As we mentioned in the previous section, banks are subject to reserve requirements. This means that they are required to hold a certain fraction of their deposits in the form of bank reserves – currency and/or deposits at the central bank. To put it differently, for every dollar banks hold in currency/central bank deposits, they can create more than a dollar's worth of regular money (deposits). This is sometimes referred to as fractional reserve banking. Prior to 2008, the US banking system overall typically held reserves that were about equal to their reserve requirements. There was little incentive for banks to hold excess reserves because reserves earned zero interest. Currency held by a bank ("in the vault") earns no interest, and by law the Fed was prohibited from paying interest on bank deposits at the Fed.

Depending on the flow of transactions on any given day, some individual banks would fall short of their reserve requirements, while others would have reserves in excess of their legal requirement. The latter group would try to convert their excess reserves into interest-earning assets, by making new loans to nonbank customers, by buying interest-earning securities, or by lending the excess to other banks in the form of an overnight, uncollateralized loan. The market in which banks and other financial institutions lent and borrowed deposits at the Fed is called the *fed funds market*, and the interest rate on such loans is the *fed funds rate*. Today, the key operating target for conventional monetary policy is a range for this overnight interest rate.

15.4   The Taylor rule

How *does* the Fed determine its target for the fed funds rate? How *should* the Fed determine this target? The first question is descriptive, the second prescriptive. John Taylor in 1993 developed a formula as a simple way of describing the level at which the Fed sets it rate target. This is called the Taylor rule. Though initially conceived as a descriptive exercise, over time, this formula has been increasingly used to assert what the Fed should do (or at least serve as a guideline).

The *Taylor rule* is a feedback rule showing how the central bank responds to deviations of inflation from the central bank's objective and of output from its potential. Like a thermostat, it alters monetary policy to cool the economy when it is running hot, and vice versa, with the goal of keeping inflation close to target and output close to its long-run norm. It consists of the following equation for the target nominal interest rate:

$$i_t = (r^* + \pi_t) + a_1(\pi_t - \pi^*) + a_2(\ln Y_t - \ln Y_t^*), \qquad (15.2)$$

In the equation, the term r^* is the neutral real interest rate that would keep a well-functioning economy in long-run equilibrium at the target values for inflation and real output, and π^* is the central bank's target inflation rate. The parameter a_1 indicates how strongly the central bank reacts to a deviation of actual inflation π_t from the target π^*, and the parameter a_2 indicates how strongly the central bank reacts to the percentage *output gap* – the deviation of real output Y_t from its potential level Y_t^*.

The Taylor rule says that three things influence the nominal interest rate that the central bank sets as its target: the sum of the long-run, neutral real interest rate and the inflation adjustment (combined, the term in the first parentheses), the reaction to a deviation of inflation from its target level, and the reaction to the output gap (which correlates strongly with high or low employment and unemployment). Note that the actual inflation rate appears in two places in the equation. This assures that a change in inflation changes the target nominal interest rate by a larger amount, so the implied target real interest rate also changes in the same direction.

The value of potential output is not directly observable. Instead, it must be estimated. For the United States, the standard source of estimates of potential real GDP are those of the Congressional Budget Office, which uses information on potential labor hours, available capital services, and overall productivity in a model based on a production function like the one we used to analyze long-run growth.

Like potential output, the level of r^* also is not directly observable. For the United States, Taylor assumed that r^* is constant at 2%, which was reasonable for the decades before the global financial crisis. In more recent years, many economists think that this neutral real interest rate has declined (to 1% or even less).

Taylor set the parameters a_1 and a_2 to equal 0.5. In the years since the global financial crisis, some Fed officials have stated that they believe that a more appropriate value for a_2 is 1. Other economists have suggested yet other changes to the Taylor rule, so today there are a number of versions. The Federal Reserve Bank of Atlanta has an interactive tool that allows you to vary different elements of the Taylor rule.

For a country whose central bank has a primary objective of price stability, more emphasis is placed on deviations in the inflation rate, so the coefficient

a_1 might be, say, 0.75 or even higher, with less weight on the output gap, so a_2 might be something like 0.25 or even lower.

So, is the Taylor rule a good description of how the Fed sets its target interest rate? Of course, one problem in answering that question is that there are actually quite a few variants of the Taylor rule. If we use the version of the Taylor rule shown in equation (15.2) and the Fed's preferred measure of inflation, based on the core PCE index (which approximates the trend of PCE prices by excluding volatile food and energy prices), then the Fed's reaction to the recession that began in early 2001 followed the Taylor rule well, as did the Fed's reaction to the recession that began in late 2007, at least through late 2008. During 2003-2005 the Fed's target fed funds rate was somewhat below the Taylor rule rate. By itself, this relatively expansionary policy was not large enough to have caused the global financial crisis that ensued, but it was arguably a contributing factor. The Taylor rule indicates that the fed funds rate should have become negative beginning in late 2008 as the recession induced by the financial crisis became severe. More recently, the Fed's interest rate target has been lower than this version of the Taylor rule suggests.

Should a central bank explicitly use a simple rule such as the Taylor rule to set its interest rate target values? No central bank is on record as saying that it slavishly follows such a rule. But a broader debate goes on about the extent to which monetary policy should be rule-bound. Should a central bank run its monetary policy by a rule, or should it use discretion to consider many inputs and react to the situation as its decision-makers see as best for the economy?

There are arguments *for* using a rule. A rule makes monetary policy predictable and transparent. The rule tells how policy will be set, both now and in the future. Using a rule can insulate the central bank from political pressures. A rule can overcome the problem of time consistency – the country's central bank can resist pressure to stimulate the economy for politically popular gains in output and employment in the short run, at the expense of high and rising inflation in the future.

There are also arguments *against* using a simple rule to run monetary policy. First, over time the economy changes, and economic relationships in the economy change. For example, if the neutral real interest rate has declined in recent years, but the Fed sticks to the original Taylor rule value, then the Fed would set the fed funds rate target too high. A second argument is that no rule can capture the complexity of the economy and the unusual circumstances that develop from time to time. A Fed that is bound to follow a rule would be severely limited in its ability to respond to such circumstances.

In practice, the Fed pays attention to a range of policy rules, and sometimes explains its policy choices in comparison to these rules. Historical experience suggests that this form of constrained discretion underpins the credibility of the Fed's commitment to price stability and helps overcome the time consistency challenge associated with a purely discretionary framework. At the same time, it provides the Fed with some scope for discretion in the face of a changing economy occasionally faced with large shocks that do not instantly register in inflation or output data (the two observable inputs to the Taylor rule).

15.5   Open market operations

How does the Fed actually implement its policy? How does the Fed's use of its instruments flow through to affect the entire economy and the Fed's ultimate objectives? The final three sections of the chapter present three different versions of this story. The first, discussed in this section, pertains to the pre-2008 era when the Fed used open market operations to control the supply of bank reserves and, through that, influence the federal funds rate. The second, described in the next section, examines the Fed's shift to using unconventional policy instruments starting in late 2008. The final section of the chapter examines instruments adopted in late 2015.

As discussed earlier in this chapter, conventional monetary policy could make use of three policy instruments – reserve requirements, discount rate, and open market operations. In practice, however, the first two were not really used to implement policy changes. Reserve requirements were seldom changed. The discount rate was updated frequently, but, given the stigma associated with borrowing directly from the Fed, few banks actually borrowed outside of periods of financial distress. Thus, the workhorse policy tool was open market operations, the Fed buying or selling existing US Treasury securities in the secondary market.

Let's see how this worked in practice. Recall that, prior to 2008, reserves were scarce – in the sense that banks typically held reserves that were about equal to their reserve requirements. Those with excess reserves would lend (at the fed funds rate) to others which fell short.

Now, suppose the Fed wanted to shift its policy to a more *expansionary* (or accommodative, in the Fed's terminology) stance by lowering its target for the fed funds rate. To implement this change, the Fed would use open market operations to buy existing Treasuries from banks and pay by increasing bank deposits at the Fed. In what follows, we will use a simple example with made up numbers to illustrate how this affects the balance sheets of the Fed and the banking system.

For the sake of brevity, we will only show items that are affected by the open market operations. Suppose these items on the Fed's balance sheet, before the open market operation, looked as follows (in billions of dollars):

The Fed

Assets		Liabilities	
Bonds	260	Deposits from banks	40

Similarly, the relevant items on the combined balance sheet of the banking system were :

Banking system

Assets		Liabilities
Bonds	650	
Deposits at the Fed	40	

Now, in order to implement the new lower target for the fed funds rate, let us suppose that the Fed buys $10 billion of Treasuries from banks. This open market operation leads to the following changes:

The Fed

Assets		Liabilities	
Bonds (+10)	270	Deposits from banks (+10)	50

Banking system

Assets		Liabilities
Bonds (−10)	640	
Deposits at the Fed (+10)	50	

The monetary base increases, as does the supply of liquidity (i.e. reserves) in the banking system, because banks now hold $10 billion more reserves than they did before the intervention. This increases the supply of loanable funds in the fed funds market, and lowers the actual fed funds rate to its new target value. Note that the open market operation does not directly increase the net worth of the banking system, it only changes the composition of its assets.

How does this policy change go on to influence the entire economy? The increase in reserves usually leads to an increase in the creation of new loans and deposits by the banking system (since they have little incentive to hold reserves in excess of the required level). Moreover, the fall in the fed funds rate spills over into other short-term interest rates (short-term rates are generally closely linked to each other). To the extent that investors expect the lower short-term interest rates to persist, there could also be downward pressure on long-term interest rates (the expectations hypothesis). As a result of these changes, the AD curve shifts to the right. Real GDP increases, unemployment falls and employment rises, and inflation increases.

Now, consider a situation in which the Fed decides to shift to a *contractionary* monetary policy stance by raising its target for the fed funds rate. The corresponding open market operations would involve selling US Treasuries and taking payment by reducing bank deposits at the Fed, which reduces the supply of liquidity (reserves) in the banking system. The effects on interest rates and on the entire economy would be the same process described above, but in reverse.

15.6   Quantitative easing and forward guidance

By late 2008, in response to the financial crisis, the Fed had lowered its fed funds rate target close to zero but the economy was still in a deep recession, with the unemployment rate hitting 10 percent. Conventional policy was close to the limits of its effectiveness. Why? Because there is a limit on how low short-term nominal interest rates can go. This limit, called the *effective lower bound*, is estimated to be modestly below zero.

Why can't interest rates go lower? Because, when nominal interest rates are sufficiently negative, everyone would prefer to hold currency rather than short term nominal assets. Of course, holding currency is costly (storage, transportation, insurance, etc.), which is why it makes sense only when interest rates are sufficiently negative (i.e. below the effective lower bound, which is slightly below zero).

What else can a central bank do to be expansionary when it has pushed its policy-target interest rate as low as it can? The answer is to resort to unconventional monetary policy. This is a collective term for a number of non-traditional instruments, including *quantitative easing* and *forward guidance*.

Quantitative easing results in a massive increase in the size of the central bank's balance sheet. QE is usually implemented using open market operations (purchases of existing government bonds or other securities) that are much larger than had been used for conventional (pre-2008) monetary policy. Sometimes, other means are also used (e.g., massive lending to banks or intervention in the foreign exchange market).

In the US, the initial increase in the Fed's total assets in late 2008 was a side effect of the Fed's efforts to attempt to stabilize and resuscitate financial markets that had frozen or were functioning at very low levels in the wake of the failure of Lehman Brothers in September 2008. Subsequently, the Fed implemented its first official quantitative easing (QE1) in early 2009, in the form of large-scale purchases of mortgage-backed and federal agency (mortgage related) securities and long-term US Treasuries. QE2 involved large Fed purchases of Treasuries in late 2010 and the first half of 2011. QE3 started in in September 2012 and ran through October 2014, with large purchases of both Treasuries and mortgage-backed securities. The Fed's balance sheet expanded from less than $1 trillion in total assets in early September 2008 to about $4.5 trillion in late 2014. On the liabilities side of the Fed's balance sheet, bank deposits at the Fed increased from about $20 billion (a relatively small amount) to about $2.8 trillion, most of which was excess reserves for the banking system. In November 2008, the Fed started to pay interest on these bank deposits.

The Fed has also increased its use of forward guidance – which refers to providing information about the future course of monetary policy. Specifically, during this period, the Fed announced repeatedly that it would continue to keep the interest rate target close to zero well into the future.

How do QE and forward guidance affect interest rates and the broader economy? Both the effects and the channels through which they operate are hotly debated in academic and policy circles. The Fed's thinking on this is that QE and forward guidance both lower long-term interest rates, and through that, boost demand by shifting the AD curve to the right. Forward guidance tries to directly influence investors expectations about future short-term interest rates while QE could also be interpreted by market participants as a signal of how committed the Fed was in pursuing expansionary policy well into the future. The combination of these two instruments led investors to expect that short-term interest rates would be lower for longer into the future, so that current long-term interest rates would decrease (recall the expectations hypothesis from Section 15.1). QE could also lower long term interest rates by influencing the term premium. By purchasing long-term Treasuries and mortgage-backed securities, the Fed reduces their effective supply. To the extent different types of bonds are not perfect substitutes (recall market segmentation from Section 15.1), a fall in the supply of long-term assets raises market prices and lowers interest rates on those securities.

15.7 Exit from QE: the new normal?

By late 2014, the fed funds rate was still close to zero, the Fed's total assets had grown to $4.5 trillion, and the banking system had over $2 trillion dollars of excess reserves (beginning in late 2008 the bank deposits at the Fed earned interest, so there was little cost to holding excess reserves). The economy was expanding at a steady rate, and the unemployment rate was falling. When it came time to shift to a contractionary stance, how would the Fed do it?

One option was to return to the operating procedure under conventional monetary policy that the Fed used prior to 2008. To do this, the Fed would need to drastically reduce the size of its balance sheet, reducing the supply of reserves and making them scarce again. This would have required the Fed to quickly sell trillions of dollars of long-term Treasuries and mortgage-backed securities into the secondary market.

Fearing that such large sales would be disruptive to financial markets and the economy, the Fed instead turned to a new set of instruments to implement the first increase in its interest rate target since 2006. In December 2015, the Fed decided to increase the target range for the fed funds rate from 0-0.25% to 0.25-0.50%. To implement this change, first, the Fed increased the interest rate that it paid on bank deposits to 0.50%. Second, the Fed set up a facility (called overnight reverse repurchase agreements or ON RRP) which allowed a range of financial institutions to lend to it against collateral (usually Treasuries). The interest rate on these ON RRP transactions was set at 0.25%.

To understand how these two instruments affect the market fed funds rate, it is important to note two key features of the current environment. First, banks hold trillions of dollars of excess reserves. This implies that the market fed funds rate (for a borrower bank with good credit) cannot exceed the interest on bank deposits at the Fed. If it did, any bank with excess reserves would find it profitable to lend at this higher rate (rather than earn the interest paid by the Fed). Given the abundance of excess reserves in the banking system, this would push the market fed funds rate back down.

Second, a number of non-bank financial institutions currently hold deposits at the Fed. Importantly, the Fed does not pay interest on these deposits, but they can be used to extend fed fund loans to banks. In practice, most of the loans in the fed funds market today come from these non-bank institutions. These loans are usually at a rate lower than the interest paid by the Fed on bank deposits. The ON RRP facility ensures that this excess liquidity from outside the banking system does not push the market fed funds rate below the Fed's target range. If the Fed accepts ON RRP loans without limit, the interest rate on such loans effectively becomes a lower bound on the market fed funds rate: no financial institution would be willing to make an uncollateralized loan in the fed funds market at a rate that is lower than what they can get from an overnight repurchase agreement with the Fed.

Thus, these two overnight interest rates – on bank deposits at the Fed and on reverse repurchase agreements – create a range for the market fed funds rate. The Fed has used these two instruments to raise the market fed funds rate several times since December 2015. Whenever it has raised the interest rate paid on bank deposits, it also has raised the ON RRP rate to maintain a 25-basis-point corridor between these two rates. The instruments have worked nearly perfectly in keeping the actual fed funds rate within the target range, even though banks have massive excess reserves. In fact, in many respects, the process has worked better and is easier to implement than the process that the Fed had traditionally used (based on controlling the supply of reserves, before late 2008). At the same time, the new framework has yet to be tested in a period of banking distress (like the crisis of 2007-2009).

But, what about the Fed's balance sheet? In October 2017, the Fed began the process of slowly reducing its holdings of Treasuries and mortgage backed securities. Specifically, the Fed stopped reinvesting the principal repayments from its portfolio of mortgages and long-term Treasuries in new securities, subject to monthly maximums (or caps) for each type of security. Now that it is largely anticipated by investors, this gradual reduction in the size of the Fed's balance sheet is expected to have little further effect on financial markets and the economy. The Fed expects that its balance sheet will have declined to a reasonable size by about 2022.

Executive summary

1. Central banks use instruments (regulations, rates, or actions that they control) to achieve ultimate macroeconomic objectives like the inflation rate, employment, or real GDP. Central banks usually have operating or intermediate targets that are more directly connected to their instruments.

2. The Taylor rule offers a guide for the interest rate target set by a central bank. The central bank tends to raise (lower) the target rate in response to increases (decreases) in inflation and output.

3. Prior to 2008, the Fed's (traditional) approach to implementing monetary policy focused on using open market operations to affect the fed funds rate. If the Fed wanted an expansionary change, the Fed bought U.S. Treasuries. The monetary base and bank reserves increased, the fed funds rate (as well as other short term rates) decreased. This also put downward pressure on longer term rates, stimulating bank lending and through that, aggregate demand.

4. When the Fed (like some other central banks around the world) had lowered their interest rate target (close) to the effective lower bound, they pursued additional expansionary monetary policy by using unconventional instruments, including quantitative easing and forward guidance. Unconventional policies may lower long-term interest rates by lowering expected future short-term interest rates or by lowering the term premium.

5. More recently, the Fed has begun using two instruments, the interest rate on bank deposits at the Fed and the interest rate the Fed pays on reverse repurchase agreements, to implement a range for the market federal funds rate. It has also started the process of exiting from QE gradually.

Review questions

1. Real and nominal interest rates.   Consider the following information about inflation and US interest rates.   If we ignore the difference between actual and expected inflation, what was the real interest rate in each year presented in the table?   When was it highest?   When was it lowest?

	Inflation Rate	One-Year yield
1980	8.75	12.05
1990	3.80	7.88
2000	2.15	6.11
2010	1.33	0.32

Answer. The real interest rates for the four dates were 3.30, 4.08, 3.96, and –1.01. The highest was 1990, but 2000 is close. By far the lowest is 2010.

2. Conventional monetary policy mechanics. Consider the US economy before 2008, where reserves earned no interest and banks held almost no excess reserves. How did the Fed increase interest rates ? What was the likely effect on money supply?

Answer. The Fed sells government bonds to banks (or other holders of the government bonds), taking payments by reducing bank deposits at the Fed. This reduces the monetary base and bank reserves. The decrease in liquidity in the banking system increases demand for fed funds and reduces supply of fed funds, so the fed funds rate increases, and other short-term interest rates follow. With reduced bank reserves, banks must also reduce deposits from their customers to meet their reserve requirements. (The reduction in bank liquidity means that banks make fewer loans, so there are also fewer new deposits created by the loans.) This reduction in customer deposits at banks decreases the money supply.

3. Taylor rule in action. If the inflation rate rises, how would a central bank following a Taylor rule respond? Why?

Answer. It would raise the interest rate target. Note that the interest rate rises by more than one-for-one with inflation. This is done in order to slow aggregate demand in the economy, to counter the rise in the inflation rate.

4. Quantitative easing. The Cleveland Fed has a beautiful chart that describes the asset side of the Fed's balance sheet since January 2007. Search: "Cleveland fed credit easing." Using the chart and/or the underlying data, identify the different phases of the QE programme, beginning with the first phase in early 2009.

Answer. The large increase in the size of the Fed's asset positions that began in September 2008 was in response to crisis conditions in financial markets. These expanded the Fed's total assets without formally being called QE. The first formal QE program implemented in early 2009 was designed to prevent the Fed's total assets from declining rapidly as these crisis programs were being reversed because the financial markets were recovering. The rapid increase in Fed holdings of mortgage-backed securities and long-term Treasuries kept total Fed assets roughly steady at $2.2 to 2.3 trillion. QE2 is the period November 2010 to June 2011, when the Fed's total assets increased from $2.3 trillion to $2.8 trillion. QE3 is the period September 2012 to October 2014, when the Fed's total assets increased from $2.8 trillion to $4.5 trillion. The program to shrink the Fed's balance sheet began in October 2017, and you should be able to see a gradual decline in the Fed's total assets on the right-side of the summary graph.

5. Policy rules. The Nobel laureate Milton Friedman advocated that the Fed should adopt the k-percent rule, in which the Fed increases the money supply by a constant k percent each year, without attention to anything else in the economy. If the velocity of money (V from Chapter 14) is constant, and the growth rate of real GDP is 3 percent on average, what

growth rate of the money supply would deliver average inflation of 2 percent? What are the strengths and weaknesses of such a policy rule?

Answer. If velocity is constant, then the policy rule is that the money supply should grow at 5 percent per year, with 3 percent points of the 5 percent supporting the growth rate of real GDP and the other 2 percent points supporting the 2 percent inflation. Strengths: policy is predictable; good average inflation performance; insulate the Fed from political pressures; avoid major policy mistakes. Weaknesses: no room for policy to respond to current conditions (compare, for example, policy in the aggregate supply (AS) and aggregate demand (AD) model from Chapter 13); changes in the economy could undermine the relationships among money supply growth, real output growth, and the inflation rate (for example, velocity could vary over time, leading to erratic inflation movements).

If you're looking for more

The Fed provides a lot of information to the public about its balance sheet and activities. For example, detailed information about its assets and liabilities are reported weekly in publication H.4.A, available on the website of the Federal Reserve Board of Governors.

For more on the art and science of monetary policy: The presidents of the regional Fed banks and the chair and other members of the Fed Board of Governors regularly give public speeches discussing US monetary policy. You can search for recent speeches using the Reserve Bank Presidents' Speeches web page of the Chicago Fed and the Speeches page of the Fed Board. Ben Bernanke's speeches are typically clear and thoughtful. See

- "Constrained discretion," February 2003.

- "The Logic of monetary policy," December 2004.

- "Implementing Monetary Policy," March 2005.

Another good source of information about the Fed's views of the economy and policy is the semiannual Monetary Policy Report from the Fed Board.

The Atlanta Fed has a Taylor rule utility, and the Cleveland Fed has a Web page devoted to Simple monetary policy rules.

For QE, see the artcile by Edison Yu in the first quarter 2016 issue of Economic Insights published by the Philadelphia Fed: "Did QE Work?".

Symbols and data used in this chapter

Table 15.1: Symbol table.

Symbol	Definition
π^e	Expected Inflation
i	Nominal interest rate
r	Real interest rate ($= i - \pi^e$)
q_m	Price of m-year bond
i_m	Nominal interest rate or yield on m-year bond
π_m^e	Expected inflation over m years
M^S	Money supply
M^B	Monetary base
P	Price level
Y	Real output or GDP
Y^*	Long-run equilibrium or potential real output
r^*	Long-run, neutral real interest rate
π^*	Target inflation rate
a_1, a_2	Coefficients or weights in Taylor rule

Table 15.2: Data table.

Variable	Source
Fed funds rate	DFF
Fed funds target rate (pre- Dec 2008)	DFEDTAR
Fed funds target rate, upper bound (from Dec 2008)	DFEDTARU
Fed funds target rate, lower bound (from Dec 2008)	DFEDTARL
3-month Treasury yield	DGS3MO
2yr Treasury yield	GS2
10yr Treasury yield	GS10
Potential real GDP (CBO)	GDPPOT
Real GDP	GDPC1
PCE price index (all products)	PCEPI
PCE price index (core)	PCEPILFE
Consumer price index (all products)	CPIAUCSL
Consumer price index (core)	CPILFESL

To retrieve the data online, add the identifier from the source column to https://fred.stlouisfed.org/series/. For example, to retrieve the Federal funds rate, point your browser to https://fred.stlouisfed.org/series/DFF

Part IV
Crises and Other Topics

Crisis Overview

This outline covers key concepts from the third part of the course: macroeconomic crises and other topics. It is not exhaustive, but is meant to help you (i) anticipate what is coming and (ii) organize your thoughts later on.

Taxes and Government Debt and Deficits

Tools: Welfare triangles; government budget constraint; debt dynamics.

Key Words: Tax wedge; deadweight loss; primary deficit/surplus.

Big Ideas:

- Tax systems should be (i) administratively simple and transparent and (ii) have a broad tax base.

- Government spending must be paid for, either now through taxes, or in the future by running primary surpluses.

- Changes in the ratio of debt to GDP have three sources: interest, growth, and primary deficits.

International Capital Flows

Tools: Balance of international payments; dynamics of net foreign assets.

Key Words: Current account; net exports; capital account; capital flows; net foreign assets.

Big Ideas:

- A current account deficit means that a country is borrowing from the rest of the world; a current account surplus means it is lending to the rest of the world. We refer to the former as a capital inflow and the latter as a capital outflow.

- A capital inflow (borrowing) can lead to problems if it does not support productive activities.

Exchange-Rate Fluctuations and Exchange-Rate Regimes

Tools: Arbitrage arguments; central bank balance sheet.

Key Words: Real and nominal exchange rates; purchasing power parity; covered/uncovered interest parity; spot and forward exchange rates; the carry trade; convertibility; capital mobility; capital controls ; fixed (pegged) vs. flexible (floating) exchange rate regimes; foreign exchange reserves; sterilization; speculative attack.

Big Ideas:

- Short-run movements in real exchange rates are largely unpredictable.

- Countries adopt different exchange rate regimes: fixed, floating, and in between. The trilemma limits our policy options: we can choose only two of (i) fixed exchange rate, (ii) free flow of capital, and (iii) discretionary monetary policy.

- Fixed exchange rate regimes must be defended through open market operations and are vulnerable to speculative attack.

Macroeconomic Crises

Tools: Crisis triggers and indicators.

Key Words: Sovereign default; bank runs and panics; refinancing (rollover) risk; leverage; conditionality; solvency and liquidity.

Big Ideas:

- Common triggers of macroeconomic crises are sovereign debt problems, financial fragility, and fixed exchange rates.

- Measures related to these triggers can help identify countries in trouble: debt and deficits, financial weakness, exchange rate regime, and so on.

- The goals of crisis prevention and crisis management are often at odds.

16

Taxes

Tools: Welfare analysis; triangles.

Key Words: Tax wedge; welfare loss; social cost; tax rate; tax base.

Big Ideas:

- Tax systems should be (i) administratively simple and transparent and (ii) have a broad tax base.

- A broad tax base minimizes the social cost of taxes.

Governments are a fact of life. They are the central player in building and enforcing the institutional arrangements that make life as we know it possible. They are also, in some cases, an obstacle to performance. The difference between good and bad economic performance is often the difference between good and bad government.

Our focus will be on the narrower issue of government revenues and expenses. Governments around the world differ in how much they spend (generally measured as ratios to GDP), what they spend it on, and how they finance their spending (taxes and borrowing).

This chapter is devoted to taxes. Taxes are mind-numbingly complicated, but these three principles describe good tax systems:

- **Tax revenue pays for spending.** A government must collect enough tax revenue to pay for its expenses, whatever they might be.

- **Broad tax base.** Most tax systems are riddled with exemptions. The problem with exemptions is that they leave non-exempt activities to finance government spending. With a narrower tax base, the rate must be higher on what's left.

- **Administratively simple and transparent.** The tax systems in some countries are so complex that people spend days or weeks of their time, or hire professionals, to figure out what they owe. Worse, some countries assess taxes in ways that seem arbitrary, leading to unpredictable tax expenses and endless disputes. The best systems are simple (it's not hard to figure out what you owe) and transparent (you know ahead of time the tax consequences of your actions).

We'll focus on the second principle, leaving the first for the next chapter and the third to speak for itself. But if you're interested in an example of a complex tax system at work, search "vodaphone taxes India."

16.1   Social cost of taxes

Taxes are a necessary evil; governments, like people and businesses, must finance their spending one way or another. Governments generally do it with taxes. However, the way in which governments collect tax revenue can affect economic performance and welfare. Our issue is not that taxes take purchasing power away from individuals. They do, but if government spending must be financed, that's really a question of whether the purchasing power they take is put to good use. We'll leave you to decide that for yourself. Our issue is that taxes inevitably discourage some activities relative to others. Taxes on labor income may discourage work, taxes on capital (or investment) income may discourage saving and investment, and taxes on cigarettes may discourage smoking. We'll leave cigarettes for another time, but the general incentive effects of taxes are worth a closer look.

More formally, taxes affect ("distort") economic decisions. They insert a "wedge" (a difference or discrepancy) between private and social costs of various activities. As a result, they generally lead to decisions that are socially inefficient: We could reallocate the same resources and raise everyone's welfare. The conditions for this invisible-hand result should be familiar from your microeconomics class: clear property rights, competitive buyers and sellers (no monopolies), complete information, and absence of externalities (no direct impact of one person's actions on another's welfare). Under these conditions, we might want to set tax rates to generate the least disruption to resource allocation: to minimize the adverse incentives built into taxes.

We can get a sense for how taxes affect decisions in a traditional supply-and-demand setting like that in Figure 16.1. The demand curve (labeled D) represents purchasers of the product; for any given quantity Q, it tells us how much buyers are willing to pay — hence the value to them (at the margin) of that number of units. The supply curve (labeled S) represents sellers. With competitive sellers, it tells us how much it costs to produce a given quantity (at the margin). The market clears at point A, where supply and demand are equal.

Figure 16.1: The social cost of a tax.

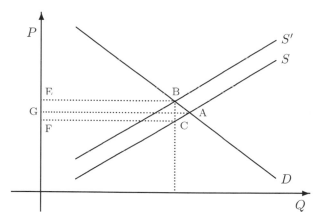

The social cost of imposing a tax that shifts the supply curve from S to S' is the triangle ABC.

Now suppose we charge a tax of a fixed amount per unit. From the perspective of buyers, the supply curve has shifted up by the amount of the tax to S'. Note that there is now a difference between the social cost (the marginal cost of production in terms of resources used) and the private cost (the price paid by buyers): a wedge, in other words. The market now clears at B for buyers and C for sellers. This difference leads buyers and sellers to reduce the quantity of resources allocated to this product, leaving them to be used elsewhere in the economy. Buyers, of course, buy fewer units, because the price has gone up. Sellers offer fewer units for sale because the price to them has fallen.

The social cost of the tax (the reduction in welfare it causes) is the area inside the triangle ABC. The upper part of the triangle is the loss of consumer surplus (the difference between what buyers pay and what the product is worth to them). The lower part of the triangle is the loss of producer surplus (the difference between what sellers receive and the cost of production). The sum is the social cost of the tax, which economists refer to as the "deadweight loss" or "excess burden." You may recall a similar argument against monopolies. Both result in fewer resources devoted to the product than we would like.

If you're not familiar with this kind of analysis, here's a more complete accounting of the welfare loss. It's not essential to our story; feel free to skip to the next paragraph. In the figure, the loss of consumer surplus is the area EBAG, the cost to them of charging a higher price. The loss of producer surplus is FCAG. Adding them together gives us an area much larger than the triangle ABC. The difference is the rectangle EBCF, which is the amount of revenue collected by the government. This revenue doesn't disappear, so it's not a welfare loss. That leaves us with the triangle ABC as the welfare loss.

There's a fine point here about who pays the tax. We could charge sellers or buyers with the same result. Governments sometimes prefer taxes on firms to taxes on people, in part because it makes the tax less visible to voters, but the impact on resource allocation should be the same.

16.2   The benefits of a broad tax base

One objective of a good tax system is to minimize the social cost of taxes: to raise tax revenue with as little impact as possible on resource allocation. We sometimes say we're looking for a resource-neutral tax system — or as close to neutral as we can get. This is a complicated issue, both in theory and in practice, but one principle is that we want a broad tax base.

The argument for a broad tax base goes like this. Think about two ways of raising the same tax revenue: a low tax rate on a broad base and a higher rate on a narrower base. Which is better? We'll give an answer using our supply and demand analysis. Suppose we have two similar markets, each like the one we described in Figure 16.1. In the broad-base system, we tax the products in both markets at the same rate. The social cost is, therefore, double what we saw earlier: the triangle ABC for each market.

Now consider a narrow-base system that taxes one market at twice the rate. We'll use Figure 16.2 to see how this works. There, we have drawn three supply curves: S refers to supply without the tax; S' refers to supply with a small tax (the broad-base system); and S'' refers to supply with a tax rate double that in S' (the narrow-base system). What is the social cost of the narrow base? Since the rate is higher, the welfare triangle is larger; it consists of the area ADE. If you look at this long enough, you'll realize that the area of ADE is four times that of ABC, which makes the social cost twice as large as in the broad-base system.

Figure 16.2: The social cost of doubling a tax.

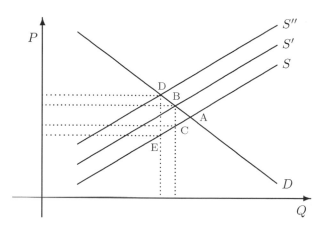

We double the tax rate by shifting the supply curve from S to S''. Note the social cost: the triangle ADE is four times as big as ABC.

The point, in general, is that broad-based tax systems are better because they allow you to raise a given amount of revenue with a lower rate and (therefore) smaller social cost. You'll hear lots of arguments for tax exemptions, but you rarely hear that they result in higher taxes on other things, which is the primary argument against them.

A corollary of this principle is that with similar goods — by which we mean goods with similar supply and demand curves — we should aim for similar tax rates. The reasoning is the same, although it's harder to show in a diagram. If we have goods whose demand curves have different slopes, similar logic would lead us to tax them differently, but that's a subtle point we'd prefer to leave for another time.

16.3   Applications

Here are some practical applications of the broad-tax-base/tax-similar-goods-the-same principle.

The underground economy.   One of the difficulties of an underground economy is that unofficial businesses typically do not pay taxes, thereby forcing all of the tax burden onto the rest of the economy. That violates our principle (low rate on broad base) and also the corollary (tax similar goods at similar rates). We've shown that this leads to an inefficient allocation of resources.

William Lewis (*The Power of Productivity*) argues that in Brazil, it may also lower productivity. His argument has several steps. Brazil has a relatively large government for a country at its stage of development (40 percent of GDP, which is above the US and significantly above what we see in most developing countries). Financing government spending requires, therefore, relatively high tax rates, which creates a substantial incentive for tax avoidance. Small firms (the story goes) are generally less productive than large firms (economies of scale), but many survive because they are able to avoid taxes. Thus the tax system protects inefficient small firms, thereby lowering overall productivity. In Lewis's story, this is a direct result of large government.

Value-added taxes (VAT). Before the VAT became popular, countries often had piecemeal tax systems in which goods were taxed at every stage of production. This led, in some cases, to very high taxes on intermediate and final products simply because the taxes at each stage added up. This violates our principle, specifically the corollary, because a product made by a single vertically-integrated firm is taxed at a lower rate than the same product made by several firms, one at each stage.

Consider a product that has five stages of production, each performed by a different firm. If each stage is charged a moderate tax of ten percent, what is the total tax paid in the production of the product? Let's say that total value added is five, with one unit of value added at each stage. The first-stage firm produces one unit of value. This costs the second-stage firm 1.10 since it must pay the ten percent tax. This firm also adds one unit of value, and sells its output for a price (including taxes) of

$$(1.10 + 1) \times 1.10 \;\; = \;\; 2.31,$$

so the implicit tax rate over the two stages is $0.31/2 = 15.5$ percent. If you work through all five stages, you'll find that the price of the final product, including all the taxes paid, is 6.71 after the last stage, so the effective tax rate is 34.2 percent [$= (6.71 - 5.00)/5.00$]. Note the large difference in tax rates across the five stages of production. The final stage only gets taxed once, so it pays a tax rate of 10%, but the first stage gets taxed five times, so it's taxed at a rate of 61 percent [$1.10^5 = 1.61$]! In contrast, a vertically-integrated firm pays only ten percent, at each stage and overall.

These differences in tax rates potentially lead to inefficient production, as firms look for substitutes for highly-taxed inputs, or integrate vertically. This is one of the arguments for a value-added tax system. With a VAT, firms pay tax on only the value-added of their stage of production, which eliminates differences in tax rates paid by different stages. A value-added tax system is equivalent to one in which we tax only the final good; we just arrange to collect the tax in pieces.

Taxes on capital income.   A high tax rate on capital income might be expected to discourage saving and investment, leading the economy to have less capital than otherwise. This, in turn, would reduce wages, since the marginal product of labor is lower if we have less capital. So, what is an appropriate tax rate on capital income? Some economists argue that taxes on capital income should be zero. People would eventually pay tax on capital income indirectly when they consume the proceeds, but they should not be taxed before then. The logic is similar to the argument for a value-added tax, since taxes on capital income are effectively taxes on future consumption and accumulate in a similar way.

Let's think about how households allocate their income over time. Suppose that we have two dates (labeled "0" and "1"). If a household earns labor income (Y_0, Y_1) at the two dates and receives a (real) interest rate r on saving, then saving is $Y_0 - C_0$, and consumption at date 1 must be $C_1 = (1 + r)(Y_0 - C_0) + Y_1$. We can put the two together in the present-value relation:

$$C_0 + C_1/(1+r) = Y_0 + Y_1/(1+r).$$

This tells us, in essence, that the price of date-1 consumption is $1/(1+r)$. If we had more periods, we'd have a similar relation, with prices $1/(1+r)$, $1/(1+r)^2$, $1/(1+r)^3$, etc., for consumption at dates 1, 2, 3, etc.

Now think about taxes. If we tax interest income, this changes the price of future consumption. For a given real interest rate r, a higher tax rate increases the price of future consumption, which you might expect to encourage current consumption. If the tax rate on capital income is τ, then the after-tax interest rate is $(1 - \tau)r$ and the price of consumption n periods in the future is $1/[1 + (1 - \tau)r]^n$. This may not seem like a big deal, but with the mythical power of compound interest, it can increase the price of future consumption substantially. Consider a numerical example with $r = 0.04$ (four percent a year) and a tax rate of $\tau = 0.25$ (25 percent). With no tax, the price of consumption one period in the future is 0.9615 $[= 1/(1+r)]$. With the tax, this increases to 0.9709 $[= 1/[1 + (1 - \tau)r]]$, a modest difference. But if the number of periods is large, the difference can also be large. Suppose $n = 25$; think of a 30-year-old consultant saving for retirement. Then, the tax raises the price of future consumption by 27 percent, from 0.3751 to and 0.4776. You can imagine that this could lead people to consume more now and less later since future consumption has become relatively more expensive. It might also lead them to work less if working now is intended to finance future consumption.

If people consume more now and less later, then they are saving less. And if they are saving less, the economy will have less capital. The cost has the same source as in our earlier analysis: The private benefits of saving are less than the social benefits, so we do too little of it. That's why some economists favor a consumption tax: a tax on only that part of income that is consumed. In practice, many countries offer something of this sort through tax-sheltered retirement and saving programs, which avoid the period-by-period tax on investment income of our example.

If a government promises not to tax capital too heavily in the future, will investors believe it? This version of the time-consistency problem can be severe. If investors doubt the commitment, they will refrain from investment even if current tax rates are low. The issue arises whenever governments are seen as willing to exhaust their borrowing capacity. As we have seen in other examples, overcoming the challenge of time consistency depends on the nature and quality of a society's institutions. In the late 17th century, for example, the empowerment of the British parliament helped persuade a rising commercial class that the King would not arbitrarily seize their wealth. The flow of savings and investment helped Britain grow earlier and faster than other modern economies. In many highly indebted countries today, concerns about future tax burdens can reduce saving and investment now, or encourage other means of tax avoidance, possibly making the government's current budget situation worse.

Changing tax rates.   Economist Edward Prescott writes (*Wall Street Journal*, December 20, 2005):

> Let's drop the word "cuts" [when we talk about taxes]. The problem with advocating a cut in something is that you are nec-essarily going to stir up political trouble from someone who will want to increase it again. So, even if you are fortunate enough to get your cut enacted, it is likely a matter of time before the political pendulum swings back and someone else gets their in-crease.

The argument against large changes in tax rates over time follows from the corollary: "Tax similar markets at similar rates." In this case, the two markets are "today" and "tomorrow." We could add the cost of the uncertainty created by the process of changing tax rates.

Deficits. The same argument gives us some insight into deficits. We should finance whatever the government spends with relatively stable tax rates. Why? Because low taxes now and high taxes later, or the reverse, violates our principle. Suppose, then, that the government is running a deficit. Should it raise taxes? It should aim at a stable level of tax rates that finances government spending. Typically, you would expect this to lead to deficits in recessions, when the tax base is small, and surpluses in booms. In practice, this is more complicated because we don't know either the level of spending (what's the present value of future commitments to Social Security and Medicare?) or the base on which tax rates will be applied (will the economy grow three or four percent a year over the next decade). The principle remains: finance government spending with stable tax rates.

Executive summary

1. All taxes have incentive effects. In the absence of externalities and mo-nopolies, the tax systems that lead to the most efficient allocations of resources (a) apply low tax rates to a broad base and (b) tax similar products at similar rates.

2. The cost of exemptions is that non-exempt products must pay higher rates as a result.

Review questions

1. Welfare triangle review. In Figure 16.1, identify the following:
    (a) The loss of consumer surplus. Why does the tax leave consumers with less surplus?
    (b) The loss of producer surplus. Why does the tax leave producers with less surplus?
    (c) Government revenue.
    (d) The total welfare loss.

   Answer.

    (a) The area EBAG. consumer surplus before the tax is the area between the demand curve and the line GA indicating the market price. Some consumers are willing to pay more; the difference is their surplus. When the price paid by consumers rises as a result of the tax, some of this surplus goes away.
    (b) The area FCAG. Producer surplus before the tax is the area between the supply curve (the cost of production) and the line GA indicating the market price. When the price received by producers falls as a result of the tax, some of this surplus goes away.

(c) The area EBCF. this is the tax (EF) times the equilibrium quantity (FC).

(d) The area ABC. This is consumer surplus plus producer surplus minus government revenue.

See also the discussion at the end of Section 16.1.

2. Tax systems. Comment on the welfare impact of these aspects of the US tax system:

   (a) Sales tax exemption for food and clothing.

   (b) Sales tax exemption for goods purchased over the internet.

   (c) Sales tax exemption for medical care.

   (d) Income tax exemption for health insurance.

   (e) Sales tax exemption for education supplied by nonprofit institutions.

   (f) Elimination of the capital gains tax.

   Answer.

   (a) Probably bad because it means tax rates on other things must be higher, which generates larger welfare losses. Remember: broad base, low rates. One common justification is that it favors poor people, since food and clothing are necessities, but it's probably not an effective way to do this. The best way is simply to give them money.

   (b) Also bad, and for the same reason. It leads to such things as sales tax on internet purchases from Barnes & Noble (since they have local outlets) but not on Amazon (since they do not).

   (c) Ditto.

   (d) Ditto.

   (e) Remember the principle: tax similar products the same way. There's no economic logic for taxing a product differently just because its producer it has a different legal structure. Remember: the NYSE was a nonprofit until recently.

   (f) To the extent that it's a tax on capital or investment income, this could be a good thing. Further, capital gains reflect inflation as well as investment income, which can result in potentially very high tax rates on real returns. The solution here, though, is to index the tax system (or keep inflation low enough that it doesn't have much effect). An important caveat is that there are no adverse incentive effects involved in taxing capital gains that have already occurred; the incentive argument works only going forward.

3. Taxes without spending? Suppose a hypothetical government has no expenditures to finance. What tax rates should it set?

Answer. Zero! Why? Nonzero taxes (even negative taxes or subsidies) generate adverse incentives; the prices people pay for products do not reflect their social cost of production. Possible exception: externalities, although even here there may be better choices than taxes.

4. Small government. Since government spending must be financed with taxes, and taxes distort the allocation of resources, should we have a small government?

Answer. This is a complex issue, but here's one take on it. First, you need a government. There are clearly important and necessary roles for government: providing national and personal security, defining and enforcing property rights, supporting competitive markets, and so on. Without an effective government, you simply can't have a productive economic system. Second, there's tremendous variety across countries in the kinds of services provided by government. In many countries, governments supply educational services, social insurance, and pensions, although the degree of government involvement varies. The evidence is mixed. Among countries with high GDP per person, those with large governments are not notably less productive than those with small governments. Sweden, for example, is a productive and prosperous country despite very high government spending. Among developing countries, the evidence is stronger: Those with smaller ratios of spending to GDP have grown faster, on average, over the last forty years. This may reflect the direct effects of government or other factors — it's hard to say.

5. Progressive taxes. Questions often come up about the progressivity of tax systems. They aren't really review questions, but this seems as good a place to put them as any.

   (a) How does a progressive tax square with taxing similar things at similar rates?

   (b) Since rich people own most of the assets, shouldn't we tax investment income as a way to redistribute income?

   (c) If we rely heavily on VAT, as many countries do, how do we make the overall tax system progressive?

   Answer.

   (a) It doesn't. For reasons we've seen, progressive taxes distort resource allocation more than a flat tax that collects the same amount of revenue. But they also redistribute income from rich to poor. If you want the latter, you're stuck with some of the former.

   (b) Maybe. It still has adverse incentive effects, but it's true that wealth is much more unequally distributed than income.

(c) A VAT is, by design, a flat tax: products and people are treated the same way. In practice there's some variation in rates by products, but it's harder to treat buyers differently. Most countries introduce progressivity through the income tax and means-tested benefits.

If you're looking for more

The analysis of welfare triangles is standard economics. See, for example, these links from Wikipedia:

> http://en.wikipedia.org/wiki/Economic_surplus
> http://en.wikipedia.org/wiki/Deadweight_loss

There's also a Khan Academy video ("Taxation and dead weight loss").

Real-world tax systems can be incredibly complicated. Some good overviews are:

- The OECD's program on taxation has an extensive set of data and analysis for developed countries:

  > http://www.oecd.org/tax/.

- The World Bank's Doing Business website includes information about tax rates and associated administrative costs for mid-sized firms. Be careful, however, of the definitions. Total tax, for example, is reported as a percentage of profit, even though some of the taxes apply to labor.

- The Economist Intelligence Unit's Country Commerce and Country Finance reports contain information about both business and individual taxes. Here's what they say about corporate taxes in the US: "Tax jurisdiction in the United States is divided among the federal government, the 50 states plus the District of Columbia, and local counties and municipalities. ... There are no uniform rules on the definition of taxable income or on the apportionment of income among the various tax jurisdictions. Hence, the advice of a tax lawyer is practically indispensable to any newcomer to multistate business."

- Myron Scholes, Mark A. Wolfson, Merle Erickson, Edward Maydew, and Terrence Shevlin's *Taxes and Business Strategy (4e)* is a wonderful, practical book on tax issues. (Earlier editions are cheaper, and probably as good for our purposes.)

Symbols used in this chapter

Table 16.1: Symbol table.

Symbol	Definition
P	Price
Q	Quantity
S	Supply
D	Demand
Y	Labor income
C	Consumption
r	Real interest rate
τ	Tax rate (proportional)

17
Government Debt and Deficits

Tools: Government budget constraint; debt dynamics.

Key Words: Government budget; government debt and deficits; primary deficit/surplus; the debt-to-GDP ratio; hidden liabilities.

Big Ideas:

- Government spending must be paid for, either now through taxes, or in the future.

- Current debt must be balanced by future primary surpluses.

- Changes in the ratio of debt to GDP have three sources: interest, growth, and primary deficits.

The first principle of government finance is that governments must finance spending with taxes. Issuing debt postpones this obligation but does not eliminate it. If a government doesn't collect enough tax revenue now, it must collect it later — or face default. Since investors like to be repaid, they pay close attention to government debt and deficits. If they're too large, investors may demand higher yields or even stop buying government securities altogether. The consequences of this sequence of events are never pretty.

Debt finance poses a *time-consistency* problem because (i) governments have an incentive to issue debt and tax future generations who do not vote today; and (ii) future governments may decide to inflate away or repudiate past debt. Countries with good governance solve this problem either through sound budget policy or institutional design. Countries with poor governance, not so much.

17.1 Government revenues, expenses, and debt

We start with a quick overview of government expenditure and revenue
decisions — what is conventionally called *fiscal policy* .

Countries differ in the size of government relative to the economy, in the
sources of tax revenues, and in their expenditures. Governments everywhere
purchase goods and services (schools, police, courts, roads, military), transfer money to individuals (social insurance, health care), and collect revenue
(largely through taxes). The distinction between purchases and transfers
is important. Only purchases show up in the expenditure-side GDP identity. Transfers are, nevertheless, a large part of total expenditures in many
economies, particularly developed economies. Governments also pay interest
on outstanding government debt, an category we track separately.

We'll look at data for each of these in class. As a rule, government spending
and revenue are a larger fraction of GDP in rich countries than in poor
ones. Rich countries also spend more on transfers. There is, however, a lot
of variation at all levels of development.

We put these elements together in a relation we'll call the *government budget
constraint.* On the expenditure side, we label government purchases of goods
and services G, transfers V, and interest payments iB (the product of the
government debt B and whatever interest rate i the government pays on it).
On the revenue side, we label tax revenue T. (Note: T is tax revenue, not the
tax rate.) By convention, all of these things are nominal: they're measured
in local currency units. The government budget constraint is, then,

$$G_t + V_t + i_t B_{t-1} - T_t \quad = \quad B_t - B_{t-1}. \tag{17.1}$$

Here, B_{t-1} is the amount of debt outstanding at the end of period $t-1$.
The left-hand side of (17.1) is the government deficit, the right the change
in the quantity of debt. The equation says, in essence, that any surplus or
deficit is matched by a change in the quantity of debt. A government deficit
is financed by issuing more debt.

The elements of equation (17.1) are often used to generate summary measures of fiscal policy. The most common are ratios of the government deficit
and government debt to GDP. We'll look at both, as well as the connection
between them.

17.2 Debt and (primary) deficits

Governments need to finance their spending with taxes. It's not quite true
— governments have other sources of revenue — but it's close enough to be

worth remembering. Issuing debt allows a government to postpone taxes, just as a credit card allows an individual to postpone paying for purchases, but does not eliminate the obligation. Delay, in fact, comes with a cost: We need to pay the original obligation, plus interest. In the rest of this section, we make the same point more formally.

We're going to take our budget constraint, equation (17.1), and use it to relate debt to past and future deficits. To make things a little simpler, define the *primary deficit* D as the deficit net of interest payments (sort of an "EBITDA" number):

$$D_t = G_t + V_t - T_t.$$

(This is sometimes reported with the opposite sign and called the primary budget balance or surplus.) With this simplification, (17.1) can be expressed as

$$B_t = (1+i)B_{t-1} + D_t \tag{17.2}$$

or

$$B_{t-1} = B_t/(1+i) - D_t/(1+i). \tag{17.3}$$

They're the same equation, but the first one looks backward from t to $t-1$, and the second looks forward from $t-1$ to t. We'll put both to work. The i in these equations is the *nominal interest rate* that the government pays on its debt. We'll assume it is constant for now — it makes the math simpler — but allow it to change in the next section.

Equation (17.2) tells us where the debt came from. If we substitute over and over again, back to some period $t - n$, we have

$$
\begin{aligned}
B_t &= D_t + (1+i)B_{t-1} \\
&= D_t + (1+i)[(1+i)B_{t-2} + D_{t-1}] \\
&= D_t + (1+i)D_{t-1} + (1+i)^2 D_{t-2} + \cdots + (1+i)^n B_{t-n}.
\end{aligned}
$$

In words: The current debt is the debt we started with n periods ago plus the current value of past deficits plus accumulated interest. It's like your credit card bill: Your current balance consists of past shortfalls plus accumulated interest.

Equation (17.3) tells us what we need to do in the future to service the current debt. If we substitute repeatedly, we find

$$
\begin{aligned}
B_{t-1} &= B_{t+1}/(1+i)^2 - [D_t/(1+i) + D_{t+1}/(1+i)^2] \\
&= B_{t+2}/(1+i)^3 - [D_t/(1+i) + D_{t+1}/(1+i)^2 + D_{t+2}/(1+i)^3] \\
&= B_{t+n-1}/(1+i)^n - [D_t/(1+i) + \cdots + D_{t+n-1}/(1+i)^n].
\end{aligned}
$$

If we assume that debt can't grow faster than the interest rate forever, then, as we continue to substitute, the first term goes to zero. [The technical condition is $B_{t+n}/(1+i)^n$ approaches zero as n approaches infinity. It amounts to not allowing the government to run a Ponzi scheme, paying off old debt by issuing new debt, forever.] The relation then becomes

$$
\begin{aligned}
B_{t-1} &= -[D_t/(1+i) + D_{t+1}/(1+i)^2 + D_{t+2}/(1+i)^3] + \cdots] \\
&= -\text{Present Discounted Value of Primary Deficits} \\
&= \text{Present Discounted Value of Primary Surpluses.} \qquad (17.4)
\end{aligned}
$$

In words: The current government debt must be matched by the present discounted value of future primary surpluses. As we said at the start, all spending must be financed by tax revenue — eventually. It's not enough to shrink the deficit. Eventually we have to run surpluses, measured net of interest payments.

Analysis of this sort often uses the term *sustainable*. We say the debt is sustainable if current debt is balanced by plans for future surpluses, as in equation (17.4). If not, we say the government's budget is *unsustainable*. In this case, we can paraphrase the economist Herbert Stein: "Something must change, so it will."

17.3   Debt dynamics

Investors watch government debt and deficits for signs that a government may not honor its debts. Even a hint of this can change the rate at which the government borrows or even its ability to access capital markets. In practice, it's common to look at them as ratios to GDP. In such ratios, we measure both numerator and denominator in local currency units, so we have (for example) the ratio of the nominal debt to nominal GDP.

So how does the debt-to-GDP ratio change from one period to the next? There's a useful decomposition of changes into components due to the real interest rate, GDP growth, and the primary deficit. It's a little complicated, so we'll work our way up to it.

Recall that debt evolves according to

$$
B_t = D_t + i_t B_{t-1} + B_{t-1}, \qquad (17.5)
$$

where D_t is the primary deficit and $D_t + i_t B_{t-1}$ is the total deficit. You should recognize this as equation (17.2) in slightly different form. Here's how it looks with real numbers.

Example (US, 2013). Consider US government debt and deficits in 2013, expressed in trillions of US dollars:

Government debt, year end 2012	B_{t-1}	13.015
Total deficit, 2013	$D_t + i_t B_{t-1}$	1.233
Primary deficit, 2013	D_t	0.693

The numbers are estimates from the April 2014 edition of the IMF's World Economic Outlook database. Given these numbers, use what we know about debt dynamics to compute debt B_t at the end of 2013. How much interest was paid on debt? What is the interest rate i_t paid on the debt?

Answer. Year-end debt follows from equation (17.5): $B_t = 1.233 + 13.015 = 14.248$. Interest payments are the difference between the two deficit numbers: $i_t B_{t-1} = D_t + i_t B_{t-1} - D_t = 1.233 - 0.693 = 0.540$. The implied interest rate on the debt is the ratio of interest payments to debt: $i_t B_{t-1}/B_{t-1} = 0.540/13.015 = 0.0415 = 4.15\%$.

Now back to the dynamics of the debt-to-GDP ratio. The bottom line is the equation

$$\frac{B_t}{Y_t} \approx \frac{B_{t-1}}{Y_{t-1}} + (i_t - \pi_t)\frac{B_{t-1}}{Y_{t-1}} - g_t\frac{B_{t-1}}{Y_{t-1}} + \frac{D_t}{Y_t}. \tag{17.6}$$

Circle this, it's important. It gives us three sources of change in the ratio of debt to GDP. The first is the real interest on the debt, which accumulates as long as the debt and real interest rate are positive. The second is the growth of the economy, which reduces the ratio by increasing the denominator. The third is the primary deficit. Each makes a contribution to changes in the debt-to-GDP ratio.

It's not required, but if you're interested in where this comes from, here are the details. We divide equation (17.5) by nominal GDP Y_t to get

$$\frac{B_t}{Y_t} = \frac{D_t}{Y_t} + (1 + i_t)\frac{B_{t-1}}{Y_t}.$$

In the last term, note that the denominator is Y_t, not Y_{t-1}. If the growth rate of real GDP is g_t and the inflation rate is π_t, then the growth rate of nominal GDP is approximately $g_t + \pi_t$. Therefore

$$Y_t \approx (1 + g_t + \pi_t)Y_{t-1}.$$

The ratio of debt to GDP then follows

$$\frac{B_t}{Y_t} \approx \left(\frac{1 + i_t}{1 + g_t + \pi_t}\right)\frac{B_{t-1}}{Y_{t-1}} + \frac{D_t}{Y_t}$$

$$\approx [1 + i_t - (g_t + \pi_t)]\frac{B_{t-1}}{Y_{t-1}} + \frac{D_t}{Y_t}$$

$$\approx \frac{B_{t-1}}{Y_{t-1}} + (i_t - \pi_t)\frac{B_{t-1}}{Y_{t-1}} - g_t\frac{B_{t-1}}{Y_{t-1}} + \frac{D_t}{Y_t}.$$

The second equation is based on the approximation

$$\frac{1 + i_t}{1 + g_t + \pi_t} \approx 1 + i_t - g_t - \pi_t,$$

good for small values of i_t, g_t, and π_t. A simpler version is $1/(1+x) \approx 1-x$ for small x. All you need to know is that the right side is simpler than the left. After rearranging terms, we're left with (17.6), as promised.

This is a mechanical analysis, but a useful one. By looking at the components of equation (17.6), we can get a sense of the origins of past changes in the debt-to-GDP ratio and the potential sources of future changes.

Example (US, 2013, continued). The numbers we saw earlier look this way expressed as ratios to GDP:

Government debt, year end 2012	B_{t-1}/Y_{t-1}	0.8012
Primary deficit, 2013	D_t/Y_t	0.0413
Interest rate	i_t	0.0415
Real GDP growth rate	g_t	0.0188
Inflation rate	π_t	0.0151

What is the ratio of debt to GDP at the end of 2013?

Answer. We apply the formula, equation (17.6):

$$\begin{aligned} B_t/Y_t &= 0.8012 + (0.0415 - 0.0151)0.8012 - (0.0188)0.8012 + 0.0413 \\ &= 0.8012 + 0.0212 - 0.0151 + 0.0413 = 0.8486. \end{aligned}$$

In words: the ratio of debt to GDP rose from 80.1 percent to 84.9 percent, an increase of 4.8 percent of GDP. The primary deficit contributes 4.1 percentage points of the change and growth drives it the other way by 1.5 percentage points.

Comment. We have two sets of numbers here that are often expressed as percentages, meaning we multiply them by one hundred. One is the "growth rates": g, i, and π. For them, *it's essential we use numbers, not percentages.* You might verify that we did this in the calculation above. You'd see the same when you calculate a present value in finance. The second set of numbers is the ratios to GDP: B/Y and D/Y. These can be used either as numbers, as in the example above, or percentages, as long as we treat them both the same way. If we use percentages in our example, equation (17.6) becomes

$$B_t/Y_t = 80.12 + (0.0415 - 0.0151)80.12 - (0.0188)80.12 + 4.13$$
$$= 84.86.$$

Evidently the equation still works when we multiply it by one hundred.

Example (Peru, 2003-2007). Between 2003 and 2007, Peru's debt fell from 47 percent of GDP to 25 percent. Using the numbers in the table below, what happened? What was the primary source of this decline?

	Debt B_t/Y_t	Interest $(i_t - \pi_t)B_{t-1}/Y_{t-1}$	Growth $-g_t B_{t-1}/Y_{t-1}$	Deficit D_t/Y_t
2003	47.1			
2004	44.3	0.2	-2.4	-0.6
2005	37.7	1.1	-3.0	-4.6
2006	33.1	1.0	-2.9	-2.7
2007	30.9	1.1	-2.9	-0.4
2008	25.0	-0.3	-3.0	-2.5
Sum		3.1	-14.3	-10.9

Answer. Between 2003 and 2008, the ratio of debt to GDP fell from 47.1% to 25.0%, a change of −22.1%. What factors were most important? You can see from the final row that growth (−14.3%) and the primary deficit (−10.9%) both played large roles. Interest on the debt pushes us the other way: it raises the ratio of debt to GDP (+3.1%).

17.4   What's missing?

Our summary of debt dynamics, captured in equation (17.6), buries some issues beneath the mathematics.

One issue is the link between the interest rate and the fiscal situation (the debt and deficit). If investors start to worry about a government's willingness to honor its debt, they may demand higher interest rates, which, in turn, raises future debt — and so on. Such credit spreads can rise sharply if the government has not shown sufficient fiscal discipline. (Here, "sufficient" means whatever is needed to reassure investors.) It can also rise because global financial markets place a higher premium on risk, as they did during the 2008-09 financial crisis. Over this period, spreads on emerging market debt of all kinds widened, even in countries with fundamentally sound fiscal positions.

Another issue is the link between growth and deficits. If growth rises, as in Peru (example, above), that reduces the debt-to-GDP ratio through the impact on g in equation (17.6). But it also generates higher tax revenues and, hence, a lower primary deficit, even if tax *rates* do not change. This, in turn, reduces future debt further. That's one reason that Peru's fiscal situation improved: The economy boomed. Growth, then, is the cure for many problems.

A third issue is hidden government liabilities. The idea behind our analysis is that the primary deficit determines how the debt evolves. In fact, current decisions often involve commitments for future expenditures that don't show up in the current government budget but are nevertheless important. In principle these *hidden liabilities* should show up in the budget when they're incurred, but in practice they don't. Here are some common examples:

- Social security and pensions. Many countries have implicit commitments to pay money to retired people in the future that are not accounted for properly. In the US, for example, the official accounts are based on the current cash flow of social security receipts and payments. In principle, there should be an entry for unfunded pension liabilities, as there is for firms. In many countries, aging populations have made these looming payments a serious concern. Healthcare payments are similar.

- Financial bailouts. We tend to treat these as one-offs, but, in fact, they happen all the time and they're invariably expensive. A country that bails out its banks may find its debt rise sharply.

- Regional governments. Relations between central governments and local authorities differ widely around the world. In the US, the precedent was set in the 1840s for state and local governments to finance their own activities without help from the central government. In other countries, debt problems of regional governments are often passed to the central government. These implicit liabilities of the central government were a concern in Argentina and Brazil in the 1990s and in Spain right now.

A serious analysis of fiscal policy should, therefore, start with equation (17.6) but go on to consider all possible sources of change in its components. It's no different from financial accounting for firms: we need to know what lies behind the numbers.

17.5   How much debt is too much?

How much debt is too much? At what point should investors be concerned? There is, unfortunately, no clear answer. Or rather there is an answer, which is that the quality of governance is more important than the debt numbers. Argentina defaulted with debt of about 40 percent of GDP, but the UK had debt well over 100 percent of GDP after World War II and didn't generate undue concern. In many cases you're stuck trying to guess how the local politics will play out.

With that warning, here are some rules of thumb:

- Debt. Worry if the government debt is above 50 percent of GDP. This is very rough, but it's a start.

- Deficits. Worry if the deficit is above 5 percent of GDP — and is expected to stay that way. The issue is not so much any particular deficit, but the long-term posture.

- Institutions. Worry if a country's political institutions are weak. An old rule of thumb is that a country's credit rating is more closely connected to the quality of its institutions than to the quantity of debt it's issued. Think to yourself: Argentina is different from the UK, and Germany is different from Greece. The institutions that matter most are those that help contain the time-consistency problem: namely, the risk that a future policymaker will repudiate or inflate away the debt. Relevant institutions would include an independent central bank (to limit inflation), a robust financial system (that promotes market discipline and limits bailouts), and fiscal arrangements that limit debt accumulation or prevent its repudiation (e.g., transparent and comprehensive long-term budgeting, pay-go or balanced budget rules, and legal requirements for prioritizing debt payments).

- Structure of debt. Worry if the debt is primarily short-term or denominated in foreign currency. Even if the debt is stable, countries may find themselves in difficulty if they have to refinance a large fraction of their debt over a short period of time. (Companies are no different; think Lehman Brothers, or Drexel before that.) In late 1994, for example, Mexico had much of its debt in short-term securities. When investors refused to buy new issues, it triggered a crisis. This despite relatively modest debt and deficits.

  Foreign debt has similar risks. Many developing countries issue debt denominated in hard currency (dollars, say, or euros), but it's a mixed blessing. Issuing debt in hard currency reduces currency risk for investors, but if a country's currency collapses, it debt can rise sharply, perhaps increasing the odds of default. We've seen this repeatedly: Mexico in 1994, Korea in 1997, Argentina in 2001, and Iceland in 2008.

Executive summary

1. Countries differ enormously in the magnitude and composition of government spending, taxes, and debt.

2. Government spending must be paid for, either now through taxes or in the future by running primary surpluses.

3. The following factors govern changes in the debt-to-GDP ratio: (a) interest on the debt; (b) GDP growth; and (c) the primary deficit.

4. Institutions that limit the incentive of future governments to inflate away or repudiate the debt can help to promote fiscal discipline.

Review questions

1. Deficits down under. Consider this data for Australia:

	2010	2011
Real GDP growth (annual percent)	2.6	2.9
Inflation (annual percent)	5.2	4.8
Interest rate (annual percent)	5.3	5.9
Government deficit (primary, percent of GDP)	2.9	0.7
Government deficit (total, percent of GDP)	4.1	2.2
Government debt (end of period, percent of GDP)	25.3	

(a) Why are the primary and total government deficits different?

(b) What is the government debt ratio at the end of 2011?

Answer.

(a) The difference is interest payments on government debt. Apparently in 2011 they amounted to 1.5 percent of GDP.

(b) We use the debt dynamics equation:

$$
\begin{aligned}
\frac{B_t}{Y_t} &= \frac{B_{t-1}}{Y_{t-1}} + (i_t - \pi_t)\frac{B_{t-1}}{Y_{t-1}} - g_t\frac{B_{t-1}}{Y_{t-1}} + \frac{D_t}{Y_t} \\
&= 25.3 + (0.059 - 0.048) * 25.3 - 0.029 * 25.3 + 0.7 \\
&= 25.6.
\end{aligned}
$$

We used a shortcut here on the interest rate, taking the number from the table (a typical market rate) rather than computing the interest rate paid on government debt.

2. How the US financed World War II. The short answer is that they issued debt, but how did they pay off the debt? Between 1945 and 1974, the ratio of debt to GDP fell from 66 percent to 11 percent. What led to the change? George Hall and Thomas Sargent (source below) computed the following:

	Interest $(i_t - \pi_t)B_{t-1}/Y_{t-1}$	Growth $-g_t B_{t-1}/Y_{t-1}$	Primary Deficit D_t/Y_t
1945-1974	−12.5	−21.6	−20.8

All numbers are percentages.

Answer. If you look at the numbers, they tell you that growth (the same debt looked smaller when GDP grew) and primary surpluses account for most of this. You also see a negative contribution from real interest payments. What does this tell us? With hindsight, we would say that investors lost money in real terms because inflation was higher than they expected when they purchased government debt. If the government had paid (say) a one percent real return, this contribution would have been positive and the 1974 debt level would have been higher. In that sense, the US used inflation to reduce the debt burden.

If you're looking for more

It's too technical for this course, but some of the material on debt dynamics was adapted from Craig Burnside, ed., *Fiscal Sustainability in Theory and Practice*, World Bank, 2005.

More user-friendly (and very good) is George Hall's summary of his work with Thomas Sargent, "How will we pay down the debt?" They describe sources of changes in the US debt position from World War II to 2008.

Most sources of macroeconomic data include the debt, the deficit, and the primary deficit. One of the best sources of data and analysis is the IMF. Their World Economic Outlook database is updated twice a year. Their historical database covers the last 200 years or more. Search: "imf debt database." And their Fiscal Monitor describes the fiscal situations in many countries around the world.

One thing to keep in mind: reported debt numbers, whether from the IMF or other source, are generally inconsistent with reported deficits. It's an

embarrassment, to be sure, but true. In our examples, we construct (total)
deficits from year-to-year changes in debt. If you ever need to know more
about this, get in touch.

Symbols and data used in this chapter

Table 17.1: Symbol table.

Symbol	Definition
G	Government purchases of goods and services
V	Transfers
B	Stock of government debt
T	Tax revenues (not a tax *rate*)
D	Primary deficit $(= G + V - T)$
i	Nominal interest rate
g	Discretely-compounded growth rate of real GDP
π	Inflation rate
$g + \pi$	Discretely-compounded growth rate of nominal GDP
Y	Nominal GDP

Note: In this chapter we have dealt only with *nominal* variables.

Table 17.2: Data table.

Variable	Source
Federal government debt	GFDEBTN
Federal government debt held by the public	FYGFDPUN
Federal government net surplus	FGDEF
Federal interest outlays	FYOINT
Nominal GDP	GDP
Real GDP	GDPC1
GDP deflator	GDPDEF

To retrieve the data online, add the identifier from the source column to `http://research.stlouisfed.org/fred2/series/`. For example, to retrieve real GDP, point your browser to `http://research.stlouisfed.org/fred2/series/GDPC1`

18
International Capital Flows

Tools: Balance of international payments; dynamics of net foreign assets.

Key Words: Trade balance; net exports; current account; capital account; capital flows; net foreign assets.

Big Ideas:

- A current account deficit implies that a country is borrowing from the rest of the world; we refer to this as a capital inflow. A current account surplus — a capital outflow — implies that a country is lending to the rest of the world.

- A capital inflow (borrowing) can lead to problems if it does not support productive activities. For this reason, analysts often focus on the reasons for capital flows as well as their magnitude.

- The dynamics of net foreign assets are analogous to government debt dynamics.

International trade in goods and assets are at all-time highs all over the world. In these notes, we describe the measurement system used to track such trades: the balance of payments (BOP), a close relative of the National Income and Product Accounts (NIPA) focusing on international transactions. This is simply accounting, in the sense that we're counting things in a consistent way and not applying any particular theoretical framework. Nevertheless, an important idea emerges: Countries that run trade deficits can also be thought of as attracting foreign investment or borrowing from abroad. This connection between flows of goods and flows of assets gives us a new perspective on issues such as persistent trade deficits.

18.1   Trade in goods, services, and income

The balance of payments starts with a measurement system for trade in goods and services and related flows of income. See Table 18.1.

Two closely-related measures are commonly reported. Net exports in goods, sometimes called the *merchandise trade balance* is reported monthly, and so is more readily available than the quarterly data from the National Income and Product Accounts, which are broader. Service trade includes such things as foreign tourists visiting the US (hotels, restaurants), consulting services provided by US firms for foreign clients, and foreign students attending US universities. The US currently runs a sizeable deficit in goods (merchandise) trade and a modest surplus in service trade. The *current account balance* is a broader concept than net exports; it consists of net exports plus net receipts of capital income, labor income, taxes, and transfers from abroad (*net foreign income* for short). Mathematically,

$$CA = NX + \text{Net Foreign Income},$$

where CA is the current account and NX is (still) net exports.

Net foreign income includes such items as payment of interest on US government bonds owned by foreign central banks (a negative entry), salaries received by consultants based in the US working in Tokyo (a positive entry), and salaries paid to Russian hockey players in the US (a negative entry).

Table 18.1: US balance of payments.

Net Exports of Goods and Services	−500.4
Net Labor Income from ROW	−11.0
Net Capital Income from ROW	193.3
Unilateral Current Transfers from ROW	−145.0
Current and Capital Account	**−462.9**
Net direct investment	30.8
Net portfolio investment	96.9
Net other investment	42.1
Net financial derivatives transactions	25.4
Financial Account (inflows)	**195.2**
Statistical Discrepancy	**267.7**

The numbers are for 2015, billions of US dollars. ROW means "rest of world." There are modest differences between these balance of payments measures and quarterly NIPA measures.

We see in Table 18.1 that the US was a net recipient of capital income and a net payer of labor income.

The current account balance is, thus, the broadest measure of a country's flow of "current" payments to and from the rest of the world. In the US, the difference between net exports and the current account usually is modest. In other countries, the flows of labor and capital income may play larger roles.

18.2   Trade in assets

There are also flows related to capital and financial transactions. You can see in Table 18.1 that the US in 2015 was the net recipient of $195.2b of capital and financial "inflows," meaning that foreigners' purchases of US assets were greater than US nationals' purchases of foreign assets by this amount. By convention, this is reported as a positive entry, even though it corresponds to an accumulation of liabilities with respect to the rest of the world. Foreigners' purchases of domestic assets consisted of direct investment (a controlling interest in a US business); purchases of equity and bonds issued by US corporations; purchases of US government and agency issues; loans to US borrowers; and some other minor items we won't bother to enumerate.

The central insight we gain from the balance of payments is that these asset transactions must match the current transactions:

Current Account + Capital and Financial Account = 0.

It's not quite true in the data, because the numbers are not entirely accurate. We add a balancing item ("statistical discrepancy" or "errors and omissions") to make up the difference. The point is that any deficit in the current account must be financed by a capital inflow: selling assets or accumulating liabilities with respect to the rest of the world. The same accounting truism applies to a firm or an individual. If your expenditures exceed your receipts, you need to sell assets or borrow to finance the difference. Firms do this regularly when they make major additions to plant and equipment. And households often do the same when they buy houses.

The interesting thing about this accounting identity is that it gives us a different perspective on current account deficits. If we run a current account deficit as a reflection of a trade deficit, as in the US right now, we're tempted to look at imports and exports as the reason. Perhaps foreign countries are keeping our goods out of their home markets, or pushing down their exchange rates to encourage exports. That's the first reaction most people have. But now we know that a current account deficit must correspond to a capital and financial inflow: Foreign investors are buying our assets. This perspective leads us to think about the investment opportunities in the US and elsewhere in the world that might lead to this. Are US assets particularly attractive? Or are foreign assets unattractive? Both perspectives are right, in the sense that they're true as a matter of accounting arithmetic, but the second one captures more clearly the dynamic aspect of decisions to invest.

18.3   Net foreign assets

The capital and financial account measures net flows of financial claims: changes in asset position, in other words. The balance-sheet position of an economy is referred to as its net international investment position (NIIP) or, simply, net foreign assets (NFA). If a country's claims on the rest of the world exceed their claims on it, then it has positive net foreign assets and is said to be a net creditor. If negative, a net debtor. The position changes over time, as indicated by the capital and financial account. Mathematically, we would say

$$NFA_t \quad = \quad NFA_{t-1} + CA_t$$
$$+\text{Asset Revaluations.} \qquad (18.1)$$

As in most accounting frameworks, there's a connection between the income statement (the "flows" in economics parlance) and the balance sheet (the "stocks").

An analogous relation for an individual might go something like this: Suppose you start with no assets or liabilities and then borrow 50,000 for the first year of your MBA. You spend the entire 50,000 and have no other source of funds, so you have a cash-flow deficit of $-50,000$ for the year. At the end of the year, you have a net asset position of $-50,000$. The bookkeeping is analogous to equation (18.1), with *NFA* analogous to your net worth, *NX* analogous to your annual cash-flow surplus or deficit, and the last two terms ignored to keep things manageable. If we added interest on the debt, that would show up in Net Foreign Income.

Why do we need asset revaluations? We measure international investments at market value, so if the value of an asset changes, we need to account for it in NFA. For international investments, asset revaluations occur both through the usual change in prices of equity and bonds and through changes in exchange rates for instruments denominated in foreign currencies.

We report recent numbers for the US in Table 18.2. There we see that the US has a net financial asset position of $-\$7,280.6b$, meaning that foreign

Table 18.2: US net international investment position.

US-owned assets abroad	**23,340.8**
Direct investment	6,978.3
Corporate equity	6,828.2
Bonds	2,777.9
Loans and other	3,977.3
Reserves & govt	383.6
Financial Derivatives	2,395.4
Foreign-owned assets in the US	**30,621.4**
Direct investment	6,543.8
Corporate equity	6,218.8
Corporate bonds	4,310.1
US govt (treasuries, currency, official)	6,148.1
Loans and other	5,062.4
Financial Derivatives	2,338.1
Net international investment position	**−7,280.6**

The numbers are for 2015 yearend, billions of US dollars.

claims on the US exceed US claims on the rest of the world by this amount. The table gives a more detailed accounting of these positions.

18.4 Sources of external deficits

We'll talk more about the difference between the trade balance and the current account shortly, but for now, let's ignore the difference and consider a trade deficit. If we have a large deficit, should we be worried? Is it a sign that the economy is in trouble? In this and many other cases, it's helpful to consider an analogous situation for a firm. Suppose that a firm is accumulating liabilities. Is that a bad sign? The answer is that it depends what the liabilities are used to finance. If they finance productive investments, then there should be no difficulty servicing the liabilities. In fact, the ability to finance them suggests that someone thinks the investments will pay off. But if the money is wasted (surely you can think of examples!), then investors might be concerned. The same is true of countries — it depends where the funds go.

Consider the flow identity that we saw in Chapter 2:

$$S = Y - C - G = I + NX.$$

If we run a trade deficit ($NX < 0$), it must (as a matter of accounting) reflect some combination of low saving and high investment (high I). If we borrow from abroad to finance new plant and equipment, and the plant and equipment lead to higher output, we can use the extra output to cover the liabilities. If the investment is ill-considered, then we face the same issue as a firm in a similar situation.

What if we finance household consumption or government purchases? We have to answer the same question: Was the expenditure worthwhile? Here there is room for concern, but a serious answer would depend on the nature of the expenditures.

The Lawson Doctrine, named after British government official Nigel Lawson, makes a distinction between public and private sources of deficits. Recall that we can divide saving into private and government components, so that

$$S_p + S_g \;=\; I + NX.$$

In Lawson's view, a trade (or current account) deficit that financed a difference between private saving and investment is fine. But if the external deficit (trade or current account) stems from a government deficit, it's worth a more careful look. In practice, emerging market crises often stem from government deficits that are financed abroad.

18.5   Debt dynamics and sustainability

The net foreign asset position evolves through time, just as government debt does. As with government debt, the focus is traditionally on the ratio to GDP, which can change through either the numerator or denominator. We've seen that NFA changes like this:

$$
\begin{aligned}
NFA_t \;&=\; NFA_{t-1} + NX_t + \text{Net Foreign Interest Income} \\
&=\; (1 + i_t)NFA_{t-1} + NX_t.
\end{aligned}
$$

Note that everything here is nominal, including the interest rate i_t on the net foreign asset position. Here, we're skipping asset revaluations and the non-interest component of net foreign income, but we could add them back in later if we thought they were relevant. If the growth rate of nominal GDP is $g_t + \pi_t$, we can write

$$Y_t \;=\; (1 + g_t + \pi_t)Y_{t-1}.$$

With these inputs, we see that NX/Y evolves like this:

$$\frac{NFA_t}{Y_t} \;\approx\; \frac{NFA_{t-1}}{Y_{t-1}} + (i_t - \pi_t)\frac{NFA_{t-1}}{Y_{t-1}} - g_t\frac{NFA_{t-1}}{Y_{t-1}} + \frac{NX_t}{Y_t}. \qquad (18.2)$$

The logic is identical to our analysis of government debt in equation (17.6).

How does the ratio of NFA to GDP change over time? The first issue is what real interest rate $i_t - \pi_t$ we pay on our borrowing. Typically the rate is positive, which tends to increase a positive net foreign asset and decrease a negative one. The second issue of real GDP growth g_t. High growth reduces the ratio of net foreign assets to GDP by increasing the denominator. Finally, a trade surplus or deficit carries over directly to the net foreign asset position.

If a country has a large current account deficit and a large and growing net foreign liability position, it's sometimes said to be *unsustainable*. But if it's unsustainable, what happens? The theory doesn't say, but we can imagine some possibilities: The trade deficit turns to surplus; the country defaults on some or all of its foreign liabilities; and so on. More commonly, this is used to project the growth of NFA over the next few years. If this leads to a large ratio of NFA to GDP, then investors may start to wonder whether they'll be repaid. How large does it have to be to generate concern? It depends on the country and its institutions — just as we learned in studying government debt in Chapter 17.

History tells us, however, that we see deficits and net liabilities in both countries on the brink of trouble (Argentina in the late 1990s) and countries that are performing well (Australia over most of its history). Most analysts would check further and find out what the deficit was financing (plant and equipment or government spending) and how it was structured (debt or equity). If debt, then the maturity and denomination are also relevant.

18.6   Big picture

The bottom line is that the current account deficit and net foreign asset position are important indicators of the state of an economy. Important, yes, but it's not always clear what to make of them. Take a current account deficit. Is a deficit is bad (it sounds bad!) or good (look, people want to invest in our country!)? We need to look at the overall picture and come up with a judgment. It's another piece of the puzzle to consider when deciding whether a country is a good opportunity.

Executive summary

1. There are several measures of current transactions with other countries:
   - The trade balance measures exports minus imports of goods and services, the same as Net exports in the GDP expenditure identity.

- The current account also includes net international factor income, taxes, and net international transfers.

We refer to them collectively as "external" balances (deficits or surpluses).

2. The current account is mirrored by an equal and opposite capital and financial account measuring net asset transactions.

3. The net international investment position measures our current net claims on the rest of the world.

4. The flow identity tells us that the external deficit reflects some combination of personal saving, government saving, and investment.

If you're looking for more

For more information:

- In the US, international transactions are reported along with the National Income and Product Accounts by the Bureau of Economic Analysis. See their International Economic Accounts.

- The International Monetary Fund's International Financial Statistics is the best single source of balance of payments and international investment data.

- International standards for BOP data are set by a working committee of the International Monetary Fund. Their web site includes discussions of both conceptual and measurement issues. The annual reports are a good overview. One of the recent highlights: In 2007, the world trade balance was \$108b, meaning that countries reported \$108b more exports than imports. Since every export must be someone else's import, this can't really be true, but it points to some of the difficult measurement issues faced by the people putting these accounts together.

Symbols used in this chapter

Table 18.3: Chapter 18 symbol table.

Symbol	Definition
CA	Current Account
NX	Net exports
NFA	Net foreign assets
S	Saving
Y	Gross domestic product ($=$ Expenditure $=$ Income)
C	Private consumption
I	Private investment
G	Government purchases of goods and services (not transfers)
S_p	Private saving ($= Y - T - C$)
S_g	Government saving ($= T - G$)
i	Interest rate on net foreign assets
g	Discrete compound growth rate of GDP

In this chapter, we have dealt only with *nominal* variables.

Data used in this chapter

Table 18.4: Chapter 18 data table.

Variable	Source
Current Account (BOP)	BOPBCA
Current Account (NIPA)	NETFI
Net exports of goods and services (NIPA)	NETEXP
Nominal GDP	GDP
Foreign-owned assets in US ($+$ equals increase)	BOPI
U.S.-owned assets abroad ($+$ equals decrease)	BOPOA
Income payments (total)	BOPMIT
Income payments on foreign assets in US	BOPMIA
Income receipts (total)	BOPXRT
Income receipts on assets abroad	BOPXR
Statistical discrepancy (BOP)	BOPERR

To retrieve the data online, add the identifier from the source column to `http://research.stlouisfed.org/fred2/series/`. For example, to retrieve the GDP, point your browser to `http://research.stlouisfed.org/fred2/series/GDP`

19
Exchange-Rate Fluctuations

Tools: Arbitrage arguments.

Key Words: Real and nominal exchange rates; spot and forward exchange rates; purchasing power parity; covered/uncovered interest parity; the carry trade.

Big Ideas:

- Exchange rates: where sensible theory comes to die. Meaning: short-run movements in exchange rates are both hard to predict and hard to explain after the fact.

- Purchasing power parity relates the relative price of goods across countries to exchange rates.

- Interest rate parity (covered, uncovered) relates interest rates to exchange rates.

- The empirical performance of purchasing power parity and uncovered interest parity is poor.

Exchange rates (prices of foreign currency) are a central element of most international transactions. When Heineken sells beer in the US, its euro profits depend on its euro costs of production, its dollar revenues in the US, and the dollar-euro exchange rate. When a Tokyo resident purchases a dollar-denominated asset, her return (in yen) depends on the asset's dollar yield and the change in the dollar-yen exchange rate. Exchange rates, then, are an essential component of virtually all international transactions.

Nevertheless, countries in which exchange rates are determined in open markets find that short-term fluctuations are substantial, largely unpredictable, and hard to explain after the fact. That's been horribly disappointing to those of us who would like to understand them better, but it's a fact of life. From a business perspective, they're a source of random noise. Heineken profits, for example, vary with the dollar-euro rate, even if the underlying business doesn't change.

What follows is a summary of what we know.

19.1   Terminology

There is a lot of jargon associated with this subject. You'll run across references to:

- **Exchange-rate conventions.**   We typically express exchange rates as local currency prices of one unit of foreign currency. In the US, we might refer to the dollar price of one euro. In currency markets, the conventions vary (every currency pair has its own), but we'll try to stick with this one. It has the somewhat strange feature that an increase in the exchange rate is a decline in the relative value of the home currency. Of course, it's also an increase in the value of the foreign currency. As a rule of thumb, remember that we quote prices in dollars (or whatever our local currency is).

- **Exchange-rate changes.** Changes in exchange rates also have their own names. For a flexible exchange rate, we refer to a decrease in the value of a currency as a *depreciation* and an increase as an *appreciation*. For a fixed exchange rate, where the changes reflect policy, the analogous terms are *devaluation* and *revaluation* .

- **Real exchange rates.**   You'll see this term, too, but what does it mean? (What's an *imaginary* exchange rate?) A nominal exchange rate is the relative price of two currencies: the number of units of currency A needed to buy one unit of currency B. The real exchange rate is the relative price of a commodity or a basket of goods. If P is the US CPI in dollars, P^* is the European CPI in euros, and e is the dollar price of one euro (the *nominal* exchange rate), then the (CPI-based) *real exchange rate* between the US and the Euro Zone is

$$RER \;\; = \;\; eP^*/P,$$

the ratio of the price of EU goods to US goods, with both expressed in the same units (here, dollars). We use an asterisk here and below to denote a foreign value.

- **Parity relations.** We generally think that globalization and trade ("arbitrage") will tend to reduce differences in prices and returns across countries. Parity relations are based on the assumption that differences are eliminated altogether. It's an extreme assumption, to be sure, but a useful benchmark. *Purchasing power parity* is the theory that prices of baskets of products are equal across countries: $P = eP^*$ (or $RER = 1$). *Interest rate parity* is the proposition that expected returns are equal for comparable investments in different currencies — think of US and Japanese treasury bills, or dollar- and yen-denominated eurocurrency deposits at major banks.

We'll see each of these in action shortly.

19.2   Properties of exchange rates

Flexible exchange rates move around — a lot. The standard deviation of annual rates of change of currency prices is ten to 12 percent for major currencies, more for emerging markets. That's less than the standard deviation of equity returns (the return on the S&P 500 index has an annual standard deviation of 16-18 percent) but a significant source of risk. With a standard deviation of 10 percent, and assuming that changes in currency prices are normally distributed, there's a five-percent chance of seeing a one-year change greater than 20 percent either up or down.

You can get a sense of recent dollar movements from Figure 19.1, which plots the price of one dollar expressed in Australian dollars, British pounds, euros, yen, and yuan/renminbi, respectively. (Inverses of dollar exchange rates, in other words.) They are constructed as indexes, with the January 2001 values set equal to 100. You can see that the dollar-euro rate fluctuates quite a bit; over the last five years, it's ranged from 50 to 110. This reflects, to a large extent, the approaches taken by the US and the European central banks: They let their currencies float freely. The yen and the Australian dollar are similar. The renminbi, however, is fixed (or close to it) by the Chinese central bank at a value of about eight yuan per dollar. More on this in the next chapter.

19.3   Purchasing-power parity

So we've seen that exchange rates move around. But can we say anything about why? We can't say much about short-term movements, but here's a theory that gives us a long-term anchor for the real exchange rate. It's a helpful benchmark.

Figure 19.1: The US dollar against other major currencies.

The idea is to compare prices of goods. Suppose that exchange rates adjusted
to equate prices across countries. The logic is arbitrage: If a good is cheaper
in one country than in another, then people would buy in the cheap country
and sell in the other, taking a profit along the way. This process will tend
to eliminate the difference in prices, either through changes in the exchange
rate or in the prices themselves.

Consider wine. Suppose that a bottle of (some specific) wine costs $p = 26$
dollars in New York, and $p^* = 20$ euros in Paris. Are the prices the same? If
the exchange rate is $e = 1.3$ dollars per euro, then the New York and Paris
prices are the same once we express them in the same units. More generally,
we might say that

$$p = ep^*.$$

We refer to this relation as the *law of one price* : that a product should
sell for the same price in two locations. An even better example might be
gold, which sells for pretty much the same price in New York, London, and
Tokyo.

If the law of one price works for some products, there are many more for
which restrictions on trade (tariffs or quotas), transportation costs, or other
"frictions" prevent arbitrage. Agricultural products, for example, are protected in many countries, leading to substantial differences across countries
in the prices of such basic commodities as rice, wheat, and sugar. Cement

faces substantial shipping costs, even within countries. Many services (haircuts, dry cleaning, medical and legal services) are inherently difficult to trade, and often protected by regulation, as well.

The Economist, with its usual flair for combining insight with entertainment, computes dollar prices of the Big Mac around the world. The idea is that it's the same product everywhere, so differences in prices reflect deviations from the law of one price. In July 2014, Big Mac prices were $4.80 in the US, $4.95 in the Euro Zone, $3.64 in Japan, $2.57 in Argentina, and $2.73 in China. These price differences vary widely over time. For example, In January 2006, Big Mac prices were $3.15 in the US, $3.55 in the Euro Zone, $2.19 in Japan, $2.50 in Argentina, and $2.45 in China. Perhaps it's no surprise that the law of one price doesn't hold — you can imagine the mess involved in trying to arbitrage price differences. But it's a good illustration of international price differences more generally.

Despite such modest encouragement, the first-cut theory of exchange rates is based on an application of law-of-one-price logic to broad baskets of goods. The so-called theory of purchasing power parity (PPP) is that local and foreign price indexes (P and P^*, say) are linked through the exchange rate: $P \approx eP^*$ or

$$RER \;=\; eP^*/P \;\approx\; 1. \qquad (19.1)$$

The approximation symbol suggests that we don't expect this to be perfect. In the most common applications, the price indexes are CPIs (consumer price indexes), and we refer to the measure of the real exchange rate as CPI-based. If this doesn't work for specific goods, why might we expect it to hold for average prices of goods? One reason is that, for any pair of countries, we might see as many products that are "overpriced" as there are products that are "underpriced." When we average, these deviations could offset each other, but, in fact, they don't. If prices of some goods are cheaper abroad, then prices of other goods tend to be, too.

What limited success we have comes in the long run. As an empirical matter, deviations from PPP tend to average out over time. Sometimes prices are higher in Paris, sometimes higher in New York, but, on average, prices are roughly comparable. Prices are lower, on average, in countries with lower GDP per capita, but here, too, large fluctuations in the real exchange rate tend to disappear with time. How much time do we need for this to work? At least several years. If you're thinking of going to Paris next month, there's little reason to expect that we'll be closer to PPP by then. Maybe we will, maybe we won't; it's a tossup.

Real exchange rates computed this way are often used to judge whether a currency's price is reasonable. If the prices are lower at home than abroad

($RER > 1$), we say the (home) currency is *undervalued*. If prices are higher
at home ($RER < 1$), we say the currency is *overvalued*. Over- and undervalued here means relative to our theory of PPP. We can do the same thing
with the Big Mac index. We saw earlier that Big Macs were cheaper in
China than in the US, so we might say that the dollar is overvalued relative
to the yuan. Over time, we might expect most of these "misvaluations" to
decline. Experience suggests, however, that any such adjustment will take
many years. Our best estimates are that about half the difference from
PPP will disappear in five years. We can do the same thing with CPIs, with
one difference: Since CPI are indexes, we don't know the absolute prices.
The standard approach is to find the mean value of the real exchange rate
(or its logarithm) and judge under- or overvaluation by comparing the real
exchange rate to its mean, rather than one.

19.4   Depreciation and inflation

We can express the same theory in growth rates, with the result that the
change in the exchange rate (the depreciation of the currency) should equal
the difference in the two inflation rates. Simply put, if one country has a
higher inflation rate than another, then we would expect its currency to fall
in value by the difference. That's not true over short periods of time, but it's
reasonable guide over longer periods of time. Countries with high inflation
rates find that their currencies fall in value as a result.

Here's how that works. The PPP relation equation (19.1), implies that

$$e_t = P_t/P_t^*.$$

(Feel free to put $\approx$ here if you prefer.) If we take (natural) logs of both
sides, we have

$$\ln e_t = \ln P_t - \ln P_t^*.$$

If we take the same equation at two different dates, we have

$$\begin{aligned}
\ln e_{t+1} - \ln e_t &= (\ln P_{t+1} - \ln P_t) - (\ln P_{t+1}^* - \ln P_t^*) \\
&= \pi_{t+1} - \pi_{t+1}^*.
\end{aligned}$$

In words: The depreciation rate equals the difference in the inflation rates.
It's simply PPP in growth rates.

Does this work? It's pretty good for long-run averages (five to ten years or
more), but like everything we know about exchange rates, not very useful
for short-term movements outside very very-high-inflation situations.

Figure 19.2: Venezuelan depreciation and inflation differential.

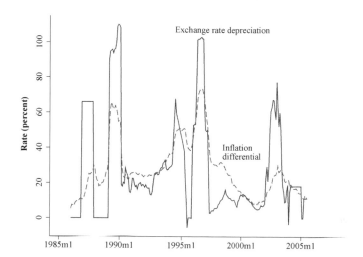

By way of example, consider the exchange rate between the Venezuelan Bolivar and the US dollar. Between January 1985 and January 2006, Venezuela's average annual inflation rate was 30 percent, as opposed to the US's 2.9 percent. In the same period, the Bolivar depreciated at the average yearly rate of 27.9 percent, i.e. only .8 percent more than implied by the PPP condition. In the short run, however, deviations from PPP are the norm. Figure 19.2 shows that this has definitely been the case for the Bolivar: There have been plenty of periods in which exchange-rate depreciation did not closely track the inflation differential with the United States. In some instances, in particular in the late 1980s, the deviations were due to the central bank's attempt to keep the exchange rate constant. In other cases (the early 1990s, for example), the deviations probably had nothing to do with central bank interventions.

In developed countries, it's not unusual to see deviations of the real exchange rate from one of 30-40 percent in either direction. Figure 19.3 shows this for the dollar-euro. This picture is typical of developed countries: Inflation differentials are relatively small, so changes in the real and nominal exchange rates are almost equal. These deviations from PPP tend to disappear with time, but, as we saw earlier, they go away slowly.

Figure 19.3: Dollar versus euro and inflation differential.

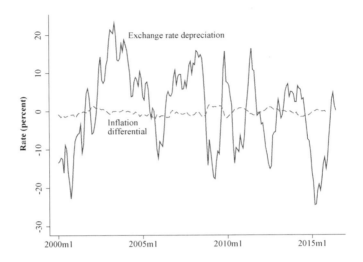

19.5   Interest rate parity and the carry trade

Exchange rates also play a role in interest rate differences across countries.
In June 2004, for example, three-month eurodollar deposits paid interest
rates of 1.40 percent in US dollars, 4.78 percent in British pounds, 5.48
percent in Australian dollars, and 2.12 percent in euros. If international
capital markets are so closely connected, why do we see such differences?
The answer is that these returns are expressed in different currencies, so
they're not directly comparable.

Let's think about how prices of currencies show up in interest rate differentials. We'll start with a relation called *covered interest parity*, which says
that interest rates denominated in different currencies are the same once you
"cover" yourself against possible currency changes. The argument follows
the standard logic of arbitrage used endlessly in finance. Let's compare two
equivalent strategies for investing one US dollar for three months. The first
strategy is to invest one dollar in a three-month eurodollar deposit (with
the stress on "dollar"). After three months, that leaves us with $(1 + i/4)$
dollars, where i is the dollar rate of interest expressed as an annual rate.

What if we invested one dollar in euro-denominated instruments? Here we
need several steps to express the return in dollars and make it comparable
to the first strategy. Step one is to convert the dollar to euros, leaving us
with $1/e$ euros (e is the spot exchange rate — the dollar price of one euro).

Step two is to invest this money in a three-month euro deposit, earning the annualized rate of return i^*. That leaves us with $(1 + i^*/4)/e$ euros after three months. We could convert it at the spot rate prevailing three months from now, but that exposes us to the risk that the euro will fall. An alternative is to sell euros forward at price f. In three months, we will have $(1 + i^*/4)/e$ euros that we want to convert back to dollars. With a three-month forward contract, we arrange now to convert them at the forward rate f expressed, like e, as dollars per euro. This strategy leaves us with $(1 + i^*/4)f/e$ dollars after three months.

Thus, we have two relatively riskless strategies, one yielding $(1 + i/4)$, the other yielding $(1 + i^*/4)f/e$. Which is better? Well, if either strategy had a higher payoff, you could short one and go long on the other, earning extra interest with no risk. Arbitrage will tend to drive the two together:

$$(1 + i/4) \;=\; (1 + i^*/4)f/e. \tag{19.2}$$

We call (19.2) *covered interest parity*. Currency traders assure us that covered interest parity is an extremely good approximation in the data, except in extreme periods of liquidity, such as a financial crisis. The only difference between the left and right sides is a bid-ask spread, which averages less than 0.05 percent for major currencies.

A related issue is whether international differences in interest rates reflect differences in expected depreciation rates. Does the high rate on Aussie dollars (AUD) reflect the market's assessment that the AUD will fall in value relative to (say) the euro? To see how this works, suppose that we converted the proceeds of our foreign investment back to local currency at the exchange rate prevailing in three months. Our return would then be

$$(1 + i^*/4)e_3/e,$$

where e_3 is the spot exchange rate three months in the future. This investment is risky, since we don't know what the future exchange rate will be, but we might expect it to have a similar expected return to a local investment. That is,

$$(1 + i/4) \;=\; (1 + i^*/4)E(e_3)/e, \tag{19.3}$$

where $E(e_3)$ is our current expectation of the exchange rate in three months. This relation is an application of the expectations hypothesis to currency prices (the forward rate equals the expected future spot rate) that is commonly referred to as *uncovered interest parity*.

In fact, uncovered interest rate parity doesn't work. It implies that high-interest-rate currencies depreciate, when, in fact, they appreciate (increase in value) on average, making them potentially good (if risky) investments.

If $i > i^*$, we invest at home. If $i < i^*$, we invest abroad, expecting to pocket not only the higher interest rate but an appreciation of the currency ($e_3 > e$). That's the essence of what is called the "carry trade." Why this investment opportunity persists remains something of a mystery to academics and investors alike.

Two fine points: (i) This feature of the data does not apply to the currencies of developing countries, where higher interest rates typically do imply future depreciation. That is, uncovered interest parity works better here. (ii) In developed countries, forecasts of exchange-rate changes based on interest differentials have an R^2 of 0.05 or less. That's still useful for investment purposes, but leaves most of the variance of exchange-rate changes unexplained.

19.6   Predicting exchange rates

Let's summarize what we've learned about movements in exchange rates:

- PPP works reasonably well over long periods of time, but has little empirical content over periods of less than a few years, and virtually none over periods under a year.

- Interest rate differentials have some forecasting power, with high-interest-rate currency increasing in value, on average, but they leave most of the variance of exchange-rate movements unexplained.

Can we do better than this? A little, but probably no more than that. It's extremely hard to forecast exchange rates better than a 50-50 bet on up or down. Interest differentials do a little better, but only a little. We may be able to do better still using more complex theory or personal judgment about policy, but years of failure suggest that it's very hard to beat a random walk consistently.

Executive summary

1. In the long run, exchange rates tend to equalize prices of products across countries (PPP).

2. In the short run, exchange-rate movements are large and unpredictable.

Review questions

1. Purchasing power parity for Big Macs. The Economist reports the following data for local prices of Big Macs and US dollars in July 2011:

	Big Mac Price (Local Currency) (A)	Exchange Rate (LCUs per Dollar) (B)
Argentina	20.0	4.13
Brazil	9.50	1.54
India	84.0	44.4
United States	4.07	1.00

LCUs are "local currency units."

(a) What is the dollar price of a Big Mac in each of these locations?

(b) In what ways is the ratio of USD Big Mac prices similar to the real exchange rate?

(c) What exchange rates for the first three currencies would equate the dollar prices of Big Macs in other countries to the US price? How is this related to PPP?

(d) How much are the first three currencies over or undervalued relative to the US dollar?

Answer. The calculations are summarized in

	Big Mac (USD) (C)	Big Mac (Ratio) (D)	Overvaluation (percent) (E)
Argentina	4.84	4.91	19
Brazil	6.17	2.33	51
India	1.89	20.64	−53
United States	4.07	1.00	0.0

(a) Dollar prices of Big Macs are reported above as column (C), computed as (A)/(B).

(b) The relative price of Big Macs is like a real exchange rate. The real exchange rate is the ratio of prices converted to a common currency:

$$RER = eP^*/P.$$

Usually we use prices indexes for P and P^*, here we use prices of Big Macs.

(c) Mathematically, we set RER equal to one (the PPP condition) and solve for $e = P/P^*$. In the table, we computed this as the ratio of entries on column (A) to the US entry in the same column. That gives us a PPP benchmark for what the exchange rate should be.

(d) If we compare our calculation of the PPP exchange rate in (c) to the actual, we can see how far off we are. In the table, we compute "overvaluation" as the percentage difference between true exchange rates and our PPP calculation: `100*[(D)/(B)-1]`. We see that the Brazilian real is overvalued (Big Macs are expensive there) and the Indian rupee is undervalued (Big Macs are cheap there).

2. Forecasting the euro. Suppose the euro is "overvalued" in PPP terms relative to the dollar (goods are more expensive in Europe) and Euro Zone short-term interest rates are slightly above US interest rates. Given these facts, how would you expect the euro/dollar exchange rate to change over the next 6 months? 6 years? How good is each of these informed guesses?

Answer. Purchasing power parity is a long-run "anchor" for the exchange rate: if prices of goods and services in the Euro Zone are higher than those in the US, when expressed in a common currency, we'd expect the euro to fall in value relative to the dollar — eventually. This is pretty much useless over a period as short as 6 months, but has some content over 6 years. More useful in the short-run is the interest differential. Since the Euro interest rate is higher, we'd expect the euro to increase in value. Neither works well: an R^2 of 0.05 would be good over periods of a few months.

If you're looking for more

FRED has exchange rates for many countries. So does the Fed; search: "fed exchange rates."

The Economist's Big Mac index (search: "big mac index") is the center of a nice web site on exchange-rate data and issues.

Deutsche Bank's *Guide to Exchange-Rate Determination* is a terrific summary of what we know about exchange rates from a bond and currency trader's perspective.

Symbols and data used in this chapter

Table 19.1: Symbol table.

Symbol	Definition
e	Spot exchange rate = home currency price of foreign currency
f	Forward exchange rate
P	Domestic price level
P^*	Foreign price level
RER	Real exchange rate = eP^*/P
π	Domestic inflation
π^*	Foreign inflation
i	Domestic nominal interest rate
i^*	Foreign nominal interest rate
$E(x)$	Expected value of a variable x

Table 19.2: Data table.

Variable	Source
USD/euro exchange rate	EXUSEU
Yuan/USD exchange rate	EXCHUS
Yen/USD exchange rate	EXJPUS
USD/UK pound exchange rate	EXUSUK
USD/AUD exchange rate	EXUSAL
Venezuela/USD exchange rate	EXVZUS
Real trade-weighted USD index (broad)	TWEXBPA
US consumer price index	CPIAUCSL
Euro area harmonized consumer price index	CP0000EZCCM086NEST

To retrieve the data online, add the identifier from the source column to http:
//research.stlouisfed.org/fred2/series/. For example, to retrieve the dollar-euro
exchange rate, point your browser to http://research.stlouisfed.org/fred2/series/
EXUSEU

20

Exchange-Rate Regimes

Tools: Central bank balance sheet.

Key Words: convertibility; capital mobility; capital controls; fixed and flexible exchange rates; foreign exchange reserves; sterilization.

Big Ideas:

- Countries adopt different exchange rate regimes: fixed, floating, and in between.

- The trilemma limits our policy options: we can choose only two of (i) fixed exchange rate, (ii) free flow of capital, and (iii) discretionary monetary policy.

- Fixed exchange-rate regimes must be defended through open market operations and are vulnerable to speculative attack.

The term "exchange-rate regimes" refers to the various arrangements that governments around the world make about international transactions. We'll see (i) how central banks intervene in currency markets to fix the price and (ii) how such fixed exchange-rate systems sometimes blow up.

20.1 A catalog of foreign-exchange arrangements

Governments follow a wide range of policies toward their currencies. One aspect of policy is whether people and businesses can freely exchange their local currency for another: whether the currency is *convertible*. The US dollar, for example, is convertible. You can walk into most banks in New

York and use dollars to buy dozens of foreign currencies. Or you can use
your credit card abroad and have the currency transaction done for you.
The renminbi, however, has limited convertibility. You need approval from
the Chinese central bank to buy or sell Chinese currency.

A related issue is *capital controls*: whether the government restricts movements of capital (funds) in and out of the country. In the US, capital is
generally free to move in and out of the country, although there are restrictions on foreign ownership of companies in some industries (banks, media,
airlines). In China, there are limits on foreign investments that vary (as
in the US) by industry and type (direct investment is easier than buying
securities). And there are restrictions that limit the amount of money that
Chinese citizens can take out of the country. These controls are typically
enforced through convertibility: since you can't convert renminbi to (say)
dollars, you can't take it out of the country.

There's nothing unusual about this. Many countries limit convertibility and
capital flows, particularly during times of stress. Malaysia imposed capital
controls during the Asian crisis of 1997, and Argentina did the same in 2002.

Another aspect of foreign-exchange policy is whether the price of the currency is set by the government, allowed to float freely, or something in
between. If the price is determined in a free market, we say that we have a
flexible or *floating* exchange-rate regime. If the government sets the price,
we say it has a *fixed* or *pegged* exchange-rate regime. A *managed float* is
somewhere in between.

20.2   Fixed exchange rates

Many countries have fixed exchange-rate regimes of one sort or other. Ecuador
uses US dollars, so its currency is fixed by design. The countries of the European Monetary Union use a common currency, the euro. Other countries
have their own currencies, but intervene to fix the price. Probably the most
prominent current example is the Chinese renminbi, which has been quasi-
fixed for more than a decade.

How does a central bank set the exchange rate if the currency is convertible?
Can it simply announce a rate? Probably not. You can state a price, but
you can't make people trade at it. You could claim, for example, that your
apartment is worth $10m, but if no one is willing to buy it for that price, the
statement is meaningless. For the same reason, a central bank must back
up its claim to fix the exchange rate by buying and selling as much foreign
currency as people want at the stated price.

Let's think through how this might work. Suppose the New York City government decided to fix the price of beer at $2 a six pack (cheap even if you live outside NYC). It supports this price by buying or selling any amount at the quoted price. Can they keep the price this low? Our guess is that at this price, beer makers would not find it profitable to make any (at least not any that we'd be willing to call beer). People would then flood the government with requests for beer, which the government would not be able to meet. When the government reneged on its promise to buy or sell at $2, the price would rise above $2 to its market level, either officially or on the black market. Unless the government has enough beer to back up the price, the system will collapse. Alternatively, suppose that the government set the price at $20. Beer makers would flood the government with beer at this price, leaving the government with a huge surplus. This is roughly what Europeans do with agriculture, where artificially high prices have left the EU with "mountains of butter," "lakes of wine," and so on. The point is that the government can fix a price only if it is willing and able to buy and sell at that price — or outlaws market transactions altogether.

The same logic applies to currencies. If the People's Bank of China were to support an excessively high price for the renminbi, then it would be flooded with offers from traders selling renminbi for (say) dollars. Its balance sheet would look something like this:

Assets		Liabilities	
FX Reserves	20	Currency	20
Bonds (in domestic currency)	180	Deposits from banks	180

We made these numbers up, but they give us the right idea. The central bank has the usual liabilities, domestic currency (the renminbi, in the case of the PBOC) and deposits from banks (the monetary base from Chapter 15). Two of the central banks assets will be relevant to our story, bonds (or other securities) denominated in domestic currency (as in Chapter 15) and foreign currency reserves, usually US government bonds that can easily be converted into dollars. The PBOC intervenes in the currency market by trading renminbi for dollars, and vice versa, depending on market conditions.

Suppose, for example, that Nike wanted to convert $2m to renminbi to build a new plant in China. It would do this through a Chinese bank. If the bank had no countervailing trades, it would go to the PBOC and exchange the $2m for renminbi at the going rate — say ten yuan per dollar, to make the arithmetic simple. The PBOC's balance sheet would then show an increase of 20m yuan worth of foreign currency and a comparable increase in its monetary base:

Assets		Liabilities	
FX Reserves	40	Currency	20
Bonds (in domestic currency)	180	Deposits from banks	200

Note that the transaction doesn't make the PBOC any richer. Its net worth is unchanged, since it has exchanged assets with equal value.

The difference, then, between fixed and flexible exchange-rate regimes is that the former obligates the central bank to buy and sell currencies at the stated price.

20.3   Sterilization

You might have noticed that when a central bank buys and sells foreign currency, the monetary base changes. In the example above, the purchase of 20 worth of foreign currency increased the monetary base by the same amount. It's automatic: when the central bank purchases foreign currency, it creates an equivalent amount of deposits from banks on the liabilities side of its balance sheet.

Central banks often want to reverse this impact of foreign exchange intervention by engaging in an offsetting open market operation. We refer to this as *sterilization*.

In our example, after the intervention in foreign exchange markets, the central bank would like to reduce the monetary base by 20, offsetting the impact of buying foreign currency. It does so with an open market operation, specifically by selling government bonds in exchange for a reduction in bank deposits banks at the central bank. Its balance sheet is now

Assets		Liabilities	
FX Reserves	40	Currency	20
Bonds (in domestic currency)	160	Deposits from banks	180

In some cases, this can happen to such an extent that the bond position is negative, turning the central bank into an issuer of bonds, instead of an investor. For example, at the end of 2011, the People's Bank of China held more foreign currency assets than the monetary base (i.e. the sum of its currency and bank deposit liabilities).

20.4   The trilemma

Exchange-rate policy is, evidently, a dimension of monetary policy since it involves management of the central bank's balance sheet. Is it another tool a central bank can use to manage the economy?

Both logic and experience tell us that the central bank's choices are limited. The sharpest example is the *trilemma*. You can choose, at most, two of the following:

- fixed exchange rate

- free international flow of capital

- discretionary monetary policy

If you try for all three, something will give, probably the exchange rate.

The US lets the exchange rate float, which allows it to have a discretionary monetary policy and free movements of capital. China limits the international flow of capital, which allows it to have a fixed exchange rate and some degree of monetary policy discretion. The UK, in 1992, tried for all three, and it blew up, driving them out of the European Monetary System, the precursor of the European Monetary Union.

20.5   Exchange-rate crises

As a matter of experience, fixed exchange-rate systems often collapse — sometimes spectacularly — when the central bank runs out of reserves.

We can illustrate the mechanics with the central bank's balance sheet. Suppose that it looks like the one above, with "fx reserves" of 40. And suppose, further, that investors would like to exchange 50 worth of pesos for the same value in dollars. Once the central bank runs out of dollars, it can no longer support the exchange rate, which becomes (more or less automatically) floating.

It's the same issue we illustrated earlier with beer: If people would prefer to buy foreign currency at the official exchange rate, and the currency is convertible, the central bank may find that its supply of foreign reserves is not enough to meet the market demand. (The market for currencies is enormous, so you need a lot of reserves.) For that reason, currency traders often look closely at the central bank's foreign currency reserves to measure its ability to maintain a fixed rate.

What invites "speculative attacks" on a currency with a fixed exchange rate? Often, it's a problem of time consistency. A fixed exchange rate is a policy promise to exchange one currency for another at a specified price without limit into the future. If investors today expect that a future policymaker will alter that price, what will stop them from selling the "expensive" currency today? In a foreign-exchange market that transacts about five trillion dollars daily, few governments have adequate foreign reserves to fend off a run on a fixed exchange rate.

One classic currency run occurred in 1992 in the United Kingdom. As part of the European Exchange Rate Mechanism (ERM), the UK had effectively fixed its currency, sterling, to Germany's Deutsche Mark (DM). But Germany was in its post-unification economic boom and needed high interest rates to limit inflation, while the UK was in a deep recession and needed low interest rates. Doubting that UK policymakers would keep interest rates high just to maintain the fixed exchange rate, speculators sold sterling. They made a fortune when the UK exited the ERM in September 1992 and sterling plunged versus the DM.

You might ask: Should the UK have considered capital controls instead of devaluing sterling? One practical obstacle was that any hint of controls would have further encouraged investors to flee sterling before they could no longer do so. Where time consistency is lacking — in this case, in currency policy — instability often follows.

There's a big-picture question lurking behind the scenes here: whether fixed exchange rate regimes reduce volatility. With flexible rates, we tend to see a lot of short-run volatility. With fixed exchange rates, short-run volatility is low most of the time, but we occasionally have spikes in volatility when the system collapses. Neither seems completely appealing, but that's the choice we're given.

20.6   Strong fixes

The tendency for fixed exchange rates to blow up has led to two competing lines of thought. One is to let them float — let the pressure off, so to speak. The other is to reinforce the fixed-exchange-rate system and nail the lid down tighter. Nothing has proved foolproof to date, but you never know.

One way to reinforce a fixed exchange rate is with a currency board. The idea is to start off with a large reserve of foreign currency and limit issues of domestic currency to this amount. That way, you should not run out of foreign currency when people trade in their local currency. Argentina set up a system like this in the 1990s, and established an exchange rate of one dollar per peso. But it was dissolved in a currency crisis ten years later. Hong Kong has had such a system since 1983, with the Hong Kong dollar pegged to the US dollar. As a result, interest rates in Hong Kong mirror those in the US: it has, in a sense, inherited US monetary policy.

A more extreme arrangement is a common currency. EMU (the euro area) is the most ambitious effort along these lines to date. But it has been under stress for years, and it remains unclear whether it will survive in its current form.

Executive summary

1. "Convertibility" and "capital mobility" refer to policies limiting foreign exchange transactions and international capital flows.

2. Foreign currency reserves are an indicator of the government's ability to maintain a fixed exchange rate.

3. The trilemma says you can have, at most, two of the following three things: (i) fixed exchange rates; (ii) international capital mobility; and (iii) discretionary monetary policy.

Review questions

1. Foreign exchange market intervention. Use a hypothetical central bank balance sheet to show how purchases of foreign currency affect the bank's assets and liabilities. What does this purchase do to the monetary base?

   Answer. When a central bank buys foreign currency, it gives the seller (typically a bank) domestic currency in return by crediting its deposit account at the central bank. The latter is an increase in the domestic monetary base. Suppose, for example, that the central bank starts with the balance sheet

Assets		Liabilities	
FX Reserves	100	Currency	140
Bonds	100	Deposits from banks	60

   The purchase of 25 worth of foreign currency changes the balance sheet to

Assets		Liabilities	
FX Reserves	125	Currency	140
Bonds	100	Deposits from banks	85

2. Sterilization. Suppose that the central bank has increased the money
   supply by purchasing foreign currency, as described above. How might it
   offset this impact on the monetary base (sterilize it, so to speak)?

   Answer. It does an equal sale of bonds, and as compensation, reduces its
   bank deposit liabilities. If it sells 25 worth of bonds, the balance sheet
   changes to

Assets		Liabilities	
FX Reserves	125	Currency	140
Bonds	75	Deposits from banks	60

   The net result of the two trades is that its liabilities are now more heavily
   weighted in foreign currency.

3. Hong Kong's trilemma. Use the trilemma to explain why Hong Kong has
   inherited US monetary policy.

   Answer. Hong Kong has (i) a fixed exchange rate against the US dollar
   and (ii) international capital mobility. The trilemma then tells us that it
   can't have its own monetary policy. Should they want their own monetary
   policy, either (i) or (ii) has to go.

If you're looking for more

The International Monetary Fund's *Annual Report on Exchange Arrangements and Exchange Restrictions* is the definitive guide to exchange-rate
arrangements: fixed, flexible, capital controls, and so on.

21
Macroeconomic Crises

Tools: Crisis triggers and indicators.

Key Words: Sovereign default; bank runs and panics; refinancing (rollover) risk; leverage; conditionality; solvency and liquidity.

Big Ideas:

- Common triggers of macroeconomic crises are sovereign debt problems, financial fragility, and fixed exchange rates.

- Measures related to these triggers can help identify countries in trouble: debt and deficits, financial weakness, exchange rate regime, and so on.

- The goals of crisis prevention and crisis management are often at odds.

Economies periodically experience *crises*: economic downturns that are not only larger than typical recessions but qualitatively different. The idea is now fresh in our minds, but similar episodes have occurred throughout recorded history. They're less common in modern, developed countries, but they can happen anywhere. Like snowflakes and business cycles, no two are exactly the same, but they share some common features.

21.1 Classic crisis triggers

There are three classic triggers of macroeconomic crises: sovereign debt, financial fragility, and a fixed exchange rate.

Sovereign debt problems. If investors fear that a government may not repay its debt, the market for debt collapses, often taking the economy with it. In the old days, wars were the standard problem. Wars are expensive, and if investors thought the expense was more than the government was willing or able to bear, they would stop buying the debt. In modern times, governments spend money on many things besides wars, but the possibility of default remains. Argentina in 2002 and Greece today are recent examples. These experiences remind us that sovereign debt need not be risk-free.

The central issue with government debts is sovereignty. If a corporation defaults, the creditors take it to court and claim the assets. With governments, there's no such mechanism, and the process is sloppier as a result.

Financial fragility. We know from centuries of experience that when the financial system freezes up, economic activity slows down sharply. We saw that in 2008, but the same thing happened during the Bank of England Panic of 1825, the Baring Crisis of 1890, the US Panic of 1907, Japan and Scandinavia in the 1990s, and many other occasions. It's a feature of even advanced financial systems that they sometimes break.

In most cases, these financial problems follow from poor investments (real estate is a common example), which put the solvency of financial institutions in question. The problems tend to snowball: Worries about the viability of one firm may lead others to reduce their lending, leading to a cycle of retrenchment that puts even sound firms in trouble. The word "panic" is apt here and stems from the imperfect information that investors have when deciding where to put their money.

Fixed exchange rates. For various reasons, the defense of fixed exchange rates by central banks periodically breaks down in ways that undermine the economy. Recent examples include the UK in 1992, Mexico in 1994, Korea in 1997, and Argentina in 2000.

Many crises combine several of these elements. The countries of the euro area face all three. In Ireland and Spain, bailing out their banks landed the governments in financial peril. In other countries, bank positions in government debt or in overpriced real estate put the banking systems in peril. Finally, the common currency eliminates exchange rate changes among the euro area countries as a possible correction mechanism.

21.2   Crisis indicators: the checklist

Crises are inherently hard to predict. Why? Think about cardiologists. We understand that they can identify risk factors (weight, high blood pressure) but cannot predict the date of a heart attack with any precision. Crises are worse. Once people see a crisis on the way, their actions tend to reinforce it: they sell government debt, withdraw funds from banks, or shift their money to foreign currency. But like a cardiologist, we can use what we know to identify signs of trouble.

Analysts differ in the details, but most would include the following in their "checklist" of crisis indicators:

Government debt and deficits. The primary issue here is the quality of governance. That aside, common rules of thumb include: Worry if government deficit is more than 5 percent of GDP or debt is more than 50 percent of GDP. Adjust upward for developed countries, downward for developing countries and for regional governments. And watch out for hidden liabilities: pensions, health care, bailouts, etc. These are often much larger than official liabilities.

Fine points: Worry further if debt is short-term and/or denominated in foreign currency. Short-term debt subjects the government to refinancing ("rollover") risk; markets may demand better terms or refuse to refinance. Foreign-denominated debt subjects government to risk if currency falls in value, making the debt larger in local terms.

Banking/financial system. This isn't something we've discussed, but analysts track leverage, duration mismatch, exposure concentration, risk-management processes, and nonperforming loans. The challenge is measuring them accurately from reported information. Some of the most troubling situations come with low-quality data.

Exchange rate and reserves. Rule of thumb: Worry if the exchange rate is fixed, or close to it, and the currency is significantly overvalued in PPP terms (Big Macs cost 30 percent more than in other currencies; the real exchange rate has risen more than 30 percent in the past 2-5 years). Worry more if foreign-exchange reserves are low or have fallen significantly.

Political situation. Crises are often more political than economic. Countries with effective governments suffer fewer crises and deal with those that occur more effectively. Analysts therefore look for signs that the political system is unable or unwilling to deal with problems that might turn into crises. Zimbabwe's hyperinflation and Argentina's debt crisis are good examples. Or the Weimar Republic in 1920s Germany.

All of these things generate more concern in countries with weak institutions. It's not an accident that Greece is in worse trouble than France or Germany.

21.3   Crisis responses

What should a government do when faced with a crisis? It depends on the trigger. Standard advice includes:

Sovereign debt crises. If the problem is that the government is borrowing too much, the answer is to stop doing it — run primary surpluses until the debt is manageable. Default is also an option, and saves money in the short term, but probably raises borrowing costs in the future. And if you go through a default, it's helpful to resolve it as quickly as possible.

IMF support is often used to cushion the blow: Contingent on progress with the deficit, the IMF lends the government money on more attractive terms than the market would provide. This "conditionality," as it's called, helps reduce moral hazard (you get the money only if you behave) and provides cover for local politicians (the IMF made us do this). Such conditional lending can be critical in a crisis, when high borrowing rates exacerbate the government's debt problems. (See: debt dynamics.)

Financial crises. If the financial system is fundamentally sound (solvent) but illiquid, the longstanding advice is for the central bank to lend aggressively. The classic quote comes from Walter Bagehot, a 19th-century businessman and journalist: "To avert panic, central banks should lend early and freely, to solvent firms, against good collateral, and at high rates."

If the financial system is insolvent, it's important to get it recapitalized and operating again. This advice comes with more than a little irony, as governments sometimes find themselves bailing out precisely those banks that triggered the crisis. The trick is to do it in ways that inflict some pain on the bank's management and creditors (incentives for the future) and don't bankrupt the government. These things happen fast, so it's hard to get everything right.

Fixed exchange rates. Let them float. A more controversial approach is to impose capital controls to inhibit the response of capital markets to a possible drop in the exchange rate. (See: trilemma.) Capital controls are a dangerous tool, because the fear of future capital controls can generate a crisis on its own, as investors rush to get their money out of the country. capital controls on inflows may, for that reason, be more attractive than controls on outflows.

Executive summary

1. The classic crisis triggers are (i) government debt and deficits, (ii) a fragile financial system, and (iii) a fixed exchange-rate system that is

increasingly under pressure.

2. Crises are hard to predict, but we nevertheless have useful indicators connected to each of the triggers.

3. Politics and institutions are central.

Review questions

1. Risk and opportunity in Ghana (May 2012). You have been asked to prepare a risk assessment for the West African country of Ghana. Ghana is a former British colony that has been growing rapidly in recent years after a period of unusually stable politics. The Economist Intelligence Unit refers to it as a "robust democracy." The World Economic Forum ranked Ghana 114th (of 133) in their Global Competitiveness Report. They continue: "The country continues to display strong public institutions and governance indicators, particularly in regional comparison."

The EIU's Country Risk Report adds:

- The December 2012 elections are expected to be close. The president, John Atta Mills, came to power promising accountability and transparency, but has struggled to maintain party unity while evidence emerges of financial impropriety of some government ministers.

- The victor faces a challenging policy environment, particularly the fiscal situation.

- Expectations among the population are high as production starts at the offshore Jubilee oil field.

- The government's decision to allow use of 70% of future oil revenue as collateral for borrowing is a cause for concern if the revenue is not managed properly.

- The Bank of Ghana (the central bank) faces the twin goals of containing inflation and fostering growth.

- The currency — the cedi — floats with occasional heavy intervention.

Your mission is to assess the risks to Ghana using the information in the table, as well as your own good judgement and analytical skills.

(a) You decide to start with a fiscal assessment. What trend do you see in government revenues and expenses?

(b) You notice that neither the primary deficit nor interest expenses are reported separately. How would you estimate them from the numbers in the table? What are their values for 2011?

(c) Using what you know about government debt dynamics, compute the ratio of government debt to GDP for 2011. What factors contribute the most to the change from 2010?

(d) Overall, how would you assess the risks to Ghana's economy over the next couple of years?

	2008	2009	2010	2011	2012
GDP growth (%)	8.4	4.0	7.7	13.6	7.4
Inflation (%)	18.1	16.0	8.6	8.6	8.5
Interest rate (%)	20.8	28.8	22.7	20.5	20.6
Govt revenue (% of GDP)	16.0	16.5	19.1	23.4	22.2
Govt spending (% of GDP)	24.5	22.3	25.5	27.6	27.7
Govt budget balance (% of GDP)	−8.5	−5.8	−6.5	−4.2	−5.5
Govt debt (% of GDP)	30.6	33.3	33.9		
Real exchange rate (index)	81.7	76.3	81.8	78.1	74.5
FX reserves (USD billions)	1.8	2.9	4.3	4.4	4.8

Data from EIU CountryData. The government budget balance is a surplus if positive, deficit if negative. The real exchange rate is the price of goods in Ghana relative to the rest of the world; the larger the number, the more expensive goods are in Ghana. The numbers for 2011 and 2012 are estimates.

Answer.

(a) Trends include: (i) revenues and spending both rising, (ii) spending still ahead of revenue (there's a deficit), and (as a direct result) (iii) ratio of debt to GDP rising a little (more on that to come).

(b) This is a tricky one. Remember that interest payments in year t are $i_t B_{t-1}/Y_t$. We get what we want from:

$$\begin{aligned} i_t B_{t-1}/Y_t &= i_t(B_{t-1}/Y_{t-1})(Y_{t-1}/Y_t) \\ &\approx i_t(B_{t-1}/Y_{t-1})/(1 + g_t + \pi_t). \end{aligned}$$

That gives us interest payments in 2011 of 5.7% of GDP and a primary deficit of −1.5% (that is, a surplus).

(c) The key relation is this one:

$$\Delta(B_t/Y_t) = (i_t - \pi_t)(B_{t-1}/Y_{t-1}) - g_t(B_{t-1}/Y_{t-1}) + (D_t/Y_t).$$

We refer to the components on the right as A, B, and C. Doing the calculations gives us

	2010	2011
Interest payments		4.0
Component A (interest)		4.0
Component B (growth)		−4.6
Component C (primary deficit)		−1.5
Total change in B/Y		−2.1
Public debt (% of GDP)	33.9	31.8

Over this period, the ratio of debt to GDP fell by 2.1%. The components contributed: interest +4.0, growth –4.6, and the primary deficit –1.5. Note especially the growth term, the result of unusually high GDP growth in 2011.

(d) This is a call to look at the checklist of crisis indicators:

- Government debt and deficits. We have deficits, but there's not much sign yet of a growth debt to GDP ratio. One future concern might be the possibility of borrowing now against future oil revenue. Will any debts incurred be spent wisely? Will the oil revenue show up?

- Banking system. No information provided.

- Exchange rate and reserves. Reserves are modest, but with the exchange rate floating there shouldn't be much concern about that.

- Politics. Always an issue, especially with a contentious election coming and the promise of money from oil revenue. It's an odd fact but a true one that revenue from natural resources is more likely to cause problems than solve them.

Update: In August 2014, Ghana asked the IMF for help. The chance of default remains low, since foreign debt is backed by oil revenue, but the promise of oil has turned into a curse, as it often does.

2. Don't Cry for Me Argentina. (We know, it's a cliche, but so is their approach to policy.) Argentina is a seemingly endless source of entertainment to economists, yet its economy has done well in the recent past. GDP growth fell to 0.9% in 2009, during the global financial crisis, but averaged over 9% the next two years. Most analysts attribute this success to favorable commodity prices and strong global demand for Argentina's commodity exports. Additional information is provided in Table 21.1.

At the same time, the government of President Cristina Fernandez de Kirchner continues to adopt policies that befuddle outside observers, including: taking over private pension funds, restricting imports and purchases of foreign currency, attacking the press, nationalizing the Spanish-owned oil company YPF, imposing price controls on electricity, natural gas, and public transportation, and subsidizing energy consumption.

The Economist Intelligence Unit reports:

- A US court case may eventually leave Argentina with the unpalatable choice of repaying the "holdouts" (creditors that did not participate in the 2005 or 2010 restructurings) in full — something that it has sworn never to do — or falling into default with its remaining creditors.

- According to official data, consumer price inflation remains among the highest in emerging markets, at 10.5% in April 2013. However, the official data are widely discredited and we are now using estimates

	2010	2011	2012	2013
Official exchange rate (pesos per USD)	3.90	4.11	4.54	5.46
Inflation (%)	22.9	24.4	25.3	20.6
Foreign currency reserves (USD billions)	52.2	46.4	43.2	32.2
Real GDP growth (%)	9.2	8.9	1.9	5.2
Govt revenue (% of GDP)	24.3	23.6	25.4	27.3
Govt spending (% of GDP)	24.1	25.3	28.0	30.5
Public sector surplus (% of GDP)	0.2	–1.7	–2.6	–3.2
Primary balance (% of GDP)	1.7	0.3	–0.2	–0.8
Govt debt (yearend, % of GDP)			44.8	
Interest rate paid on debt (%)	4.0	5.5	6.7	6.5
Money market interest rate (%)	9.1	10.0	9.8	12.7

Table 21.1: Economic indicators for Argentina. Source: EIU.

produced by PriceStats, which estimates that inflation in 2012 was 25%.

- Double-digit inflation has generated real peso appreciation. Foreign-exchange controls have failed to prevent an erosion of foreign exchange reserves, heightening the risk of an eventual devaluation.

- The Argentine peso floats in principle, but the central bank intervenes to limit its rate of depreciation. In addition, foreign currency transactions are subject to a variety of controls. For the past couple of years, the government has been gradually tightening the "clamp," an unofficial policy of discouraging purchases of dollars. As a result, the peso's official decline has been modest, but the unofficial "blue market" price of the peso is considerably lower.

- The poor banking sector risk rating reflects weak economic activity, expansionary monetary policies that contribute to credit risk, high risk of exchange-rate and interest-rate volatility, and increased currency convertibility risk.

- The ruling party fared badly in the October midterm election, leaving the president without enough support in Congress to change the constitution and run for re-election. Focus will now shift rapidly to the 2015 presidential race. The president remains alienated from almost all of the country's most influential groups, including the unions, the media, the Catholic Church and the traditional leaders of the Peronist party. In this context, risks to political stability will be high. An additional risk to stability is the president's health.

The question is what happens next: Could another crisis be on the way, or has Argentina put its problematic past to rest? Use the information provided, including Table 21.1, to assess the risks to the Argentina economy over the next 2-3 years.

(a) By "real appreciation" we mean an increase in the price of local goods relative to foreign goods — what is sometimes called a decline in the real exchange rate. Use the numbers in the table to demonstrate (or disprove) real appreciation of the peso.

(b) Why do you think the central bank's foreign exchange reserves have declined?

(c) How do you see government debt evolving? Compute, in particular, the ratio of government debt to GDP at year-end 2013. What factors contribute the most to the change in the ratio?

(d) Overall, how would you rate the risk of a macroeconomic crisis in Argentina? What are the biggest sources of concern?

Answer.

(a) The issue is the real exchange rate $RER = eP^*/P$, where e is the exchange rate (the peso price of one dollar), P is the price of Argentine goods, and P^* is the price of American goods. So how is the real exchange rate changing? In words: the combination of high inflation and more modest currency depreciation has made Argentine goods expensive (equivalently, foreign goods cheap).

How would you show this? Inflation is the rate of increase in P, and we see the price of Argentine goods going up rapidly, roughly 20% a year. In contrast, eP^* is going up less: P^* is roughly flat (1-2% inflation in the US) and e is rising (if we compute its rate of change) 5% in 2011 and 10% in 2012. Thus RER is rising, as Argentine goods get relatively more expensive.

(b) Evidently people want dollars, not pesos, and the central bank supplies them to maintain a relatively stable exchange rate. One possible reason: Argentine prices are rising, and a substantial depreciation is one way to get that. That makes pesos less attractive, since you'd lose (relative to dollars) if the peso falls in value.

(c) The debt dynamics equation is

$$\Delta(B_t/Y_t) \;=\; (i_t - \pi_t)(B_{t-1}/Y_{t-1}) - g_t(B_{t-1}/Y_{t-1}) + D_t/Y_t.$$

The three terms are

$$(i_t - \pi_t)(B_{t-1}/Y_{t-1}) \;=\; -6.3$$
$$-g_t(B_{t-1}/Y_{t-1}) \;=\; -2.3$$
$$D_t/Y_t \;=\; 0.8.$$

Their total is –7.8, so the ratio of debt to GDP will fall to 37.0. Note for later the negative contribution of the real interest rate: they're getting a very good deal on their debt. It's not hard to imagine that changing.

(d) This is a call for the checklist:

- Debt and deficits. (i) The calculation shows the debt ratio is falling. But the US court case could lead to default, which isn't a good thing. And the negative real interest rate is unlikely to continue. If they paid a modest 2% real rate on debt, the debt ratio would go up about 4% this year, and higher rates are certainly possible.
- Banks. The EIU suggests that banks could suffer from a weak economy.
- Exchange rates and reserves. The real exchange rate continues to appreciate, making Argentine goods more expensive. At the same time, they're losing reserves as they sell dollars to support the peso. Both point toward a decline in the value of the peso.
- Politics. Always an issue in Argentina. There's some uncertainty given the president's lame duck status and health. On the other hand, a change could make things better.

The fiscal situation, including the court case, the exchange rate and reserve position, the banking system, and the political situation all shows signs of trouble. Overall, they'll probably muddle through, but there's a chance of serious trouble.

Update: Argentina defaulted in July 2014. It's not clear how this will play out, but "muddle through" seems to be the likely outcome. This hasn't had a large impact to date because Argentina was already locked out of international financial markets for new issues. The default doesn't change that, although it does make some international transactions more difficult.

If you're looking for more

You can find similar analyses in many places. One of our favorites is the Economist Intelligence Unit's Country Risk Reports. Another is the IMF's Vulnerability Indicators.

There's no end of good descriptions of crises. On the most recent crisis, Ben Bernanke's testimony to the crisis commission is a good overview from the perspective of the US (search: "Bernanke testimony crisis causes"). Michael Lewis's Vanity Fair pieces are works of art (search "michael lewis vanity fair"). Among the many books about crises, we recommend

- Robert Bruner and Sean Carr, *The Panic of 1907*. Good read, and short; you'll think it's about 2007.

- Carmen Reinhart and Kenneth Rogoff, *This Time is Different*. The recent bestseller, covering 800 years and the whole world.

- David Wessel, *In Fed We Trust*. Terrific book from the *Wall Street Journal* writer.

- Paul Blustein, *And the Money Kept Rollin In (and Out)*. Wonderful review of Argentina's 1999-2001 crisis. He has another one, *The Chastening*, about the Asian crisis and the IMF.

Index

Made in the USA
Middletown, DE
30 November 2018